wo
8.

—
ſ

SURVIVING
MICHAEL WINNER

SURVIVING
MICHAEL WINNER
A Thirty-Year Odyssey

DINAH MAY

The Robson Press

First published in Great Britain in 2014 by
The Robson Press (an imprint of Biteback Publishing)
Westminster Tower
3 Albert Embankment
London SE1 7SP
Copyright © Dinah May 2014

ISBN 978-1-84954-703-1

10 9 8 7 6 5 4 3 2 1

A CIP catalogue record for this book is available from the British Library.

Set in Plantin

Printed and bound in Great Britain by
CPI Group (UK) Ltd, Croydon CR0 4YY

To my mother

CONTENTS

CONTENTS

INTRODUCTION

I FIRST SAID TO MICHAEL THAT I was thinking of writing a book as an off-the-cuff remark when he was being particularly horrible. It was really as a kind of defence. I thought it might just make him think twice before behaving so badly in future, or at least give me time to get my strength back. It worked. Well, at least for an hour or so, anyway. After that, he picked it up as an idea which at first amused him and then I think even quite impressed him, and he began announcing it to the world. It became almost annoying that he grew more and more enthusiastic about my writing something of my times with him. But I should not have been surprised. After all, it would be about *him*, one of his favourite subjects.

Over the last two years or so, the idea of this book cropped up more and more in our conversations. One of us would remember some incident or drama and Michael would say excitedly, 'Put it in, put it in.' I would test him occasionally and mention some happening I thought he may prefer the world to remain oblivious to. But his attitude never changed. 'Put it in, put it *all* in, dear,' he would say. 'Tell them everything.' When I looked incredulous, he once roared with laughter and said, 'People might not *believe* some things, dear,' and another time simply beamed at me mischievously and said, 'Who cares, darling, who cares? Put it in, put it in.' Without those conversations I don't think this book would exist. Firstly, the idea of it as a real possibility might very well have evaporated, and secondly, I'm sure I could not sit comfortably and tell the good, the bad and the possibly unbelievable without feeling that Michael's enthusiasm was with me. In the early months of writing, when I wavered now and then and doubts niggled at me, a friend pointed out a comment in a psychology book.

'Biographies should show people in their undershirts. Goethe had his weaknesses, and Calvin was often cruel. Considerations of this kind reveal the true greatness of a man. This way of looking at things is better than false hero worship!'

That was Jung's view and I saw good and healthy common sense in it. Michael might not be a saint but neither was he a devil. Like most human beings he was multifaceted, with perhaps an extra dollop of contradictions dropped into the mix for good measure. He also enjoyed being in the spotlight. If shining my own particular torch shows something more of the roundness of his character then I feel it can only be for the good.

And if any of the stories entertain or amuse someone then I'm sure Michael will be happy too.

He was also quite a help when the time came to actually start putting words on a page. I was at a loss as to how to begin. Again, I remembered our conversations. When I had doubted my ability to write a book he had said, 'Just tell the stories, tell the stories, that's all there is to it, of course you can do it.' I had never imagined that I would attempt to write any kind of scholarly biography. I'm not sure I had seriously imagined I could write anything at all. But by concentrating on the word 'story' I gradually felt less intimidated. However, let me be clear. I have not written this as a story because Michael told me to. It's just that it seemed the only way open to me. And it felt like the friendliest way too. I began to jot down memories and get them in order.

The next thing I realised was that I would have to say something about myself. I had been in the background, usually presented as Michael's long-suffering assistant, but no one knew much about me or what I was like. I was always perfectly happy with that. But if the book was to make sense as a story I was going to have to be in it. There was no getting away from it, but I have tried to keep that part brief. And sometimes it felt only fair that while showing the ups and downs of Michael's life, I also said something of the ups and downs of my own. The same is true of all the people who worked for Michael. They made up much of his day-to-day world and were also central to my experience of working for him. I have introduced them as they appear. Mostly I was very lucky to be part of a good team and I don't think it any coincidence that some of my most stressful times came just after some key person had moved on. Michael's sudden furies could erupt at any time and, although everyone had to find their own way to get through, a bit of understanding and support from the other staff made life much more bearable. I'm happy to say that over the years I worked beside lots of very lovely people and many remain friends to this day.

So this book is an account of my thirty-year association with Michael Winner, from the first time I met him in June 1982. He was in his prime as a famous and successful film maker and was just beginning to be known as a 'character', a 'personality'. We may dislike such controversial people for the upset they cause or the damage they may leave in their wake as they seem to push their way through their privileged lives. And we may love them because they have the courage or simply the opportunity to do or say what we would dearly like to have done or said. I saw the wreckage he could cause, just as I also saw his generosity and humour. He was often unpredictable, I realised, even to himself. He never quite knew what he might do next, so God help those around him.

To say my job was varied is something of an understatement. I might be told I had ten minutes to get ready for a helicopter flight for lunch in Paris, or be sent a memo reminding me that, as an employee, I was not entitled to eat a banana from the fruit bowl. The journey continued for over thirty years and I witnessed, or was involved in, all the different sides to his life: film making, public appearances, romances, daily office work and the minutiae of running the house. He employed me as an actor, a hair stylist and, for the last twenty years, his assistant. I played my part in looking after him throughout his long illness and was with him when he died. Throughout that time there were of course many extraordinary events, and many ordinary ones too, which he would often manage to turn into nightmares, opportunities, absurd dramas or comedy gold. And throughout those decades, as happens to all of us, his life was changing and the world was changing too. And I was perhaps one of the most constant touchstones in a life that was much more of a roller-coaster than a merry-go-round. To be with him, whether for dinner or a day's work, usually meant being strapped onto the same fairground ride as him. Friends could get on or off more easily, but being an employee usually meant clinging on for as long as you were willing or able. I'm still not always sure how I managed to do it for so long. At least now I will be able to read this book to remind myself, and I hope it will offer some kind of explanation to my family and friends as well.

When it came to choosing what things to include and what to leave out, Michael was no help at all. Whatever I thought of, I could usually hear him saying excitedly, 'Put it in, put it in, put it in the book.' There is not room for everything, but in telling the story of some of the major events in his life I have also included quite a few of the little things, the details that I feel can help to show something of his many sides. I'm not sure how possible it is to ever fully understand a character like Michael's but I hope the stories and descriptions serve to give more than an inkling of what he was like. For instance, any stranger who walked into the hallway of Woodland House, his grand Victorian home, and made their way up the stairs to Michael's office could learn a great deal about the man they were about to meet. There were clues, beautifully framed and lining the walls for all to see. Some of the most fabulous illustrations to some of the most wonderful children's stories ever written. Jenny Seagrove was quick to spot the childlike side of him and was quoted in the papers as saying: 'Michael Winner behaves like a three-year-old. I remember him once wearing a yellow and black shirt and doing an extraordinary bee impersonation. I thought, "Anyone who can do that is worth getting to know better."'

His tirades were also in some way reminiscent of the tantrums of a child, particularly one in their notorious 'terrible twos'. And sometimes I wondered if that was also why it was often possible to quickly forget it and move on. He triggered some maternal instinct in people, perhaps. I felt he could sometimes act like a child testing the boundaries, behaving badly and then being very disappointed if he was not almost immediately forgiven. But I liked some of that childlike side to him. Not the tantrums, but the schoolboy mischievousness and the playful imagination and the humour which were an important part of who he was. And Michael's comic talent was of course one of the vital ingredients of his newspaper columns and books, and often had a childlike or absurd quality. He found another platform for that when Twitter appeared and enjoyed the spontaneity it allowed him.

> My asst Dinah who was blown away and lodged in a tree yesterday is adapting well. She leaps from tree to tree. Ate 4 squirrels + woodpecker

Michael's short temper and screaming fits were one of the most difficult sides of him to cope with. They became widely known about over his long career and so have been experienced first-hand by many people. These tirades were part of life when working for Michael for any length of time and so I have simply included them as they crop up, although generally in shortened form. In 2009, when Christian Bale had a noisy rant at the director of photography for walking through his line of sight on the set of *Terminator: Salvation*, it caused quite a stir. Being known for that kind of outburst himself, Michael was invited to talk on Radio 4 and give his opinion. Of course he supported Christian Bale and said the DP deserved to be shouted at for acting unprofessionally. Christian, however, did make a full apology.

Michael had occasionally experienced what it was like to be on the receiving end of an explosion. The most famous example, I think, was when Burt Lancaster screamed obscenities at him and held him over a cliff edge. Michael was very frightened at the time but he took it in his stride and remained friends with Burt. Among the staff at Michael's we had a points system for his tirades. A 3 or a 4 could shake someone up but would be forgotten in a day or two. Anything over a 6 could lead to tears. A 9 was pretty disturbing and could take a week or two to recover from. Mostly it was women who were reduced to tears but I did see Michael make grown men cry too. The force of his anger could carry an extraordinary weight and was not to be measured by volume alone. But Michael's outbursts remained quite a mysterious phenomenon to me. It became possible to predict them sometimes from his mood but I could never really know what level they might rise to. Often they seemed to surprise Michael as much as anyone, and unless he knew the person well he would frequently regret his outburst and tell me afterwards he had been a 'bloody idiot'. But he usually reserved his most terrifying outbursts for his longest-serving and most liked and trusted employees.

As the decades wore on, his attacks of shouting seemed to me to be increasingly out of place in the modern world. Michael often said it was all an act and sometimes I think it was. Very occasionally he had winked as he bellowed at me, before turning to deliver the real tirade to someone else. But whether an act or not, it was no comfort to the person on the receiving end, of course. All I can really say is that his screaming fits were as varied and contradictory as his character.

Michael's generosity towards friends was perhaps his most straightforward quality, and he delighted in seeing people he liked being happy and successful. He could be unshakeably loyal, and with two girlfriends with health problems he was hugely financially supportive, too. When it came to giving advice to people going through difficult times, I saw him at his most thoughtful and helpful. If problems were financial or legal, he was quite an expert, and if he needed further opinions he would pick up the phone to Doug Stoker or John Burrell, who had been his accountant and his solicitor for many years. Just as I witnessed his care for others, I was also on the receiving end myself. When times were hard or I was at a low ebb he could be a very great help with his advice and had the gift of bringing a fresh perspective and humour to almost anything. In short, he was a fine friend.

Working for Michael meant that I had always to focus on the moment, on the latest drama, or sometimes just on getting through the day. There didn't seem much time to reflect on things. Recently I have had some time for that. I have had time to meet up with girlfriends of his I still know well and with people who worked at the house over the years. I have had time to sift through diaries, notebooks and the photographs I have collected. Time has passed, some eighteen months since Michael died, but in terms of memories that is no time at all. As I write I am in a room in Farley Court that for many years was one of his offices. And I'm writing a book that centres on *him*. It's understandable perhaps that now and then I get the feeling I'm *still* working for Michael. But this time he won't be getting it all his own way.

CHAPTER ONE

MEETING MICHAEL

'THAT'S MICHAEL WINNER,' SAID CECIL under his breath, leaning over the table and rolling his eyes towards the door. I turned to see a girl in a pale fur coat clinging to a very suntanned man. They made a striking couple in a 1970s glamour kind of a way. It was 1982 and we were in an Italian restaurant called Trattoo just off Kensington High Street, London. I was with Cecil Korer, a television producer who, over the ten years or so I had known him, had become a good friend. In the early 1970s a photographer called Harry Ormisher had introduced me to him. Cecil was Channel 4's first head of light entertainment and was responsible for several new shows including *Countdown*. The random number generator used on the show was nicknamed Cecil after him. Through Cecil I began to audition for television roles and found work on several TV shows. He was also involved in commissioning a new series to be filmed in America for Channel 4 called *The Optimist*, and I had rattled down to London in my Spitfire (a kind of small car, not the plane) to have dinner with him. I remember he was talking about the casting and details of the part he had in mind for me and I was thinking about America and the excitement of maybe actually *going* there.

This was the early 1980s in central London and everything seemed very sophisticated. But when I look back now, I remember it as a simpler life when time passed more slowly. From old photographs it appears to have been rather a shambles of styles. There were straight trousers and afghan coats from the 1960s and wedge heels and flares and purple ties from the 1970s. I was always a country girl at heart and very happy with that. I wasn't particularly excited by London and its fine restaurants and influential people. But I did see it as important and sophisticated. Through my work I had got used to being expected to know who everyone was. And I had learnt to deliver the appropriate expression to show that I was suitably amazed or impressed. On this occasion, I don't think I had given it my best effort.

'He is a very famous film director,' said Cecil lowering his voice, as the couple were now standing very near our table and the waitress was rushing to greet them.

There was a bit of a commotion as they were ushered to a table behind me, with Michael's raised voice and then laughter and the scrape of chairs as they were seated. When the lady in furs wandered off to the loos I was surprised by Cecil calling a greeting to Michael. Then I cringed as he continued, 'And my lady is more beautiful than yours.' With hindsight I'm sure it was a kind of private joke and he knew it would irritate Michael.

I twisted in my chair to nod and smile in the right places as they talked. But Cecil, my second best promoter, outclassed only by my mother, was listing my acting credentials and passing on my telephone number. 'In case you have a part for her in one of your films,' he said, or words to that effect. He went on to tell him that if he did ever take me out to dinner he'd have to make sure it was a place that served scampi, chips and peas.

'You can't be fucking serious,' barked Michael, his eyes bulging at me as I grew ever pinker.

'Oh yes,' said Cecil. 'Apparently they go down easiest if she has to talk at the same time as eat.' They both roared with laughter and I rushed off to find the fur lady in the lavatory. We introduced ourselves and she told me her name was Sylvia Sachs. This must have been a year or so before she appeared in the television series *Never the Twain*.

I composed myself before returning to the table.

I was thirty and Michael was in his late forties and at the peak of his film-making career. He had directed many films in both Britain and America and his recent box office hits, *Death Wish* and *Death Wish II*, had given him international recognition. It was a month or more before my phone rang and I heard his voice again.

CHAPTER TWO

MY BACK-STORY

I WAS BORN IN IRBY ON the Wirral. My father was a captain in the Merchant Navy and before I was two my mother had had enough of his heavy drinking. I have very few memories of him.

My brother Stuart is three years older than me, and our mother Shelagh brought us up while also working full time as a secretary. Shelagh was a force to be reckoned with. She worked hard and loved a good party. Among family and friends she was renowned for her cooking and frequent dinner parties. These were often impromptu and usually very lively. During school holidays she had to continue her job, so Stuart and I would often stay at Gran's house in Holyhead, or Welsh Wales, as we called it. The bus would take us on a rather alarming journey back in time. We would leave our home in the 1960s to arrive, jolted and shaken, at our gran's house in the 1890s. Turning the corner past the laundry house and into George Street was somewhere between magical and terrifying.

Gran was a good woman but often stern and always dressed in black and carrying a knobbly stick. She liked to make tea almost constantly. This was mostly served with brown bread and butter, which she would chew frantically for what seemed like hours as we fought back our giggles. A cobblestone path led down a short alleyway to the sea and local bearded fishermen would bring rustling parcels of fresh fish up to the house. At dusk we would watch the long shadows as a man with a ladder moved past outside, lighting the gas lamps. Gran would stoke up the black stove to keep the kettle with our wash water hot. I didn't mind washing from a small china bowl, but going outside and across the yard to the toilet was frightening after dark. There was one real luxury in her house and after a long day I would float warm and safe on the thickest, softest goose-down mattress.

During the days Stuart and I would make up games on the shore or around the harbour. They usually involved him laughing delightedly and me getting very wet and cold. But water always held a fascination for me and I never minded falling in, which was just as well as it happened quite a lot. I was far more concerned about Gran seeing my wet clothes and shaking that stick at me. Soon I became expert at creeping past her unseen, but it was a small community and everyone would have known who we were and what we were up to. The corner shop was the centre of our world and was run by Diana and

Carol, a mother-and-daughter team. They still sold 'loosie' cigarettes but Stuart and I were more interested in exchanging big copper pennies for bags of sweets from the colourful glass jars. As someone walked in a voice would often shout, 'Shut the fuckin' door, Ethel.' To the newcomer it would seem to be the lady at the counter but was in fact a parrot in the alcove behind. This was a source of endless hilarity – except to Gran, who was not at all amused by the 'dirty bird'.

My mother's sister, Auntie Peggy, lived nearby on the Wirral, and this was the other home we spent a great deal of time in. Our cousins Angela and Nicholas, or Nicky as we called him, were similar ages and we all got on well. As the youngest, I felt I had to be something of a daredevil to make sure I was included. I used a lot of plasters in those days and I think most of my early childhood smelt of TCP. Stuart, my brother, was often very boisterous but Nicky was an altogether gentler soul and I adored and admired him and knew he would protect me if needed. My mother would make or buy me lovely clothes, but very often they were ruined by my tree climbing or den building. However, I did love ballet, and Angela and I would go to classes twice a week.

By the age of nine I knew that I wanted to marry a farmer and have seven children and look after all the animals. I already kept over twenty rabbits and many mice in our small rented house and garden. As Mum did not drive we went on camping holidays by bus. What I best remember of this is seeing the horses and bottle-feeding lambs on a farm. This was true happiness and my future was clear. But then Desmond arrived.

Des had been around for a while, but I suppose at first I had not really noticed.

He didn't stay at the house, or so we were led to believe,

but one night I had stayed up. The Rover remained until just before Mum came to wake me for school. I was only eight but over breakfast I confronted her about it. I said he must be her boyfriend, while she insisted he was just a 'friend'.

But things were about to change. Des had got a divorce from his wife and a new bungalow was built with an outdoor pool. We moved in. Mum was convinced that this would be good for all of us and it could have been very exciting but Des had a wicked temper and I was wary of him. There had been frequent arguments and I remembered walking in from school one day as a broken bed was settling at the foot of the stairs. In our new home, that side of things stayed the same. We might be having tea when, in a sudden fit of rage, the plates would be thrown. Mashed potato and gravy would drip from the ceiling.

But I loved the swimming pool and one day Desmond bought me a horse. Well, technically Candy was a pony and a very young foal at that. I was ecstatic and walked him for over a year as he was not yet old enough to be ridden.

But all this magnificence and mayhem was to be short lived.

Candy needed breaking in before I could safely ride him. Although Des knew little of horses he was certain he could do the job. It was an exhausting ordeal but all seemed to have gone well. The next day he and my mother drove to town. They had got married just before we moved to the new house but he had never bought her an engagement ring. As they were returning with a diamond ring, Des complained of chest pains. The following day, while in hospital, he died of a heart attack, aged just forty. And that was the end of an era.

Mum was a strong woman but she was devastated and there was still more bad news to come. Des had recently changed jobs and died just a week before his life insurance policy was due to begin. Now there was no income but a huge mortgage to pay on the house. Things had to change again, and quickly. Lodgers appeared and I moved into Mum's bedroom to free up another room. She went back to work and I was needed to help with the washing, cooking, ironing et cetera. The lodgers tended to be men who needed a room during the working week and would return to Scotland, or wherever home was, at weekends. There were plenty of mishaps, and good times too. Richard Nesbitt and George Bloy, the two who stayed longest, are close friends to this day. After school I would make all the beds, light the fire in the living room and then iron shirts and sheets. I had a lot to learn, like not washing white shirts with yellow dusters, but by the age of twelve I could cook a full roast dinner for six. Domestic science became my best subject at school. I had to work hard but it was a cheerful house, and Mum was becoming the happy matriarch.

My thoughts of life on a farm had started to fade in favour of becoming a nurse, but as I began my last year of school I realised just how many exams that would involve. I started helping at the local hair salon and felt quickly at home. By sixteen I was training as a stylist and had a boyfriend called Bob May. My plan was to work towards having my own salon and move in with Bob. My mother, despite her generally modern outlook on life, was not having that. She had nothing against Bob, but we were to do it properly, so by seventeen I was married.

At about this time Mum had noticed an ad in the local paper for a beauty contest. She thought that I should have a go. It involved getting all the right clothes and from what I remember she did everything. The one thing she had not found was a pair of white stilettos, and these, apparently, were crucial. On the morning of the big day she rushed off and returned with a pair of black stilettos and a bottle of white shoe paint. My heart sank as I watched her sponging the stuff on the new shoes and I pictured myself looking a terrible mess. But when she was done they actually looked good. She put them outside the front door to dry in the morning sun. A little later I heard piercing shrieks and looked out of an upstairs window. My mother was chasing after a child who was hobbling strangely. A little girl, one of our neighbours' children, had seen the white stilettos and, slipping her own small shoes inside them, had made off towards town to show them off. No damage was done and with shoes unscuffed we headed off to see which local girl would be chosen to be 'Miss Chester'. The judges were the Black Abbotts, a well-known band at the time. I was very shocked when they announced me the winner. Mum had put in all the work and arranged everything, to the extent that it hardly felt much to do with me. I was dumbfounded and made up all at the same time. I had never seen myself as beautiful. I was only just out of school, where I had been used to being laughed at for my curly hair or buck teeth or whatever was being picked on at the time. I had found a way to survive by being quite a tomboy and also by simply being practical and useful.

I did not look at this as the beginning of something, but carried on my hairdressing and the long walks I so loved with my dogs. It was my mother who saw an opportunity and lost no time in looking for more competitions.

In those days there were quite a few and I began to enjoy it. There was prize money too.

In Liverpool there was a club called the She Club, where

Bob and I sometimes went for a night out. The owner, Roy Adams, saw me dancing and offered me a job as a DJ in a new club he was opening in New Brighton, on the Wirral. I did not feel I knew enough to do that kind of work but said I would think about it.

The next day he phoned and I went over to see his new venture, which was called Chelsea Reach. He held out a wad of money and said he would like me to go out and buy all the records I liked and also any clothes I wanted to dance in. It was an offer I couldn't resist. Bob knew a lot about the music scene and between us we quickly put together a good set of records. Within a week the club was open and was a huge success. All I had to do was announce records and then dance crazily to them on a stage built out into the dance floor to look like the bow of a boat. On special occasions Pete Price, a DJ from a local radio station, would appear and do a guest slot. He was a larger-than-life character and brilliant at all the patter. While he looked after the music I would do my own freestyle go-go dancing. It was not exactly ballet, but I was eighteen and being paid a small fortune to have fun. It was to last three years and I did really enjoy the dancing. I started entering dance competitions and felt much more at home with those than in the beauty contests. For a while I travelled all over the north-west of England and won so many prizes that I started to get banned. That just felt so unfair and was upsetting at the time.

But the dancing and disc jockeying, together with the various competitions, had also led to my finding lots of work as a model.

With all this going on there was now no time for hairdressing work. I was reluctant to let it go, as it was so satisfying and

I enjoyed it. And it was a skill I had really developed, which I can now see was important for my self-confidence. I resigned myself to putting it on the back burner and continued to keep my hand in by being hairdresser to friends and family.

Through the modelling I had worked with many photographers, and one of them was Harry Ormisher. Through him I met Cecil Korer. That was a very lucky introduction for me, as he quickly put me forward for television work.

The first was a TV quiz show called *Where in the World* starring Michael Parkinson and later Ray Alan and then another quiz called *Password* with Esther Rantzen. Cecil was to prove a brilliant agent for me. More work followed on other shows including *The Liver Birds*, which became a very popular comedy series starring Nerys Hughes, Polly James and Pauline Collins.

Most of the photography jobs I had done up until then had been editorial fashion and advertising. However, I had been naive and also posed topless.

When I saw the possibility of acting work, I woke up. At about that time I discovered that my own mother was arranging for me to appear in *Playboy* magazine. She may have had my best financial interests in mind but she did get a very clear *no* to that one. I had realised I wanted to be taken seriously as an actress and, although I didn't see exactly how to achieve that, I had begun to see what might be harmful.

My mother was still seeking out beauty contests and putting me up for them.

For me, the best times were going shopping with her and other friends and coming back with fabulous outfits. The cash seemed to come in so easily and it flowed out the same way. Often I would hardly know what was happening until we arrived at the venue and mum would bring out the clothes she had chosen for me. I especially loved the theatrical fashions and long flowing gowns and sometimes life seemed like one long dressing-up party. But I didn't ever have great confidence in my looks. It was only really when I felt the clothes I wore were very beautiful that I could start to feel more comfortable. One beauty competition my mother organised was in a Birmingham nightclub. She knew very well that I hated wearing anything less than a full swimming costume for these contests. I walked onto the stage in a silver bikini with a gold chain around my waist. This was the 1970s, but I could have killed her. The judges were the comedy duo Mike and Bernie Winters, and after the judging I got talking to Bernie. We chatted for hours and I really liked him. I mean I *really* liked him. He invited us to their show in Crewe and Mum and I went. We met up with him backstage.

Again, he was charming and very funny and such a gentleman too, and again I could feel just how much I was drawn to him. Mike and Bernie offered me work as a compère and I went on a short tour with them, introducing the acts.

It included going to Germany and Belfast with a show to entertain British troops.

The life I was leading, that seemed to be shaping itself, meant that I was often away or not getting home until the early hours of the morning. Bob was studying engineering and following his own interests. We were good friends but we were growing apart. Perhaps you could just say we were growing up. We had married so young and now it felt like our paths were heading off in different directions. I didn't like being away for days at a time on my own. I was about to travel down to Torquay one day and tried to persuade Bob to come with me. I had become the major breadwinner but he didn't want to be part of the kind of erratic life I was leading. Even when I made it clear how much I liked Bernie and told him that something might happen that could spoil our marriage he would not budge. I don't blame him; our worlds were becoming so different. Grabbing a duvet and a few clothes, I went to stay at my mum's. The friendship that had been growing with Bernie was soon a romance. He encouraged me to keep entering beauty shows and with his knowledge of the world of show business he was my teacher and guide. It was Bernie who showed me how to navigate safely and not get caught up in the seedier side of the industry. He taught me how to be sociable and have a good time but stay safe. When he was not at my side I was, after all, a girl on her own. A girl on her own could be quite vulnerable in the world I was entering. Bernie showed me how to walk that tightrope. I knew he was married and was risking everything but he included me in his life as much as was possible. He did not have to do that but he was nothing if not kind. Maybe that was the thing with Bernie: behind his humour he was a kind and good-hearted man. After his shows we often went to Blinkers, a club owned by George Best. I got to know George quite well and also met stars such as Tom Jones, Bruce Forsyth and Des O'Connor. As Bernie was so known and well respected, an introduction from him was always valuable. In turn I was taken seriously and generally well treated. My confidence was growing.

The affair with Bernie lasted a few years. For me they were important formative years. He had often said he would leave his wife and I continued to believe that might happen. One day a large envelope landed on my mother's doormat. Bob was filing for divorce and citing Bernie as the reason. That evening Bob was at the house and I was trying to persuade him not to go ahead like this. It was clear how distressing it could be for so many people if Bernie's name was involved. I was to blame for letting things get into such a mess and now I just wanted to try to minimise the damage. Life is so strange, as in the middle of all this the phone rang. It was Bernie telling me he had walked out on his wife and was on his way to see me. I told him what was happening. We could not see a way forward together that looked happy. He returned home. When, later, I spoke on the phone to Ziggy, his wife, she made it clear that Bernie was with her and she would not be letting him go. I knew she meant exactly what she said and there was no room for any delusion after that. It was a very sad time for me but somehow my friendship with him remained.

In 1976 I was crowned Miss Great Britain in the nation's favourite beauty competition. I was twenty-four. I had got into the final twice before. The first time I came third and the next year a scandal blew up about the selection of one of the candidates. I felt it was starting to feel much too competitive, to put it politely, and I didn't want to do it again. But the following year my mother put the application in without telling me. She and I were accompanying another girl to the preliminaries in Crewe and Nantwich and my name was announced. I assumed there was some mistake until my mother produced the costumes she had secretly packed in her case. I was furious but not totally unused to her surprises. Once again I got through to the final, a three-day event in Morecambe. As far as I was concerned there was really no chance of me winning but it did seem a good thing to do, if only for the publicity, which could help my TV and promotional work. Mum was there on the last day. Unbeknownst to me, her friend Penny

Jones had driven her up. And then that announcement came: 'The winner is number three, Dinah May from Little Neston.' For a while I was stunned. Then I heard my mother's unmistakable shrieks of hysteria from beside the catwalk.

When I turned and saw her and the delight in her eyes I burst into tears.

Photos of me standing in my bathing costume were splashed across the newspapers the next day. I think I was the first Miss Great Britain to be in tears at the crowning. One of the headlines read 'Weeping Beauty'.

Life became immediately more hectic. The first place I was flown to was Jersey Zoo. I was photographed with a baby gorilla. I held him in my arms but the commotion of photographers alarmed him, I think, and he gradually began to tighten his grip on my hair. Thankfully the keepers calmed the situation or my beauty queen days might have been very short lived.

It took a while for me to get used to the media. I got into trouble straight away.

The winner of Miss Great Britain was always loaned a car for a year; traditionally this was a British-made Rover. These were times when the British car industry was struggling to compete with the rising sun of Japanese technology and let's just say that some corners of society had not yet come to terms with their increasing success. As it happened I had been doing a lot of modelling for Honda and already become a central figure in their advertising campaign. My mother, on my behalf, took it upon herself to ask Honda if they would supply me with a new car. A brand-new Honda Civic arrived and the next day the papers had stories like 'Miss Great Britain Goes Japanese'. My mother was very good at seeing an opportunity. Not so good at diplomacy.

Increasingly, the work I was doing was in London. I had friends with a flat in Palace Mansions near Olympia. One of them was Bob's brother John May and another was Gilda Conchie, who kept the place in order. I had known them both since school days. I rented a room there so I could avoid staying in hotels on my frequent trips south. George Best would call sometimes. He would turn up out of the blue if he knew I was in London. Friends in the flat found it quite a thrill if someone as 'known' as he was turned up. Once I got a whispered call, 'George Best is here and he's waiting for you in the living room.'

He would take me to dinner sometimes or to a club such as Tramp. Often I was among some of the celebrities of the time. Now and then there were big egos or outrageous clothes and behaviour but mostly I met good people and laughed a lot. I remember meeting Rod Stewart a few times and always liked seeing Ringo Starr too. Often we would just sit and chat over bangers and mash. He especially could be such good company. But I did like George. He seemed shy and was funny but always polite and gentlemanly. I was wary as he had a reputation for being something of a womaniser, but I hoped that could have been mostly press stories. One night we were about to leave a club and he casually asked me back to his flat. By now I had gotten to know him quite well and agreed. It was a time when he was just about to have a book published and a moment later I overheard him talking to a group of friends. They were roaring with laughter and asking if the story of the boys watching out of the bedroom cupboard was going to be in there. I didn't quite know what that was about but it made me nervous. If that was the tone of things, I was keeping away. I made my excuses and got a cab home. Some friends thought I was mad not to jump at the chance of a night with George Best. But real life was not quite like that. The constant attention from fans and media had battered him. I think he was tired of it and also quite lonely. I was beginning to see what that level of fame could do to some people. But we kept in touch for quite a while. I always liked him and was sad to see how increasingly troubled he was.

In 1977 a friend and fellow 'beauty queen' invited me on a blind date with her and her husband and a man called Bob Manoukian. It turned out that he was a multimillionaire and her husband's brother. We met at his enormous house on Cheyne Walk, Chelsea. I was stunned by the vast rooms filled with paintings and antiques. Bob had started out selling Christmas trees and then moved onto cars and then houses. He was only in his late twenties and had started from nothing. I admired him. We started to see each other regularly. He would pick me up at the flat near Olympia in a blue Rolls-Royce. I wouldn't have known, but my friends told me that each time it was a different model of Rolls. He had a fleet of them, all in sea blue. He was happy for me to stay at his house when he was away but each time it led to some kind of drama. Several times I set off the alarms accidentally. The worst incident was when the toilet broke and water began pouring out of the cistern and all over the floor. I was terrified that it would ruin the antiques in the rooms below. Pulling off the cistern lid I spent the evening with a toothbrush holder bailing the water into the toilet.

Bob Manoukian owned some garages behind Harrods where he kept all his cars. He also had two mews houses there which he was having refurbished.

One was for his mother and the other he offered to my

mum to stay in or live in if she wanted. He had just bought a colossal house in Cadogan Square and was suggesting to me that this could be our new home. I remember wondering at the time if this was really what the future held for me. I had stumbled into an existence of luxury and wealth that I simply had not been looking for. I began to feel more panic than excitement.

It had been decided that I would go with Bob to France and we were to stay at the Majestic Hotel in Cannes. But before this I would take my mother on a two-week holiday to Greece. It was one of the many prizes I was given as Miss Great Britain. As the coach pulled into the Pontinental Club in Loutraki a band was playing to welcome the new arrivals. When the music finished the keyboard player came up to me and introduced himself. His name was Takis and with his blue eyes and jet-black hair he was very handsome. He insisted on taking us to our holiday bungalow and showing us around and it was pretty clear he was interested in me. He made a point of being very charming to my mother, too. Over the next few days we saw each other often. One night, after Mum had gone to bed we met up on the beach. I had no idea that the *News of the World* had sent photographers out to follow me. They gave the front page over to photographs of Takis and me kissing by the sea with the headline 'Miss Great Britain Falls in Love with Penniless Greek'. I returned home the day after this announcement and Bob was not particularly amused.

The holiday in Cannes was cancelled.

I remained based at my mother's, now in Little Neston on the Wirral. Three months later, Takis moved in too. Most of the money I had earned had been spent, shared with family and friends. We had just enjoyed it. My husband Bob May and I had divorced amicably and as I had been making a good living I had been happy to sign our house over to him. Suddenly there was not much coming in. I borrowed enough from his mother as a deposit for a small house in Little Neston. Takis was determined to carry on trying to make a success with his music. I knew Lynda McMurray, a well-known local singer, and together they formed a new band. I was enjoying a quieter life and had dreams of opening a hair salon somewhere near home. Really, I just wanted to start a family. But money was short and Takis and my mother were trying to persuade me to go back to the television work I had been doing. I had been working on a show called *It's a Knockout* with co-presenters Eddie Waring and Stuart Hall. I agreed to go back to that. I also continued to model for Honda. The fees they paid were very generous and they had given me the title of 'Miss Honda'. Over several years I became the face that went with the name and was pictured with everything from the little run-around mopeds to the huge touring Goldwing.

I had got to know the sales team well and it had all become very enjoyable. The displays and presentations were amazingly imaginative and lavish and I was booked to appear at shows up and down the country. Honda were riding the crest of a huge wave of success and I was very lucky to be part of it for a while. I remember it as all laughter and champagne during the day and pints of lager after the shows. Eric Sulley was the sales director, and the managing director of Honda UK, Kay Shimizu, would be at the most prestigious events. Together with a field manager or area manager I would appear on the stage. They would do most of the talking about the motorbike and I would do most of the dancing and posing.

It was good teamwork and the atmosphere was always so cheerful. Some names I remember – Ian Catford, Gerald Davidson, Harry Harper, Mike and Peter Shaw, Reggie Gilbert, Joe Ritson – and many faces, too, from the press cuttings I kept from those heady days.

The TT (Tourist Trophy) races on the Isle of Man were always the highlight of the year. Of course, I was not competing but I would often do laps, sometimes at absurd speed, on the back of the champions' bikes. The first time I hadn't yet realised that the route had been closed to other traffic so hurtling into blind corners on the wrong side of the road was more than terrifying. But once that little misunderstanding was out of the way I grew quite addicted to the excitement of it all. Oulton Park Circuit near Manchester was often the venue for race meetings and of course publicity pictures. The top riders of the day such as Barry Sheene and Bill Smith were usually there. It was Bill Smith who took me on a near full-speed lap round the track. Even in the rather lackadaisical 1970s that was seen as crazy behaviour. He ignored the marshals' shouting and waving of flags and just laid the bike flat into the next corner. It was fantastic. But he did get quite a severe ticking off afterwards.

In 1979, two years after getting married, our first son, Daniel, arrived. Takis was still struggling to find work as a musician so I was soon back to modelling. I never felt happy about signing any long-term contract with an agency and with my mother always sending out my photographs and tear sheets and generally promoting me, that never became a problem. Cecil did the same and work kept on coming. When he mentioned a part in a television series I was excited and rushed off to London to meet him for dinner at Trattoo.

CHAPTER THREE

GETTING TO KNOW MICHAEL

TWO FRIENDS IN PALACE MANSIONS were peering out of the window and pointing down at a little blue open-topped Mercedes sports car in the street below. The man in the car was shouting into his mobile telephone. In those days this was more like a military radio with its 1940s-style handset and a curly lead which disappeared into a large black plastic suitcase. 'I'M WAITING OUTSIDE IN MY CAR, I'M WAITING OUTSIDE IN MY CAR, WHERE ARE YOU, WHERE ARE YOU?' Michael Winner was about to start casting for his new film and I had accepted an invitation to dinner. When I got to the car he bundled all the radio telephone equipment onto the back seat to make room for me in the front. The sports car didn't really seem to fit him particularly well. It was as though he had borrowed his wife's car. I knew he wasn't married and had heard various rumours that he was gay. As I looked at him now, that seemed quite possibly true. He was in good spirits and we sped off into oncoming traffic. We were surrounded suddenly by idiot drivers and the open car made it easy for him to point this out to them all very clearly.

Fortunately the restaurant he had chosen was only a few streets away.

What Cecil had told him about my fondness for scampi had clearly been remembered. We were seated in a fish restaurant and he was immediately making fun of what he regarded as 'northern' eating traditions. Michael was handed the wine list and after a few moments he pointed to the white wine at the bottom of the page. The waiter looked a little startled at this choice and stepped slowly away from the table. Then he turned and, giving a rather embarrassed cough, he leant over and whispered to Michael that the Sauternes he had chosen was more often served with dessert. 'Oh, the next one up then,' he said and the waiter nodded, more out of relief than approval, and rushed off. We both laughed and Michael admitted he knew nothing about wine. He told me he often just picked the one at the bottom of the list as, being the most expensive, he assumed that simply meant 'best'.

There had not been much talk of films or acting or even his next project. We were either laughing at my accent or he was telling me of his close friendships with some of the biggest stars of the day. He didn't invite me back to the house 'for coffee' or anything like that. Instead he just drove into his garage and pressed a red button to make the metal doors rattle closed behind us. He told me he really wanted to show me 'the best house in London'. I learnt later that he had lived there as a child when it was divided into flats. He had gradually bought them all and now owned the whole thing. With great pride he pushed open door after door to show me the many, rather gloomy, rooms.

The only exceptions were the living and dining rooms, which had recently been redecorated by Tessa Kennedy in pinks and creams.

'So, what do you think?' he asked as we arrived back in the lounge and found the coffee that the housekeeper had just made for us.

'Too much brown and cream for me,' I told him quickly. He looked confused.

'You don't like the coffee?'

'No, the house. Way too much brown. And you must hate not having a decent bathroom,' I went on. I realise now he had expected me to be very impressed. Stunned, even. But it was him, I think, who was stunned. His readiness to laugh at himself as well as at me had made me feel comfortable enough to be very straightforward with him and be myself. I noticed his slightly perplexed expression.

'It's OK,' I reassured him. 'It'll be fine, you can just get some nicer-coloured paint and put it on.' He had just taken a sip from his cup and when I said that he froze for a split second in a look of panic, his cheeks bulging. Then he exploded, spraying a mist of coffee across the table. He shook with laughter and I was not exactly sure why. We were very different people and we had only just met.

The next subject he wanted to talk about was my 'bosoms', as he called them.

Now it was my turn to be stunned by his straight talking, which was somehow both funny and ridiculous. He had got it into his head that I would take off my top when he asked me to. It seemed a genuine surprise to him when I told him that was not going to happen. Oddly, I did not feel threatened, or insulted, even. He seemed neither lecherous nor seductive.

Maybe it was the general absurdity of the whole situation. He seemed more like a small boy asking for some kind of treat. It was almost as though he was saying 'Please may I have some sweets now?' or something like that. Again there was a lot of laughter, but he wasn't giving up. He went off and returned with a blue jacket that had come from the Beverly Hills Hotel. Having told me how rare and valuable it was, he went on and on saying he wanted to take a picture of me wearing it without my shirt. Eventually, just to get him to quieten down and stop jumping about, I went out to the loo and put it on. He took a few Polaroids but of course he then tried to persuade me to take the jacket off. I kept refusing and eventually he gave up and said I could keep it.

That was the first time I set foot in his Holland Park home. Having seen his driving, I would rather have walked round the corner to my flat in Palace Mansions but he insisted on taking me by sports car. I didn't really expect to hear from him again. And he might very easily have been killed on his journey home.

It was three months before Michael called again. This time it actually was about an acting role. His next film, *Wicked Lady*, was in production and he told me there would be a small part in it for me. By then I had landed a role in the

Channel 4 comedy series *The Optimist* and was focusing on preparations for that. But *Wicked Lady* was to be made first. The location was Baslow, near Bakewell in Derbyshire. I was met at the station by the chauffeur in Michael's Rolls-Royce Phantom. On arrival at the hotel I discovered that he had not booked me a room. His plan was simply that I would be in with him. I had to make quite a scene before I was found a room of my own. In my short career I had seen a few things but not quite this kind of behaviour. Even with the added fact that he knew I was married to Takis he still seemed amazed at my resistance and I could only think that here was someone who took it absolutely for granted that he would always get his own way.

I had not worked on a film drama before and so the next few days were a great education for me, and enjoyable too. My part was rather small. I was the wife of Lord Marwood, played by Dermot Walsh. The other big names in the cast, who were there for those few days, were Denholm Elliott, Faye Dunaway, Alan Bates and Glynis Barber. The famous photographer Terry O'Neill was doing the stills. I had worked with Glynis Barber before on *Blake's 7*, a science-fiction series for television that became quite a cult show. She was very talented and professional and easy to get on with and we had great fun. I was only in one episode but Glynis was in lots and went on to star in *EastEnders* and *Dempsey and Makepeace*. I did not expect to see much of Michael or any of them as I knew it was rare on a film set for the stars or director to mix with the rest of the cast and crew.

However, Michael had other plans and made a point of introducing me to everyone. He always added that I was Miss Great Britain, which embarrassed and irritated me. I had respect for actors and their skills and felt that being intro-duced as a beauty queen would not help my chances of being taken even a little seriously. But I didn't exactly improve those chances myself over dinner the first evening. Michael, Alan Bates, Denholm Elliott and Dermot Walsh were asking each other what their favourite films were. I heard titles such as *The Third Man*, *Citizen Kane* and, I think, *Vertigo* being put forward.

I'm not sure I had seen any of them at the time. But then one of them turned and asked me the same question. I felt myself going a bit pink. I was aware I was not quite as knowl-edgeable as them on this subject, but summoning up all the confidence I could, I said quite seriously, 'Well, I think *Towering Inferno*, it's got everything.' There was a pause as their eyes widened. Then they all sagged with laughter. I would happily have forgotten those few minutes, but I was to hear Michael telling that story quite regularly in the future. That became doubly annoying when he had later confessed that *his* favourite films were really the cheerful and light-hearted ones with happy endings. He also really liked Walt Disney and espe-cially the Bambi movie.

On set, I saw for the first time how Michael worked and how he got on with people. He was confident and often very impatient with the crew and more lowly cast members. He seemed very clear about what he wanted and with the big-ger names he could turn on the charm and even be tactful. Alan Bates was often flirtatious with any women who were around, but I always found him easy-going and cheerful. Den-holm Elliott was altogether more quiet and thoughtful but also very charming. It was Faye Dunaway that Michael strug-gled with sometimes, I think. Perhaps she was goading him, but she could get away with contradicting him on set and he would be attentive and considerate and very polite at all times. But I don't think he enjoyed being diplomatic at all. He could just about manage it and knew when he had to. I saw later that the more he had to bite his lip in any situation, the more dangerous it was to be around him. The pressure would build up and he would explode at someone. Sometimes there would not even be an identifiable reason. Pin or no pin, the balloon was going to burst. I never got used to that side of him and I can't pretend, even after all these years, to really understand where it came from. Those explosions could be anything from the small and quickly forgotten to the huge and utterly devastating.

My first experience of this kind of behaviour was as we were leaving to drive back to the hotel in his Rolls. It was pouring with rain and I noticed Glynis Barber holding up her dresses, as she was still in costume, and tramping down the muddy track. 'Get the chauffeur to stop,' I said, pointing her out to Michael.

'Fuck her,' he screamed and launched into a stream of unrepeatable language. Unusually, this was not directed at me or her but was just an explosion of temper. That turned out to be quite a gentle introduction to what he could be like, but I found it very shocking. There was something or other he said she had done which had annoyed him, but nothing that could begin to explain that kind of outburst.

A bit later, on the same film, there was another little explosion. This time it was more typical of what I was to see many times. It was not the anger that most worried me; it was his need to humiliate and belittle people that was most disturbing. Occasionally the incidents could appear quite funny afterwards. But not at the time. I had suggested John May, my flatmate and ex-husband's brother, for a small part in the film. He was an aspiring young actor and I'm sure Michael only hired him when he heard he had recently been working with the Royal Shakespeare Company. Michael cast him as the village idiot. In one scene John had to peer into a barn through a double door and spy on a couple in the hay. This involved opening a door with his right hand and closing another with his left in a very specific movement. It was not a help that John had always suffered a little with dyslexia. He was getting his left and right hand confused. Michael, holding his head in his hands and groaning, was not helping John to keep calm and focused.

By the fifth or sixth take, all the cast and crew had seen the growing tension and, from his tall director's chair, Michael yelled, 'CUT'. John froze and everyone was silent. 'Mr May,' he said, his voice growing louder. 'Mr May, you have worked with the Royal Shakespeare Company. YOU HAVE WORKED WITH THE ROYAL SHAKESPEARE COMPANY AND YOU CAN'T EVEN OPEN A FUCKING DOOR. YOU ARE A FUCK-ING IDIOT AND AN INCOMPETENT C***.' That may not have helped settle John's nerves, but the take was achieved eventually. The next scene was two peasants and John the Village Idiot chasing the girl from the barn. John was still seething from being ridiculed in front of everyone, although they were probably just relieved it had not been them. Still in his high director's chair, Michael gave out instructions. 'Right, you three fuckers, when I give the word I want you to run in the order I tell you to run. Is that perfectly clear?' A little later when everything was ready he barked, 'ACTION.' The two peasants ran off and John stayed motionless. 'CUT,' yelled

Michael, his face reddening. 'Mr May, you are a Shakespear-ean actor, A FUCKING SHAKESPEAREAN ACTOR, CAN'T YOU EVEN FUCKING RUN?'

'Yes, Mr Winner,' said John. 'I can run but you haven't told me which fucker I am. If you tell me whether I am fucker number one, fucker number two, or fucker number three then I'll know when to fucking run.'

Just then, a voice from the side said, 'Quite right, dear boy.' John Gielgud, who was also in the film, had been watch-ing from the shadows. Lucky for John, I think, as he may have got another roasting. It was never easy to know with Michael. Generally, if anyone so much as tried to speak dur-ing one of his tirades he would just increase the volume and even fire them. Just occasionally he would quieten down if someone was justified in putting their case, or had just the right comic tone.

It was while working on *Wicked Lady* that I first saw Cath-erine Neilson, a strikingly beautiful actress. I learnt then that she had been Michael's girlfriend for some time. When he arrived at the premiere of the film, Catherine was on his arm. John May and I were invited to the screening but not to the drinks party beforehand. However, Jean and Cecil Korer were there and, seeing us standing outside the VIP area, they ush-ered us in. We had hardly picked up a drink when we were spotted by Michael and Catherine.

Neither of them looked at all pleased to see us. I sipped at my glass of champagne a little sheepishly but very soon they appeared at my elbow.

'What the fuck are you two doing here?' he half shouted. And then told us quite simply to get out.

I was soon packing and getting ready to fly to Los Angeles

to start work on *The Optimist*. Originally I had been cast as a posh lady with a pet poodle.

This would have been quite a challenging role considering my background and character. I think the casting director then saw the Honda publicity shots in which I was either dancing on the back of a large motorbike in a bikini or posing in close-fitting leathers. I was recast as a racing driver. This meant that it would be useful if I knew how to drive a racing car. Arrangements were made quickly and I rushed off to the Formula Two circuit at Aintree. I had driven fast cars before and enjoyed it, and thought my days hurtling up and down the country in a draughty little Spitfire would pay off now. Maybe they did, but there was really no comparison. Having slid down inside the car, I seemed to be sitting only an inch off the tarmac. After a rather brief lesson the instructor jumped into another car and said, 'Follow my track.' Off we went, very fast at first but then faster and faster and faster and faster and when it was impossible to imagine that you could go any faster we went still faster. I remember the smell. The smell and the concentration. Pure concentration and pure joy. That was such a beautiful day.

Now, I was feeling a bit guilty about how excited I was to be going to America.

I had been apprehensive before and knew how much I would miss my little son Daniel, who was now three. I knew he would be safe with my mother, but I had to be away for a few weeks and that was going to be very hard. Takis was in London in a band and the distances between us all were unsettling. I consoled myself with the fact that we needed the income.

I arrived in Marina del Rey, Los Angeles. It was not at all like Little Neston.

It was not at all like anywhere I had ever been before. I was amazed by everything but there was not much time to go exploring. When I did have a day off from filming I skipped out of the hotel to take a look around. Almost immediately I felt a hand on my shoulder. A security guard dressed in black and with a gun at his hip told me that I was mad to think of walking about the area on my own. I realised I was not going to get to see much of Los Angeles so resigned myself to staying near the hotel pool on my free day. I got chatting to a friendly couple and they offered me a cookie. 'Space cookies', they called them. They were very nice and I ate quite a few. I remember feeling slightly dizzy and then being vaguely aware of two hotel porters carrying me to my room. My naivety had lost me my only day off but by call time the next morning I had regained consciousness and it was back to work.

The episode of *The Optimist* that we were filming was called 'Burning Rubber'.

And that was mostly what I did for those few weeks. But they were more like go-karts than racing cars. It was strange, as there was no dialogue and so no script to learn. It was made in a kind of silent movie style and I really enjoyed it. The star of the series was Enn Reitel and the man playing opposite me was an actor called Robert Davi. I found him a little bit arrogant. Several times he assured me he would be very famous one day. It turned out that he was right about that. It wasn't many years before he appeared as the villain in *Licence to Kill*, and he has continued to find big success in high-profile roles.

My acting career was to move on, too. Soon after getting home I was offered a part in the then very popular soap opera *Brookside*. I was very happy I only had to get to Liverpool for work, as it meant I could be back home each evening. Takis was often in London but my mother was nearby and looked after Daniel whenever needed.

Throughout this time Michael had started calling me up regularly and we would have long conversations. He would happily talk through all the minute details of his life. He was ringing almost daily. While I was auditioning for *Brookside* I noticed they were impressed that I had appeared in *Wicked Lady*, however briefly, and there was great interest in any stories I had about Michael. It's very likely that's why they gave me the part. I was to play Samantha Davies. Dicken Ashworth was Alan Partridge, whom I ditched at the altar but then later married – in the series, that is! Paul Usher, Sue Johnston and Ricky Tomlinson were the main stars of the show. It was a happy family and everyone was welcoming and helpful. With no formal training, the only thing I could say I was getting quite used to was the feeling of being out of my depth.

Sue Johnston was a great lady. I had so many questions and insecurities and she would give me all manner of help and advice. Some actors might have done the opposite and just watched me make a fool of myself. But with her help I could start to feel more confident and that was so vital to me at the time. *Brookside* had been conceived by Phil Redmond, who had also devised *Grange Hill* and then later, in 1995, *Hollyoaks*. He directed me himself in quite a few scenes and he was demanding but I enjoyed it and learnt a lot.

Michael was often asking when I would next be in London but with work on *Brookside* there wasn't often the time. He had nicknamed me 'the Wicked Witch of the North' because he said he found me forthright and difficult, presumably because I didn't kowtow to his demands. But I did manage sometimes to make the journey and it was on one of those London trips that I had first met Charles Bronson and his wife Jill Ireland. Another time, Michael said he was going to a cocktail party at 10 Downing Street and asked whether I would like to go too. When we arrived, Michael introduced me to Kenny Everett, a huge star in comedy at the time, Lynsey de Paul, the singer-songwriter, and then Margaret Thatcher herself. I was very surprised by how friendly she was and she fascinated me immediately. I remember asking her if, as Prime Minister, she was finished for the day or always felt she was working. She said she was leaving for Germany in an hour and often didn't even have time for sleep and went on to say how she had found a way to keep going by having a nap for a few minutes when possible. She made quite an impression on me.

When I caught up with Michael a bit later I found that he and Kenny Everett were giggling and trying to persuade Lynsey de Paul to fill her handbag with the silver cutlery. Maggie was the first to leave and, as you might imagine with someone like Kenny around, things just got sillier and sillier. We were nearly the last people to go and just before we walked out Kenny whispered to me that he was going to pretend to be horribly drunk. He said to get ready to catch him when he collapsed. Sure enough, when that big black door opened, he staggered out, head rolling from side to side, his tongue hanging out of the side of his mouth. Then he stopped, swaying gently to the clicking and blapping of the press cameras, before toppling over backwards.

Fortunately he had warned me and he fell into my arms. I managed to keep hold of him as the cameras moved in and the next day he was in all the papers.

On *Brookside* I also met Diana Morgan. She was in the PR

department and responsible for press reports and publicity. Apparently my first words to her were, 'Oh dear, you've put your blusher on all wrong, can I have a go?' I had a habit of saying things before taking a moment for editing. She must have realised that I was not trying to be unkind and didn't slap me across the face. Instead we quickly became firm friends. But I must have had a point, as after that, if we were going out, she would often ask me to help her with hair and make-up. It was just something I had become quite good at. Most of the cast would try to avoid the press calls and publicity events, which was understandable but could make her job rather difficult. Through modelling work I had grown quite used to all that kind of thing and was happy to be there when needed, so I had soon got to know Diana well. *Brookside* days were often long, as they would start at five when I dropped Daniel off with my mother. Sometimes I would not be home until eight or nine and I would still have to go through the script ready for the next day. I did that for about a year and a half. Good times, but pretty tiring too.

When my part in *Brookside* ended, so did our income. As well as doing his music, Takis had been working during the week in a clothes shop in London. That stopped too at about the same time. I had stayed friends with my ex-husband Bob and he and Takis also got on well. Bob had been in various bands and when he formed a new one, the Point, with his brother Peter, they asked Takis to join them on keyboards. There were two singers, Josie and Debbie. In September 1985, Radio City, a local radio station, chose them to represent Liverpool in a competition held in Helsinki. I went with them as their manager. The Fine Young Cannibals won first prize. The Point got second place.

As manager, I was now back to making frequent trips to London. My friends had moved on from the flat in Palace Mansions so I would stay on any settee I could find. I booked as many London gigs for the band as I could but that meant we needed places to stay. Often it was sofas or cushions on the floor somewhere. Years before, through my work with Honda on the Isle of Man, I had met someone called James Lane. He was a man of great wealth and very kind too, but romantically I had felt it was not going to take off. We remained friends and we still meet up now and then. The girls in the band and I would often stay at his magnificent flat in Knightsbridge and leave the men to slum it. They seemed happy to be more rock 'n' roll in a smoky basement somewhere.

It was about this time that I first met Jenny Seagrove. My agent had got me a casting for a Hammer House of Horror production called *Mark of the Devil*. I so wanted to find a way into more serious and challenging acting roles. I was cast as 'sexy blonde'. Not quite what I was hoping for but it was something. A name would have been nice. Jenny Seagrove and Dirk Benedict played the leads. One of Dirk's most famous roles was as Faceman in *The A-Team*. My son Daniel had become a big *A-Team* fan so it was nice to be able to get his autograph for him. I forget what was said when I first met Jenny. It was really just a hello. But I do remember that my dressing room was next to hers and I overheard her talking about her forthcoming marriage. She seemed rather unsure about it and I felt guilty that I could hear some of her conversations. In fact, if I stayed quiet I found I could hear every word. I was able to confess all this to her a few years later and I'm pretty sure that she forgave me.

Michael said there was a part for me in the film *Claudia*. At the time it was to be called *Claudia's Story* and he was only directing some additional scenes. I was to be the hostess of a party. He said he would pick me up from his house at four and take me to the film set. This was a bit surprising as he was filming next to Leighton House, a three-minute walk away. When he arrived he went straight to get a bottle of champagne. I imagined that was for the party scene.

He opened it and poured two large glasses. That was very unusual as he hardly ever had a drink apart from wine at dinner and I had never seen him drink when he was working. We had soon drunk more than half the bottle.

The rest he poured into a flask to take with us. His cheeks were flushed and he seemed very jolly and even slightly tipsy as the chauffeur drove us the hundred yards to the set. The party scene involved a little more drinking but was soon over. Michael had said he would take me to dinner that evening and so we went back to his house. He then wanted to show me around again, which was also odd as nothing much had changed since the first time I had been. When we got to his bedroom he went and sat at his desk in the bay window and I looked out at the garden. That was when he first asked me to marry him. He did not go down on one knee or anything like that. It was quite matter-of-fact but he did say he loved me. I reminded him that I already had a husband and that we also had a son and I loved them both. As I watched the trees outside rustling and waving in the wind he went into a long speech. He explained why I would be foolish to refuse and talked about a life of luxury, the famous and wealthy people I would meet, the places he could take me and the financial security I would have. All I could do was repeat the fact that I was actually married already. Michael told me that a divorce could be arranged and he seemed disappointed that I clearly did not quite have the imagination or intelligence to understand what he was offering. Over dinner he continued to try to help me to understand what a mistake I was making until eventually I got a bit irritated. I had already told him clearly that I enjoyed his company and really appreciated him as a friend. I kept saying that but because he just wouldn't let it go I did eventually go on to tell him that his temper frightened me. I was not quite sure how Michael might react to that comment but the conversation turned at last and he seemed happy to shrug his shoulders and forget his mission. I was relieved when the laughter returned.

He continued to call as often as before and showed no sign of being hurt or angry with me. Instead he would occasionally taunt me if I was having any problems at home or needed money for something. He would enjoy reminding me that it was my choice and I'd better just get on with it. Not long after, knowing I was in London, he invited me for dinner. I arrived at the house at the appointed time and was shown into the hall by the receptionist.

Before she could announce my arrival I was shocked by Michael bellowing from the top of the stairs. 'WHO THE FUCK IS THAT? YOU ARE TOO FUCKING LATE. THE AUDITIONS ARE OVER. DO YOU UNDERSTAND? FINISHED. FINISHED.'

For a moment I was stunned. And I thought he was sending me packing. 'It's me, Dinah,' I called back, a bit apprehensively. 'And you told me six-thirty.'

There was silence. Then I heard laughter and the stomp, stomp, stomp of feet as he ran down the top flight of stairs.

'Ah the Wicked Witch of the North, come up, come up darling, leave your broomstick by the door.' I was very glad I was not an actor arriving late.

He had been auditioning for *Death Wish III*. I was to have a small part in the film as a nurse, and the scenes in which I appeared took place in Lambeth Hospital. During lunch on the first day the caterers had set up a table in a shabby, but, in earlier times, probably very grand, room with high ceilings. There were thick, starched double damask tablecloths and the waiter was lifting the silver domes to reveal an amazing spread of food. But Michael was finding things to complain about loudly and sprinkling his sentences with obscenities. I noticed Charles Bronson, always the archetypal gentleman, seemed to be grinding his teeth. Then, taking his wife Jill Ireland's elbow, they both stood up. He turned to me and said, 'Dinah, please come with us.'

Michael looked confused. Charlie told him calmly that his language was foul and totally inappropriate when there were ladies present. As he led us to the door he went on to say that we would not be returning until he had made a full apology. The situation was already awkward for me and made worse when Michael's first reaction was to bark at me to sit back at the table. But Charlie was not having it and we all left. We had not gone far before Michael caught us up. He was red faced and stuttering and addressing Charlie as 'sir'.

He went on to offer a very full apology to both Jill and myself and looked very relieved when Charlie said, 'Ladies, are you happy to return to the table?' Lunch was resumed and the tension in the air soon evaporated. Later that afternoon a scene involved Charlie carrying a heavy gun and running quite a distance along a street in pouring rain. Michael kept calling for another take and I wondered if he might just be trying to get his own back.

I always had great respect for Charlie. Jill and I always got on very well too and, knowing that, Michael often asked me to join him if he was taking them to dinner. One evening we had gone to the club Tramp, and after the meal Charlie and Jill and I would get up occasionally to dance. Michael was sat tight in his chair and made it clear that dancing was not something he did. After a while Charlie went up to him and, gesturing to me, said, 'Get up, Michael, the lady would like to dance.' Poor Michael, he did get up and we shuffled around together, with him muttering his unhappiness under his breath. It was many years before I saw him obliged to dance again. In 2005 at Julie Cowell's birthday at the Savoy, Philip Green insisted he got up onto the dance floor.

He was between girlfriends and I found myself his partner once again as reluctantly he showed his moves. But he did manage a smile.

These were strange times, as I was still struggling to promote the band, and my income from acting was erratic to say the least. There was only just enough to put food on the table and it felt strange then to sometimes find myself in one of London's finest restaurants. I remember going to a place in Mayfair, a restaurant and club called Les Ambassadeurs, again with Jill and Charlie, and we ate in the beautiful conservatory there. It was a fantastic night out but the bill came to nearly £4,000. I had to bury the thought that just a quarter of that would have kept the family for months.

The set for *Death Wish III* was vast and very impressive. It had been built in south London to look like a street in America. My friend Diana from my *Brookside* days was interested to see it and Michael said I could bring her to watch when the days filming were nearly over. Before we found him she had discovered his tall director's chair and climbed up into it. She was enjoying herself, calling out 'Action!' and 'Cut!', and I winced when I saw Michael appear. I knew him well enough now to never quite know what to expect.

Luckily he was chuckling to himself. 'If you want action,' he said, 'I'll show you some action.' There were a few of the crew around and they were setting up a tracking shot. When it was ready he let Diana play at being a tyrannical director. On her command the camera zoomed off silently on the metal rails. She shouted and waved her arms and generally impersonated Michael as everyone fell about giggling and laughing.

*　*　*

Michael was flying to Los Angeles early in the New Year of 1986 to attend various production meetings and arrange finances for his next film.

He asked me to go as his assistant. My eyes must have widened as I pictured paperwork and complicated business talk. I mentioned my doubts but Michael was quick to reassure me. 'No, no, other people do all that. I want you to be like you are, dear. You know, tell me when my armpits stink and help with my bags, that kind of thing – and you are Miss Great Britain, darling, you can do anything. Well, surely you can write down a fucking phone number, anyway.'

Before the trip he would have his usual Christmas holiday in Barbados. Michael had been seeing the actress Stephanie Pitt, but by the time he was arranging the trip to Sandy Lane his new girlfriend was Lorraine Doyle. She could not stay for

the whole holiday as she had to be back early to continue filming with Benny Hill. Rather than meet in LA as planned, he
said if I wanted a few days in Barbados first I could come for
the New Year. In all honesty, my first thought was that it was
an opportunity to get a slight tan. I did not like the thought
of being white from an English winter when I arrived in Los
Angeles. But even more importantly I saw an opportunity to
spend a lot of time in the sea. As a small child I had discovered
that one of my greatest pleasures was being in water. You could
almost say it was a need rather than a treat. My mother was
very patient with this peculiarity. Many times she would wait in
the car with my clothes and my brother while I swam about
in some water I had spotted. Often it was the beach we passed
near Anglesey when Desmond drove us to Gran's. It could be
summer or winter, day or night. When I think back it seems
crazy. I would return, sometimes out of the darkness, often blue
with cold, but very happy. She knew just how much I loved it.

After a family Christmas I didn't really want to go anywhere. I knew I had to and luckily my mother shook some
sense into me. She realised the week in Hollywood was important and could lead to anything. Arriving in Barbados, I got
a cab to the Coral Reef Club, where Rita Tushingham and
her husband Ousama Rawi greeted me as planned, and we
sat drinking cocktails in the warm evening. Michael turned
up in an open jeep, which he called 'the beach buggy'. Sandy
Lane was just a mile away.

Even in the darkness you could feel the magical beauty of
the place. In the morning I was stunned. This was a tropical
paradise beyond anything I had imagined. There was a great
calmness too. Even the pale blue sea was restful, flopping
lazily now and then on the smooth white sand.

'Where's my bag? WHERE'S MY BAG? DINAH!' Michael was calling from his room as I sat waiting on the terrace. He had gathered his essential knick-knacks into a hotel laundry bag and was getting ready to take me to see his friend's house somewhere along the beach. 'It's here by the chair,' I called back. Reaching down, I peered into the small and slightly stained cotton sack. In one corner was a comb, a screwed-up handkerchief and various tubes of ointment. Nearby was a compact camera with more sand on it than I would have been comfortable with. In the other corner was extra sand.

'Why do you carry so much sand?' I asked when Michael appeared. 'It looks like there is plenty around if you needed some urgently.'

'Oh, you are really fucking funny,' he said, sitting down at the white painted table. 'Well, empty it out. But mind the camera, my camera's in there.'

I picked out the gold-coloured compact. It had even more sand on it than I had first realised. 'I think we should clean this and find something else to put it in,' I said, holding it up for him to see.

'It's fine, it's fine, it's a fucking Leica.' He was getting impatient and I sensed we would soon be on the move.

As I emptied the bag and began wiping and shaking each item, Michael marched off along the terrace and down towards the beach. When I caught up with him I held out the bag but he wouldn't take it. 'Oh, you carry it, darling,' he said. It was a conspicuously grubby-looking bundle in the beauty of the gardens of Sandy Lane. I explained that I had made a point of bringing nothing so I was free to run in and out of the sea. 'Just keep hold of it,' he snapped. 'Every girlfriend I have ever brought here has carried the bag.'

'Maybe, but not a dirty laundry bag and anyway I'm not your girlfriend,' I reminded him.

As we made our way onto the white sand beach, the bickering continued. I pointed out that the bag a girlfriend of his might carry would be beautiful and have a Chanel logo or something on it too. And what worried me most was being introduced to people as I clutched this grey knobbly sack. 'Yes, well, it does look a bit like a camel's scrotum,' he admitted. 'But no one cares, darling, no one cares, just carry the fucking thing.'

But I was not giving up. 'Yes, well, it's OK for you. It's OK for you to look any way you want. Smart or scruffy or nuts. You are Michael Winner.' That little sideways compliment did it and he snatched it from me. I was free of it for now, but he would soon be using the story to illustrate what a difficult and ungrateful woman he thought I could be.

He was walking briskly, and after the bag episode I dared not ask if I could have a quick swim. I was trotting to keep up with him. He pointed to distant deckchairs and named their famous occupants. 'That's Bob Monkhouse; look, there's Cilla Black.' Some people I had never heard of, so he would tell me what they did or owned or which company they ran. There were producers, musicians, studio owners and people from all walks of life. But all were the most famous, the most talented, the most successful in their field. Michael was in paradise. It was not so much the place, but who was around – and who he might discover. Who he might meet. 'Good morning, Albert,' he said as we approached Albert Finney. We stopped and Michael introduced me. We were to meet up again later. Albert had a sort of wisdom and kindness and I always felt very happy sitting and chatting and smoking a few cigarettes with him.

'Here we are.' Michael had stopped suddenly and pushed through what looked like a leafy hedge and I thought he was going into some kind of plantation. But within a few steps we heard splashing and children screaming and through the foliage came upon a large azure-blue pool. John Cleese was sitting on the edge cooling his feet and people of all ages were wandering about or jumping into the water. We sat in the shade and chatted with John and his wife, Barbara Trentham, and cool drinks appeared as if from nowhere.

Kevin Kline and Phoebe Cates were there too. The children were having a great time and I joined in with them. The youngest was Camilla, who must have been about two. We played a good game of peep-bo in a heap of colourful towels. I wished little Daniel could have been there.

Before long we were off again and at last I managed to get into the crystal-blue sea. When I emerged and walked towards Michael and the sun loungers I thought I saw a face I recognised. 'Is that Jack Lord from *Hawaii Five-0*?' I said casually as I picked up a towel.

'Where what where?' he said, his neck stretching up and his head darting from side to side as he scanned the beach.

He looked for a second like Rod Hull's Emu. I pointed. 'Look, over there, he's too far away now. It might be him going into the hotel, I'm not sure.'

But Michael was off before I could finish the sentence. I didn't know he could run so fast. He returned a few minutes later and stood doubled over, hands on knees as he got his breath back. 'It … aah … it wasn't … aah … it wasn't him,' he panted, disappointedly. I felt a bit mean. Like pretending to throw a stick for an excited retriever.

When we wandered further along the beach we came across

Jon and Jenny Anderson. Jon was lead singer in the band Yes, which rose to fame in the 1970s. They invited us to call and see them after our dinner.

Their house was just a few hundred yards from Sandy Lane. It was not so much grand as warm, ramshackle and homely, with a long wood terrace along the front. I found them such good company and could have stayed all night talking with them and their friends in a sea of glowing candle lamps. They knew Michael very well and Jon had recently worked on the soundtrack for Michael's film *Scream for Help*. In fact, they knew Michael well enough to tell me that I was welcome to drop in any time if I wanted to get away for a while.

His friends saw how he could be tiring, with his constant busy itinerary and the long conversations he would lapse into with people. I could never just wander off, of course, but over the next few days they would find some pretext to give me a short break. Their daughters Deborah and Jade were having their hair plaited with beads one afternoon. It was fascinating and took hours. I really wanted to have a go but Michael was definitely not going to have the patience to let me get involved in anything like that.

The business part of the trip came all too soon. Flying to Los Angeles meant changing planes in Miami and Houston. As we arrived in Miami there were long queues. Michael said simply, 'Stay close and follow me.' With that he put his head down and strode off. We pushed through the waiting passengers and passed barriers and control desks as officials called out for us to stop. When some gave chase we picked up speed. They caught up with us when we arrived at the departure lounge for our connecting flight and, having checked our papers, all was well. Somehow or other he seemed to get away with that kind of thing.

We were joined for breakfast in the Beverly Hills Hotel by Michael's friend Peter Falk. I knew and loved him as *Columbo* and he seemed so much like his famous character. He even wore a slightly crumpled raincoat. Sometimes I would get a strange feeling, as though there had been a terrible murder and he was investigating. But he was a lovely man; very open and friendly and a real pleasure to meet.

Yoram Globus and Menahem Golan, 'The Nosh Brothers' as they were often called, were big names in film production at that time. They had invited Michael to the premiere of *Runaway Train* and we went on to the after-party, where we met many actors, including Jon Voight and Michael York. I was introduced to Shirley MacLaine and was immediately fascinated by her magnificent red hair, and we talked for some time. What I most remember is her infectious laughter. Michael was in LA to get backing for his next film and I was waiting for the real business side of things to begin. The next day he told me we were off to see Lee and Angela Rich. Lee had been a producer of *The Waltons* and also *Dallas* and I knew he had worked with Michael too. I agreed to carry the briefcase. As we drove into Bel Air it felt like we were on the *Dallas* film set. Arriving at their gate I got quite a shock. It was just like a *Dallas* mansion. It took several minutes just to drive from the gate to their house.

The house was vast and luxurious. It could have been a little intimidating but luckily they were charming people. I felt immediately comfortable and they showed us around the house. They had no airs or graces and in many ways it felt just the same as looking over a friend's new bungalow in Neston.

That week we were to have dinner with them several times. Even after Sandy Lane in Barbados I was amazed by how extraordinarily glamorous this world I had stepped into now seemed. I had begun to feel rather underdressed. Michael said I could get something from the hotel boutique. It was quite a shop. I spent most of the afternoon in there, and everything was so amazing it was difficult to choose just one dress.

I spent the next few days either taking phone calls back at the hotel or making notes while in meetings with Michael. All was going well and when it was time to leave he was cheerful. His next film could go ahead.

Back in Little Neston, life was not quite so glamorous. There were auditions to go to and now and then I would land a part in a commercial. I was finding some acting work but they were small roles and I was only earning just enough to feed the family. I was also doing my best to promote the band but it was not proving easy. Really I just wanted to be at home looking after Daniel.

But that was still not looking like an option. Michael knew my situation and began to put forward any names he could think of to try to get the band's music heard. He also offered me a room at the top of his house whenever I needed it as an office or bedroom. He said I could ask his secretary, Val Chamberlain, for help too. Val helped me to organise myself and type the letters correctly. Michael knew how to find the right people and I would then concentrate on how to get them to listen to a demo tape. Things started to move faster and before long I was negotiating a contract with EMI. This in itself was a complicated process, but things were looking good. Then I discovered that there was another baby on its way. With the band very close to being signed by a major record label I thought the timing might actually be good. However, when the lead singer, Josie, announced shortly afterwards that she was expecting twins, well, for the band that was not so good. She told us she was leaving and things quickly started to fall apart.

Michael had made it clear that he thought I was foolish to be having another baby. He said it would seriously curtail my chances of having a busy acting career. I did not tell him that I had thought about that. In fact, I had only waited so long because Takis wanted to concentrate on his music. Daniel was already seven. Michael continued to call me regularly and if I was out and my mother answered he would talk to her for hours. Shelagh, as everyone called her, got on well with him. I overheard her assuring him that once the baby was born she would look after it and I would be free again to work. I was angry. But I couldn't see how else it could be. I was grateful to her as well.

But she and Takis were at home with the children and I was always pushed out to work. I was having some good times, some interesting times, but really I still just wanted to have lots of children and look after them. I had hoped that if the band were signed they would have earned enough to take the pressure off me. But that was now looking increasingly unlikely.

It was a sunny afternoon and I was cooking dinner when someone began thumping on the front door. As I went to answer it I noticed two men were running about in the garden. Opening the door, I was shocked to see three more men and one was holding out a plastic wallet and showing me a small picture of himself. I heard him say he was a policeman but had no idea what was happening. My first thought was that some kind of trouble was going on outside and they had come to warn us or protect us. I wish it had been.

Instead, men in plain clothes ran around the house opening cupboards and rummaging in drawers. They found a dry marijuana plant hanging on the upstairs landing. That was what they had been looking for. Takis had grown it from seed in a big pot in the hall and with all the light from the long window it had grown into a beautiful plant. Takis accompanied the policemen to their station.

Michael was very helpful when he heard the news about the marijuana. But first I had to wait until he controlled his coughing. That amount of laughter would make anyone choke. He knew I was very worried and kept assuring me that it was not a major drama. In my times of worry Michael had a knack for getting me to see the funny side. Sometimes he would be a practical help but more often his help came in the form of giving me a lighter perspective on things. There would be a fine to pay, but not a huge one, he thought. The next time I spoke to him he said he had told his friends what had happened and asked them to guess the amount the penalty might be. The person who was closest would receive a cheque from him for the same amount. As it turned out, two people won the bet: Geoffrey Sebag-Montefiore, who was working for Michael and had been a runner on his last film, and my mother. Both had said £400 and Michael promptly wrote out two cheques. He would not have been at all impressed if he'd known Mum gave the money to Takis to pay the fine. That was the way it often worked with Michael. He would not always be straightforwardly helpful but instead, through various convolutions, it would sometimes just settle out that way. And he told me afterwards that the entertainment he had got from it had been worth every penny.

My second son, Luke, was born in April 1987. A few weeks earlier Michael had asked me how long it would be after having the baby before I could work again. Without really thinking I had said about six weeks. The date on the ticket he sent me was exactly six weeks later. I was to fly to Israel to work on his next film, *Appointment with Death*. I was horrified. I needed the work but I could not imagine being away from my new baby. Not even for a day. Michael wanted me to work for six weeks but I found that unthinkable so eventually it was agreed that I would do two weeks. My mother and my niece Samantha would look after Luke. The film had a star-studded cast: Peter Ustinov, John Gielgud, Piper Laurie, Lauren Bacall, Jenny Seagrove, Hayley Mills, Carrie Fisher and David Soul. It was a remake of the Agatha Christie novel, with Peter Ustinov as Hercule Poirot. Michael wanted me to do the hair. I had trained as a stylist but I did not feel remotely qualified to create the complicated styles of the 1930s. We argued again and I agreed to do the dancers and the extras. Even that seemed impossible. Fortunately, when it came to it, I got on well with the stylists, Stephanie Kaye and Paula Gillespie, and they helped me through it. They were already labouring under a huge workload and often the big names would expect lots of attention, so they were glad of an extra hand. The tension was quite often high and I was very relieved that the focus was not on me.

Michael seemed keen to explore the history of the Jewish culture when he had free time from filming. One afternoon he disappeared to visit a village on Mount Carmel in Haifa called Yemin Orde, which had become renowned for raising and educating immigrant and at-risk youth from around the world. Michael's parents had paid for a synagogue to be built there and though he didn't announce the fact, he wanted to see it. Michael had a very ambivalent attitude to his Jewish background, never wanting to really acknowledge or discuss it. But when he got to the very striking and unusually designed synagogue he shouted at everyone to get out and then spent quite a bit of time there alone. I only discovered this afterwards from the director of the youth village, who had shown him around. Michael never mentioned it himself. One day he told me he would take me to the Church of the Holy Sepulchre where, according to tradition, the body of Jesus was placed after the crucifixion.

However, when we arrived I was not allowed in, as I was wearing shorts which did not cover my knees. I was disappointed, but Michael was not giving up yet.

We moved away from the crowds and he revealed his plan. He got me to untuck my baggy orange shirt and then lower my shorts until my knees were fully covered by the dark blue linen. To prevent them dropping further down my legs, he offered me his belt. This looked just about all right when I was standing still. When I tried to walk I could only take very small steps. 'Well, you'll just have to fucking walk slowly then,' he said when I tried to object. He gave me an old red paisley neckerchief to tie over my head too. 'Just to make sure', as he put it. Yes, just to make sure I look a completely weird idiot, I thought to myself. I began the long walk back to the queue. For Michael it was only a few paces but I had to employ a careful mincing movement to prevent my shorts from slipping lower. As the queue moved forward his final words of advice were to keep my head down and not catch anyone's eye. We got inside. I assumed it was because he looked as though he was caring for a rather mentally challenged relative.

I stood gazing at the place where it is said that the resurrection of Christ took place. Under any circumstances I think the immense significance of this would be very difficult to fully grasp. It was certainly very strange for me, shuffling about in such ridiculous attire. When we emerged and I was pulling my trousers up he told me our next stop would be to have tea with nana. He must have caught my look of amazement and he asked why I looked so stunned. I said I had no idea he had relatives in Israel.

He had just about managed to stifle his laughter in the church but now he released it as a long howl accompanied by tears. 'It's a kind of fucking mint tea, you idiot,' he said in a high-pitched voice as he was trying to catch his breath.

By now the heat was almost unbearable and sipping the piping-hot sweet mint tea was surprisingly cooling. Nana, as I will now always remember, is a traditional Israeli tea made with spearmint and often orange as well. It was beautiful. The food was good, too. I had no knowledge of Jewish cuisine so the menu was rather mystifying. Michael told me that he had found it best to ignore the menu and just ask to be served whatever they recommended. That evening we tried this approach again and were served amazingly delicious food. Quite often he would arrange dinners with all the stars of the cast.

Although he was not starring in the film I remember it was on one of those evenings that I first met Steven Berkoff and his girlfriend Clara Fisher. There were a lot of us so we would occupy several tables in the restaurant. I had noticed that Jenny Seagrove would often glance over at Michael when he wasn't looking. I mentioned to Michael that I felt she was somehow fascinated by him. He said he didn't think that at all likely and mumbled something about her looking a little too thin. I told him straight away that she would be his next girlfriend. He told me straight away that I was ridiculous. When we had finished eating I went over to her and persuaded her to join our noisy table. When Steven and Michael were together there was usually a lot of laughter. It was a lovely evening and Michael got over his initial shyness and managed to talk to Jenny.

My two weeks in Israel had seemed like an eternity away from my new baby, but at the same time it had all been a fantastic experience. And I had learnt so much about hair styling and film work, too. After that, the head of the hair and make-up department for Cannon Films kept offering me work as a stylist. In many ways I would have loved to have said yes. I found the work interesting and was feeling more and more comfortable with it. But with children back at home I couldn't even consider it.

A day or two after returning, I got a phone call from Michael. He sounded very excited. 'Darling, you were right, you were right,' he kept repeating. He and Jenny were getting on well and he seemed surprised and delighted. It was good to hear him so buoyant and he chattered on, even telling me that one night he had dared her to run naked down the hotel corridor. I think he was very surprised when she had taken up the challenge. Jenny had quite an air of refinement and I suspect that Michael had wondered how readily she would shrug it off. From what I remember, he said only one lucky guest glimpsed her as she sped back to the room. One of his most likeable sides was his zany and boyish sense of fun.

Not long after the filming for *Appointment with Death* was completed, Jenny Seagrove moved into Woodland House with

Michael. I would see them occasionally on my trips to London and Michael seemed to be becoming a little calmer. He was happy. I was going to as many auditions as I could and these were mostly in London. Also, my husband Takis had formed a new band with Paul Usher, who played Barry Grant in *Brookside*, and I was doing my best to promote them. Jenny was often working and so if I was around I would sometimes go for dinner with Michael. I knew that he had begun work on *A Chorus of Disapproval*, and on one of those evenings I met the author, Alan Ayckbourn. There was no mention of work for me. I was half relieved, as Luke was still tiny.

The filming was soon to begin. I was at home and my mother had picked up the telephone. She only lived round the corner and it was around the time that I was trying to get her to teach me some of her baking recipes. I always enjoyed cooking, but had never really learnt how to make pastry or even a good cake. I would do the dinner and she always made the desserts. She had been chatting for a while and I didn't know who it was until she handed me the phone and said it was Michael. He said he had six weeks' work for me in Scarborough. I was to work with another stylist called Liz Michie. As I was starting to remind him that my experience was still a bit limited and I did not have the necessary equipment, he interrupted.

'My dear, you must have a fucking comb,' he said.

'Yes, for men I don't need much, but for women it's…' I began to explain.

'Fuck the women, you only have to do the men,' he said reassuringly. 'Darling, you are brilliant. It'll be easy. Just don't forget your fucking comb.'

I was getting used to his brief instructions. He told me where to be and when, and that was it.

I got to Scarborough the day before filming was due to start and headed straight to the room in the hotel where the hair and make-up department were setting up. When I found Liz Michie, the hair stylist, she told me that I was responsible for all the men and also Sylvia Syms, Barbara Ferris and Patsy Kensit. She would concentrate on Prunella Scales and Jenny Seagrove.

Telling her about my conversation with Michael about bringing a comb and just doing the men did not help. I was in panic. I phoned Michael. He assured me that I was fully capable and just to get on with it. I told him that I had no dryers, no hot brush, no nets, no scissors et cetera et cetera. He said I should go out immediately and buy whatever was needed. Liz showed me what she wanted me to do and Sue Wain from the wardrobe department found me a Polaroid camera and gave me a lesson on how to do a script breakdown and keep track of continuity. Then off I went to the shops. I didn't sleep too well that night.

At six in the morning I set to work.

Sylvia Syms and Barbara Ferris were needed first and as they sat chatting I just got on with it as best I could. Liz was helpful whenever I was in doubt and Sylvia knew exactly how she wanted her hair so everything gradually began to fall into place. My experience before with dancers and extras had been much more straightforward. Once they were ready they skipped off and I would not see them again. But this was very different. I had to know exactly what each actor's hair was like from scene to scene throughout the story as well as making sure that nothing moved or dropped or changed during each scene. With one actor that was not so difficult. Keeping an eye on several at once was a little bit mind-boggling.

Sue Wain would give me little lessons, when she could make time, on how to keep the Polaroids clipped into the script as reference, and Alan Boyle from Hair and Make-up showed me the ropes on set. It was one thing to see when something needed doing but quite another to know how and when to get in and make those changes. Alan guided me through it all so I could avoid embarrassing myself, irritating people or causing havoc. Gradually I was getting the hang of it. When I saw Michael and Jenny those first few evenings after filming they knew I was struggling. They could see I was stressed. But Michael would make fun of my nervousness and reassure me that he had complete faith in my abilities. He would even go as far as to say that it was not even that important and so what if it was not always perfect. He had put me in a difficult situation but I did realise I was very fortunate. I knew there were plenty of people who would have loved to have been given that kind of opportunity.

On set things were not shaping up so well for Michael in those first few days.

It was about the third or fourth day of filming and he started shouting at a young actor. He started and he did not stop. Crew and cast looked at their toes as he bellowed insults and obscenities at the poor man. There was nothing comical about it. And it was so shocking and humiliating that there could be no argument that it might somehow be designed to improve the actor's performance. It looked like a demonstration of power. Two of the film's main stars, Anthony Hopkins and Jeremy Irons, approached Michael. When I saw him a few minutes after their conversation he was still red in the face and clearly fuming. He told me that they said they would like him to apologise to the actor and also assure them that in future

he would treat everyone involved in the production, whatever their status, in the same manner. I think they must have
made it clear that filming could not begin again until he had
carried out their requests. Michael paced up and down and
I'm sure he felt it was him that was being unjustly treated.
He must have stewed for over an hour. I was not on set when
he made the apology. Work commenced but the atmosphere
remained tense and gloomy.

Then I noticed another growing tension. And this time I
realised that I was at the centre of it. I was getting on well
with Liz, the hair stylist, and keeping on top of my share
of the work; however, Michael would occasionally pull me
out of the styling department and have me dressed up as an
extra when it suited him. I think that is what triggered the
unrest. All the time I was not there Liz had the impossible
task of covering for me. I heard rumours that the crew had
discussed the fact that Michael felt it acceptable to employ
friends who did not hold a union card. They did not share
his opinion. I found those rumours upsetting because I was
a qualified stylist and, although nowhere near as knowledgeable as Liz, I did have some experience with film work. On
the first day, Michael had in fact given me a membership
card to BETA – later to become BECTU – but had told me
to keep it safe and not mention it to anyone. We were filming outside a pub one day and I heard that a man from the
union was arriving that afternoon to look into my situation.
I was very nervous. Michael told me to not tell anybody
about my card and not to produce it until confronted by
the union official. He was yet to become known for saying
'Calm down, dear', but that was basically what he was telling me when he saw how panicked I was. When the man

arrived, filming was stopped and we all went into the pub. On cue I produced the little green card. The union man was happy and the crew were irritated and embarrassed – just as Michael had wanted them to be! But once again work could continue.

I naturally felt awkward about the whole episode, but gradually over the next week or so, as I got to know people better, the atmosphere improved. From day one I really liked Sylvia Syms. A beautiful woman, she had become a big star at an early age with such films as *Ice Cold in Alex*, *Woman in a Dressing Gown* and *The Tamarind Seed*. She had helped me feel immediately at ease and I was enjoying doing her hair. I lacked confidence but she had enough for both of us. We had a great time. And by treating me as someone she had complete faith in, she brought out the best in me. She even said I was the best stylist she had worked with, which I took as a great kindness.

Looking back, there are some key people who stand out. The ones who were understanding or sympathetic or perhaps just naturally kind and helpful when I was most vulnerable. In the brief time that our paths crossed they somehow helped me forwards and gave me something invisible but of huge value. Sylvia was definitely one of those people.

Of course, on a film set the people you work with most tend to be the ones you get to know best. Even at the end of the day there is often preparation work to be done. It never really stops. Sometimes during breaks I would go for walks along the seafront with Antony Hopkins. He was good company and always stayed in character. I had not come across that approach to acting before and found it fascinating. The work I had done, even on *Brookside*, I had never felt was the really proper serious kind of acting. On film sets I was always watching the actors to see what I might learn. I'm sure I questioned Tony pretty relentlessly.

During the filming of *A Chorus of Disapproval* I spent quite a lot of time with Jenny. From the first time we met we seemed to like each other and now it was starting to feel like we were old friends. I had met some of Michael's girlfriends before and they could be quite frosty towards me. It was never like that with Jenny. She was uncomplicated, cheerful and good natured and didn't regard me as some kind of threat simply because I was a woman of similar age. Even before meeting her the first time, I knew of her as an accomplished and beautiful actress. At the time she was most famous for her portrayal of Emma in Barbara Taylor Bradford's *A Woman of Substance*, and already I had great respect for her. She had a remarkable natural grace and elegance and was open and approachable too. I liked her immediately and we quickly fell into an easy friendliness which was to be very important for me over the coming years.

Back home, Takis was getting the occasional paid gig with the band and finally my mother seemed to have accepted that what I really wanted was to be at home with the children. She stopped trying to badger me into looking for acting work that would always mean I would be away for long periods. I searched for any job I could find locally. Jackie Brassey, my best friend from teenage years, knew someone who had a business supplying hair products. I got a job driving a van. In the morning I would pick up from the warehouse and then make deliveries, mostly to north Wales. It was a big van and I found it quite alarming to drive. I had never done anything quite like it before. I felt like it was a horse that was too large for me and knew I was frightened. It would lurch off, taking me with it, and for the first few days I did not feel very much in control. Within a week or two I had begun to get the hang of it and started to enjoy the freedom on the open country roads.

CHAPTER FOUR

FIRST YEARS AT WOODLAND HOUSE

'YOU ARE DOING WHAT? YOU'RE driving a fucking van? Are you completely fucking mad?' were Michael's first questions when I mentioned my new job. I told him that it meant I had a regular income but he wanted to know more. 'How long have you been interested in vans? I never knew you liked vans. I thought you wanted to be an actress or a stylist. I've seen you reading *Vanity Fair* and *Vogue*. I've seen you reading *Cosmopolitan*. But I didn't know you had a copy of *What*-fucking-*Van?* tucked inside it. You're so fucking secretive.' I said that I was still able to go to auditions but for now what I most wanted was to be with the children.

This was the beginning of the conversations that were to lead to me working at Woodland House. He said if I wanted a regular income he would employ me as a receptionist. I knew he had just taken on a girl to answer the door and he made it clear that the job was mine if I wanted it. It was a good offer but I would only be home for the weekends and I just couldn't face that.

Michael tried to persuade me.

'All you have to do is sit in the kitchen and just answer the door when the bell rings. You can read all fucking day. You can read *What Van?* for all I fucking care. Do you understand, dear? It's a marvellous job.'

He was right, it was a marvellous job, but I knew how long a week could feel when I was away from Danny and Luke.

With Jenny now living there, the house felt much more homely. I had stayed quite a lot because of my frequent trips to London. Mrs Hickey the housekeeper was an energetic Irish lady who cooked breakfast and lunch and did the cleaning downstairs too. She always looked immaculate in a cream or white blouse with a brooch at the collar and a pleated skirt. She had ash-blond hair which she would curl to perfection each morning. I remember seeing her one day at the top of a very tall ladder doing the huge windows in the dining room. She must have been in her sixties and I was horrified that Michael would let her. When I mentioned it he just said, 'Oh, you try to fucking stop her.' Mrs Hickey had been there for years and was a housekeeper of the old school. Her lunches were magnificent and beautifully presented. When I stayed she would produce a roast dinner as if from nowhere and carry it right up all the stairs to my room. She would put a cloth on the table and lay out silver cutlery. It was only after I had got to know her well that I managed to persuade her not to go to such effort on my behalf. I could not get used to being treated like royalty and was happier when she let me eat in the kitchen with her. She lived in two lovely rooms at the top of the house, and before retiring at the end of the day she would prepare a salad and leave it in the fridge with a large steak. She would also leave half a melon on the kitchen worktop. Michael would cook the steak himself and that was his dinner every night unless he was going out. May was the maid who came to the house each day to clean the upstairs rooms, change the beds and do the laundry. She was in her fifties and became known as Maymay, to avoid confusion with me. One day I was at the house when Mrs Hickey and Maymay were arguing over something and Michael stepped in and screamed at the maid and told her she was fired. When it had quietened down I said to Michael that it was a shame as she was always such a cheerful and kind lady.

He laughed and said, 'I know, I know, don't worry, dear, I often fire her, she'll be back, she'll be back.' After that I noticed that being fired was all in a day's work for Maymay. Another figure who would appear from time to time was Mrs Boardman. She was in her seventies and only came to help out when needed, such as when Michael had guests for dinner.

During the week, Val Chamberlain, the secretary, worked from 9.30 to 6.00 in an office at the back of the house. John Fraser worked the same hours in an office in the basement. John had known Michael from school days and was his oldest friend. He was called the executive assistant and did all the research needed on film projects. If any document or file or phone number was needed, John could reach into a filing cabinet or spin a Rolodex and produce it. He could usually do this in less than three seconds. Any longer and Michael's shouting would turn the air blue and rattle the crystal chandeliers.

I did not often see the chauffeur. He was a Yorkshireman called Michael White and spent the days in the garage at the far end of the garden. He would run errands and keep the cars spotlessly clean and polished. At that time there was the black Rolls-Royce Phantom, the blue Mercedes sports, a dark-blue Ferrari and a silver-grey Bentley. Michael White was given a flat to stay in nearby during the week and returned home at weekends on a huge motorbike. He kept to himself but I had heard he was a very skilled man. He had trained as a panel beater with Aston Martin. I remember when the doors on the Ferrari had rusted he said he could make stronger, better-quality ones. Sure enough, he made perfect new doors from flat sheet metal.

Michael did seem to find some remarkable people.

On my next trip to London I saw that things were changing. The 1980s were drawing to a close and Michael was moving into the modern world. Mrs Hickey had announced that she was retiring and disappeared back to Ireland. Lily was the new housekeeper. She was from the Philippines and was very striking in her crisp green uniform with her thick, glossy black hair tied in a ponytail. John had been moved out of his office in the basement and into Farley Court, a few hundred yards from the house in Melbury Road. Where his desk had been there was now a huge muddy hole. A conveyor belt was clanking away and carrying soil and rubble from beneath the house, across the garden and dropping it over the wall into waiting lorries. The man in charge of the team of workmen was Mr

Edwards; he had worked for George Winner, Michael's father, and was clearly well known and trusted by Michael. A swimming pool was being installed.

My van-driving days were to be short lived. I had only had the job a few weeks when, late one night, my telephone rang. I answered it, but the person at the other end hung up. It rang again a little while later, but the same thing happened. When my mother arrived that morning, we talked about who the mystery caller might be. It felt ominous. Over breakfast, the phone rang again. It was Duncan, an ex-boyfriend of Diana from *Brookside*. He had been too distressed to speak when he had called at night, and was barely able to say anything now. I managed to decipher that Diana had been in a terrible train accident and was in intensive care in St George's Hospital, London. My first reaction was to call Michael. He said immediately that a car would be waiting for me when I got to Euston.

Arriving at the hospital, I found Diana. She was out of intensive care, and her mother and sister were with her. I was relieved to find her alive and out of danger. But her mother took me to one side and told me the full extent of the tragedy. She had fallen between the train and the platform and lost part of both legs. One just above and the other just below the knee. I could not really grasp what I was hearing. Of course, with the morphine and other drugs from intensive care, Diana was not fully lucid. We were all in shock. I think we needed the first few days just to begin to come to terms with everything. We had better get a grip. If I was going to be any help, I had better just keep focused on the practical side of things. And the important things. She could have been killed. She was alive and there would be ways to help. I just tried to focus on that.

That evening I went to Michael's and he did everything in his power to lift my spirits. He could see I was pale with shock and chattered away, listing all the positive things he could think of and offering anything he thought might help. His attitude gradually began to rub off on me and I started to see a flicker of light again through the dark cloud. He really hammered it out clearly. There would be no moping about. The future must be optimistic and bright. I think he really helped me to carry that into the hospital each morning in those early days. That was probably one of the most precious things anyone could have taken Diana. He said his chauffeur would take me back and forth to the hospital whenever needed.

The next day, Diana was emerging from the morphine haze. She wanted her hair washed, and the nurse thought that a very encouraging sign. She had the headboard of the bed removed so that Diana could more easily put her head back into the bowl of warm water. I was horrified as with bowl after bowl I washed the dried blood from her hair. But before long it was done and the hospital air was filled with the scent of jasmine conditioner. Her boyfriend was on his way but she had no top to wear so I swapped mine for her hospital gown. A little perfume and make-up and she was looking beautiful again. It was amazing. The nurse said it was the best medicine. In fact, her mother was so relieved to see Diana's radiance returned that she burst into tears. Things were getting better. And I knew Diana. She had strength – she was showing it already.

Back at Woodland House, Michael stared in amusement and disbelief at my hospital gown. Before he would let me go and change he wanted to know how she was and how the day had been.

'Yes, yes, good, good, yes, yes, good, good,' was really all he could say as I told him how very hard it all was, but that she was awake and facing it. When I got back to the kitchen he had opened champagne and put another bottle out for me to take to Diana the next day. As he poured it, he told me to make sure she always had a bottle to hand. He said it was a good medicine for lifting the spirits, and that was going to be very important. The chips were down and Michael was an impressive friend.

'Goals, she needs to set goals,' he kept repeating firmly. I was still rather dazed, and the champagne was going to my head, but he kept on with his thoughts and advice. And he was right, setting a goal and achieving it would be the key to Diana moving forward over the next few weeks and months.

I spent most of the week going to and fro between Michael's house and the hospital. They were dark and difficult days. Jenny was often not back until the end of the evening as she was in a play in the West End. Michael would take me to dinner, and his humour and optimism helped to recharge my batteries ready for the next day. I needed to keep my strength up so I could be as cheerful and helpful as possible.

British Rail had presented the incident to the press as Diana's fault for trying to board a moving train. They were proposing to sue her for trespass. The reality was very different. As she was getting onto a stationary train, it had lurched forward suddenly. In fact, it had done this twice in quick succession. Most of us have experienced those sharp unexpected jolts that sometimes occur just before a train pulls away. If they catch you as you are lowering yourself gracefully onto a seat, they can send you sprawling over a stranger's lap. They often lead to discomfort, annoyance, embarrassment, even laughter. But they can also cause terrible injury.

Michael had studied law at Cambridge and he knew the power of the press too. He had seen immediately what was happening, and the injustice that could result from this kind of twisted story. Diana was only just out of intensive care and in no position to defend herself yet. He wrote to the *Evening Standard* with the real version of the events, and as she began her recovery he encouraged her with the legal proceedings. This was the start of a long road, but the outcome would be her winning the case against British Rail after a harrowing five-year battle.

My conversations with Michael had often drifted back to the subject of my working for him as a receptionist in the house. It was starting to look like the only option. It would mean being away from the family a lot, but if I was to continue visiting Diana regularly and also going to auditions then I would be away from home for several days a week anyway. We looked into moving to London, but that would be a big upheaval and would tie me to an even bigger mortgage. And I could not know what the future might bring. Every possible scenario was talked through. Round and round we went. Finally it was decided. I was to do two weeks 'on' and two weeks 'off'. I could travel home for the middle weekend so would only be away for four nights at a time. This seemed possible and a good solution to all problems. There was nothing to lose by giving it a try.

Jenny had been fighting through a difficult divorce, and that was finally in the closing stages. Michael helped her significantly, from what I remember, and always seemed very at home poring over legal documents. When her divorce was finally settled, Jenny bought a flat a few minutes' walk from Woodland House, and she would go there in the morning at

9.30, when Michael's working day began. John Fraser would arrive promptly at 9.20 and would stand like a soldier outside Michael's office. At 9.29 he would be ushered in and stand quietly for ten minutes while Michael danced about shouting, screaming and swearing at him. Sifting through the expletives, John would methodically note down his instructions for the day. Then he would make his way slowly along Melbury Road to his own more peaceful office in Farley Court. He had suffered from polio as a child, which had left him with a limp and perhaps also an ability to calmly accept whatever day-to-day dramas that life – well, mostly Michael – threw at him.

On the morning I arrived to start work, Lily, the new house-keeper, answered the door. I had only met her once or twice before and we didn't know each other well. She said she would go and tell Michael that I was here. 'Oh, that's OK,' I said cheerfully, 'I'm just going to take my bag up to my room.'

'No, no, please, wait, madam, I will tell him,' said Lily.

I was halfway up the first flight of stairs already before I noticed the pleading tone in her voice. 'Really, it's OK,' I called back. 'He knows I'm coming.'

Lily ran up the stairs behind me and continued imploring me to stop. 'No, no, madam, please, madam, please come back.' I could not understand the fuss. 'I am Dinah, I'm work-ing here today,' I said, thinking maybe she had not recognised me. 'Yes, yes, Dinah madam, but please, please, madam, Dinah, you must come back, please come back, please wait downstairs, please, please, he kill me, he kill me, he fire me.'

Turning, I saw that there were now tears running down her cheeks, and it dawned on me that she must be desperately try-ing to carry out some new instructions. 'I'm sorry, I'm sorry,' I said. 'It's my fault, I'll tell him it's my fault.' And putting my bags down, I went and found Michael and explained the commotion. All was well this time, but he said that in future any callers must wait at the door until their arrival had been announced to him.

I had spent quite a lot of time in the house over the past few years, and was used to hearing Michael's shouting. In the morning it was usually at John, and during the day Val the secretary would get a similar treatment. They were used to it, but I could see that they did still find it alarming and upsetting. I'm sure Lily found his bellowing quite frightening, and if it was directed at her she would often burst into tears. He took to writing her memos. He said he didn't think she could understand English very well. Her English was very good, but I agreed with him anyway as I thought it might give her some protection from his outbursts. Fiona, the receptionist, showed me the ropes.

Apart from running out to pick up the newspapers, collecting post or taking files up and down to Farley Court, I was to stay in the kitchen and listen out for the doorbell and the intercom buzzer. The intercom took some getting used to. It would buzz repeatedly in an erratic staccato rhythm. It was a sound that left no doubt that the jabbing finger at the other end of the line was attached to someone of very limited patience. Fiona sat at the end of the kitchen table so she could stand up and reach the intercom in less than two seconds. That was just about acceptable. Any longer and there was likely to be an angry bellow from upstairs and the sound of stomping feet.

FIONA, WHERE ARE YOU? WHAT THE FUCK ARE YOU DOING? CAN'T YOU HEAR THE FUCKING BUZZER, FOR FUCK'S SAKE? WHAT'S THE FUCKING POINT

OF HAVING A RECEPTIONIST IF YOU CAN'T EVEN
ANSWER A FUCKING BUZZER WHEN I NEED YOU?
IF YOU ARE SUCH A FUCKING MORON ... OH, THERE
YOU ARE, WHY DIDN'T YOU ANSWER THE FUCK-
ING BUZZER? TAKE THIS LETTER TO THE POST
OFFICE, IT'S FUCKING IMPORTANT, AND MAKE
SURE YOU GET THERE BEFORE FIVE. YOU'VE GOT
SEVEN MINUTES, YOU CAN GET THERE IN SEVEN
FUCKING MINUTES, IT'S ONLY ROUND THE COR-
NER FOR FUCK'S SAKE, AND NEXT TIME ANSWER
THE FUCKING BUZZER. I SHOULDN'T BE HAV-
ING TO RUN UP AND DOWN MY OWN FUCKING
STAIRS. I'M NOT YOUR FUCKING RECEPTION-
IST, I THOUGHT I WAS PAYING YOU TO RUN UP
AND DOWN THE FUCKING STAIRS. DON'T JUST
STAND THERE LIKE A FUCKING IDIOT, YOU'LL
BE LATE. I'VE JUST TOLD YOU. YOU'VE ONLY
GOT SIX MINUTES NOW AND DON'T PUT IT IN
THE BOX ON THE CORNER IT HAS TO GO TO THE
POST OFFICE, DO YOU KNOW WHAT A FUCKING POST
OFFICE IS? PUT IT IN THE POSTBOX ON THE WALL
OF THE FUCKING POST OFFICE, IS THAT CLEAR?
IT'S FUCKING IMPORTANT, AND RUN, YOU BET-
TER FUCKING WELL GET THERE BEFORE FIVE...

If I was standing by the sink when the buzzer went, I had to
spin round and lunge across the wide worktop. If Lily the
housekeeper was nearer than me, she would grab the receiver
and pass it quickly to me. Even a trip to the loo involved a
fair degree of trepidation. There was a lot to learn in those
initial few weeks.

In the first months I worked at Woodland House, I would often get the bus to Queen Mary's Hospital in Roehampton to see Diana. She had been moved there to continue her recovery. Michael had asked Lily to prepare meals for me to take, and she would package them up beautifully and often put in a bottle of champagne, too. We would chatter through the evening and I would get the last bus back at around midnight. Her injury meant that she was faced with the huge task of adapting to a different way of life. She had to come to terms with things mentally as well as learn to become mobile again. I had quickly discovered that the English language is full of expressions that it might be more tactful not to use. It was easy to stick your foot in it. But carefully filtering my sentences before speaking was never a skill I possessed or could even realistically aspire to. Diana would greet each faux pas with a howl of laughter. At first I had felt clumsy, but she assured me it was such a relief that I did not tiptoe around her.

She lived near Wilmslow and was determined to be ready to leave hospital in time to have Christmas at home with her family.

One goal we agreed on was that she would visit me in Little Neston and walk into the house. She had only a couple of months to get used to her 'pretend legs', as I called them. Sure enough, just after Christmas, she arrived with her sister. Not only did she make her way rather elegantly into the sitting room, but she also looked extraordinarily glamorous in her black and coral outfit. My mother had gathered all our family and friends and we had a huge and noisy party. It was a fabulous celebration.

Diana's accident had really been the main catalyst for me

starting work in Woodland House. Working for only two weeks in the month meant of course that my income was not very big, but it was just enough to support the family.

Also, Michael had agreed that I could take time off to go to auditions when I needed to. I was happy with the arrangement; having two solid weeks at home with the children was fantastic. I had never been able to do that before. And I didn't have to worry so much about finding acting jobs. Saying goodbye at five o'clock on a Monday morning was not so fantastic. Friday afternoon would seem horribly distant as I sat on the train speeding towards Euston. I never got used to those Mondays.

Michael's day began at eight o'clock. A switch next to his bed controlled the swimming pool cover. This meant that he did not have to wait at the poolside as it slowly rolled back. Soon after eight he would emerge from the bedroom in his swimming shorts. He had a selection of quite colourful ones. For twenty minutes he would swim up and down, doing the breaststroke at a leisurely pace and looking at the television mounted on one wall. Then he would sit in the Jacuzzi for ten minutes. As far as he was concerned, when he was in the pool he was exercising and while in the hot Jacuzzi he was looking after his weight. Having completed this ritual, he would wrap a thick white towel around his waist and divest himself of the swimming shorts. These would be retrieved later by the maid. Lily would prepare a breakfast of freshly squeezed orange juice, toast and coffee. The toast had to be made from his favourite Hovis loaf and was served with coarse-cut marmalade. She would carry it to his bedroom on a large tray, with the newspapers too, and leave it on the desk in the bay window for him to discover on his return from the pool. Michael would usually remain wrapped in the towel as he ate breakfast and read through the papers. From the desk he had a good view across the back garden.

Michael was king of the castle. There was never any doubt about that. And the working day was strictly regimented. He appeared at his desk at 9.30 every morning. His lack of patience meant that if there was something to be done it had to be done immediately. The atmosphere in his office was usually tense. Often it was very tense. A man rushing to meet a very important deadline. Sometimes he was. Sometimes he just wanted a brown envelope or a piece of string. But it didn't matter. If he wanted string it was my job to get string. And to get it as fast as humanly possible. All the staff knew that it was safest to treat everything as urgent. If a paper clip was needed it was probably needed immediately. And if the instructions were to clip it to the top right of the paper it was better just to do it and not ask why.

Michael had countless idiosyncrasies, and they had to be remembered and pandered to. The quietest way forward was to listen carefully to any instructions. I also quickly discovered that timekeeping was of utmost importance. Lunch was from 1.00 to 2.00 and the working day ended at 6.00.

God help anyone who put their coat on five minutes early.

Actually, it was all very similar to working on one of his film sets. He certainly worked hard. I had noticed that when filming there were times when he would be up at 6.00 or earlier and sometimes he would not stop until 10.00 at night.

In the office he always started at 9.30 and usually had a busy schedule. There would be articles to write and film scripts to work on and all manner of things to arrange. He often gave interviews on the telephone, and hardly a week passed without him being interviewed on film. These usually took place in the garden, winter or summer, unless the weather was very bad. He was not keen on having film crews in the house. He thought they were often clumsy and would chip furniture, scratch walls and wander about in muddy boots.

Michael had very clear ideas about how these interviews were to be set up. Most importantly, he wanted the camera set just above his eyeline. Over the years I noticed him become increasingly particular about this and other details. When a crew arrived he was usually welcoming and would talk briefly to the director or cameraman. If he was too busy he would send me to pass on any instructions. Once the camera was set up and everything made ready, one of the team would come and let me know. Michael would put on a clean shirt and I would check his hair.

In those early years he didn't pay much attention to his appearance, but as time went on he would get me to dab some foundation on various marks he had on his face. I also got him some button-down collared shirts, as often he had been filmed with one side of his collar sticking up. Perhaps because some people found him rather intimidating, they would not always want to stick their neck out and mention details like that to him. When he was ready he would stride out and sit in his chair. He could go straight into an interview without any preamble. Most times all would go smoothly and he would get up, nod his thanks and march back into the house. Quite often it did not go smoothly. The problem was invariably the camera height. If the crew had taken it upon themselves to ignore instructions and set it at eye level or lower he would stand up again. Before he was back on his feet the tirade would begin.

HOW DARE YOU WASTE MY FUCKING TIME? IF YOU CAN'T EVEN CARRY OUT A SIMPLE FUCKING TASK AND SET UP A FUCKING CAMERA, YOU IGNORANT MORONS, IT'S FUCKING UNBELIEVABLE, YOU CAN GET ALL YOUR FUCKING RUBBISH AND FUCK OFF OUT OF MY GARDEN. DO YOU UNDERSTAND? I SAID GET ALL YOUR RUBBISH AND FUCK OFF, NOW GET OUT, FUCK OFF, GET OUT OF MY FUCKING GARDEN, YOU ARE A BUNCH OF FUCKING IDIOTS…

As he yelled out his disgust he would already be storming across the lawn. Sometimes one of the crew would trot behind him, apologising profusely, but that usually just led to him upping the volume as he screamed back. Pale faces would stare at each other, blinking in disbelief, as Michael disappeared back through the glass-panelled terrace doors. Occasionally, if one of them came to the front door and gave me a message of apology to pass on, he would return and do the interview. But this was quite rare. It depended on how genuinely remorseful he thought they were, and also perhaps on how important the interview was for him.

But at six o'clock Michael would snap out of 'work mode'. It was like flicking a switch. Humour was no longer dangerous, and often he would even apologise for any screaming and yelling that he had indulged in during the day. With Jenny there now, the house felt more and more lived in. The last part of her divorce battle had been over Tasha, her spaniel. It was a very happy day when she was returned to Jenny. Tasha would follow her round the house, her wagging tail slapping the furniture. Michael accepted her and grew quite fond of her, but she was not allowed on the sofas and spent the nights in the downstairs bathroom. I adored her, and when I was there she slept up in my room. I had always had dogs, and missed them when I was in London. Tasha had a rug on the floor of my bedroom, but that was really for appearance's sake. Just before going to bed, Jenny would run upstairs and Tasha would come bounding up behind her and leap onto my bed with great excitement.

In the morning Dina, the new maid, would hoover the bedcover to remove the brown-and-white dog hairs in case Michael was wandering around. He would probably not have approved, and it was better not to risk him knowing.

There was a sound system that now linked all the rooms, and when Jenny came in, usually just after 6.00, the house would fill with music. From what I remember, film soundtracks were often played, with *Out of Africa* as a favourite. They also both liked singers such as Dean Martin, Frank Sinatra and Tony Bennett. Because of the size and layout of the house, it was not easy to find someone without running up and down a lot of stairs or calling out.

Jenny would impersonate Michael and his way of constantly swearing.

Against the background of some film score, it was comical to hear this calling and swearing until they found each other.

Quite often, before dinner, we would all go down to the pool and splash about. It had only been when the swimming pool was actually finished that we had discovered Michael had never learnt to swim. Jenny and I gave him lessons and he seemed to quickly pick it up. He wasn't particularly confident, but he would swim slowly and carefully around the pool. We were fooled for quite a few weeks, but one day I noticed the ludicrous truth: Michael had one foot on the bottom. He was using his arms to disturb the water around him and so hide the offending leg. His big colourful shorts, ballooning with air, were providing him with extra buoyancy. We had to go back to the beginning. Lessons started again. This time it was a much noisier process. Michael didn't really have the patience for 'learning'. To get information he only had to shout or pick up the phone. Developing a skill such as swimming was different. Jenny and I made sure he kept trying, but when he gulped water he would make quite a fuss.

Once, Lily rushed in, thinking he was drowning. It was all a bit of a drama, but he kept at it. If Michael became determined to do something, there was no stopping him. He drank quite a lot of the pool, but finally he got the hang of it.

I thought, as a Scorpio, he would have been more of a natural in the water, but I noticed even on holiday he never went out of his depth. He preferred to be near the sea rather than in it.

Mrs Hickey had occasionally cooked dinner when asked. Lily, on the other hand, always had to cook dinner unless Michael was going out. Jenny and I would do the honours if Lily had a day off or was on holiday. However, Michael always set the menu. He usually wanted sautéed potatoes and spinach with either steak or roast chicken. Once, Lily had bought a stewing chicken, thinking it was simply a Jewish name for a regular bird. She had no idea that it was in fact a mature chicken intended only for chicken soup, when it would be simmered for five hours. She roasted it and served it to Michael.

After chewing for a while on what must have seemed like an old boot, he erupted suddenly and stormed into the kitchen, holding up the tough old bird by one leg. 'WHERE DID YOU GET THIS FUCKING CHICKEN? IT IS A FUCKING

DISGRACE. A STARVING DOG WOULD NOT TOUCH IT.
WHAT HAVE YOU DONE, WHAT THE FUCKING HELL
HAVE YOU DONE...'

There was quite a hullabaloo until the mix-up was discovered, and Michael threw the scorched carcass onto the worktop. It bounced onto the floor and round the kitchen like a leather football, with Lily begging forgiveness. 'Please, please, I sorry, I sorry, sir, I bloody foreigner, I bloody foreigner, I sorry I not know all these things,' she screeched, trying to corner the bouncing bird.

Michael couldn't help but start to chuckle at the scene. I had been about to go out when the rumpus started, and Lily and I found a steak to cook up in place of the football. He liked his steak quite rare, so within a few minutes all was calm again.

In those days he would be glued to the television between 6.00 and 7.00 watching the news. Jenny told me she was invisible until he had caught up with world events. We often mixed cocktails in the kitchen and if the weather was good we would sit on the wooden terrace looking over the back garden.

Bloody Marys became the favourite and Michael liked to mix in a dollop of horseradish sauce. Jenny loved gardening and often spent the day mowing the lawns and weeding. She would buy bedding plants from Rassells Nursery in Earls Court Road and brighten up the beds either side of the front path.

The flower bed just below their bedroom window was also kept full of colour.

I really enjoyed gardening too, and if she was still busy out there, I would go and help her after work. Michael kept gloves and a pair of secateurs in a drawer in the lounge and would sometimes come out and set to work pruning something. This was irritating as he never picked anything up. Instead he just shouted excitedly as he loped off branches. 'Quickly, quickly, catch it, catch it.' We would have to stop what we were doing and scurry about after him gathering up his clippings. If we managed to persuade him not to 'help' he would sit on one of the teak garden chairs, smoking a huge cigar. The cigars were part of his life then and he usually had one in his hand.

Smoke hung permanently like low cloud in his office. There were always a few big yellow boxes of Montecristo in the fridge. He didn't smoke them to the bitter end. They would be abandoned when still a few inches long and lie on a nest of matchsticks in ashtrays around the house. I thought they looked rather creepy. Like the pupae of enormous moths.

* * *

In the early days, I thought Michael quite mean to Jenny when it came to buying clothes for special occasions. I wouldn't say he had a mean streak so much as that he could be just plain insensitive or thoughtless. They often attended premieres and other glamorous events together. He would phone Bruce Old-field and try to get a discount on one of his creations, or even ask to hire something for her. I never heard her complain, but I felt she was uncomfortable with his attitude sometimes. If I saw an opportunity, I would try to rattle him a bit over it. Michael always pushed to get value for money, and that might be fine when producing a film or having work done on the house. I would point out that this was not the same and remind him that he was Michael Winner and could probably afford to buy her a fine dress now and then. I don't know if it was my doing, but he did start to be more generous. Jenny was like me in being perfectly happy in a T-shirt and jeans most of the time, and she certainly didn't spend time hankering after designer clothes. But when the occasion arose, Jenny could look so fabulously elegant and beautiful, it felt only right that Michael should be properly proud and appreciative of that. I think perhaps he needed to find the courage to be kind sometimes. In some ways, kindness might have made him feel vulnerable. If it was not properly valued he might feel he was foolish or deluded. It certainly seemed to take a very long time before he could begin to trust someone.

Michael rarely threw a big party, but he often had dinner with friends. Sometimes they would come to the house first for a few drinks. The most regular visitors in those days were Kenny Everett and Jon and Jenny Anderson. One of the reasons he didn't have many parties was that he hated people disturbing the order of his house. He would run around making sure that glasses were on mats and cigarettes were not dropping ash on the carpet.

Kenny thoroughly enjoyed making fun of this fastidiousness and would cause as much havoc as possible. Wandering about as one of his outlandish characters, he would move the furniture and knock things over. Michael loved it. Kenny could work him up into a hysterical frenzy. And it just didn't stop. Walking to Cibo or the nearby Belvedere, the mayhem always continued. Kenny would make a big show of complaining about everything before Michael could get a look in.

In fact, he would start making ridiculous complaints before we had even sat down. He could impersonate Michael or send him up until we all ached from laughter. Jon Anderson, normally quietly spoken, would join in and together they were like three lunatics out for the day. Those nights were incredible fun and brought out the lighter side of Michael.

I often saw Lewis and Hylda Gilbert when they called in for afternoon tea. Michael clearly had great respect for Lewis. He had directed *Alfie* with Michael Caine, as well as several James Bond films, *Shirley Valentine*, *Educating Rita* and many others. Sometimes Michael and I would walk through Holland Park to their house. When Michael and Lewis were talking I would often get chatting with Hylda. She always showed an interest in my family and what I was doing. She was a kind and motherly character but a strong woman too.

I would be questioned about Michael and his girlfriends. They really liked Jenny, and Hylda's hope was that he would settle down and start behaving a little better. John Cleese and his new wife Alyce Faye were regular visitors too. Alyce was a psychologist and John was working on another book with Robin Skynner called *Life and How to Survive It*. They would embroil Michael in long discussions about mental health. Jenny and I would tease him and say we hoped he was learning something.

Those years were perhaps the happiest in Woodland House. Perhaps even some of the happiest of Michael's life. He and Jenny had fallen into a natural closeness and adored each other. They both had busy lives which seemed to intertwine almost effortlessly. There was rarely a cross word spoken. Most evenings a log fire would crackle in the hearth of the big sitting room, and as Tasha snoozed the air would be full of music, quiet conversation or laughter. The house and garden were lit by a hundred warm orange lights. Approaching from the street at night it looked quite a fairy-tale castle. In those times with Jenny, the house had got the nickname 'Toy Town'.

The late '80s and early '90s were very good years.

I had no job title or contract and was paid for the days I

worked. Often there was another girl working as receptionist, and I acted increasingly as Michael's assistant. It just evolved that way. He would call me to his office and talk about things he was engaged in or planning to do. It was not like a business meeting, it was more like the phone calls we used to have. He would mull things over – anything from a film script to a new washing machine. I suppose he found me to be the right kind of sounding board, although I didn't think of it that way at the time. He had a secretary and PA to type his letters, John to take care of most administrative work and he had a partner. There were builders and cleaners, accountants and lawyers; someone for everything. My role was to be more like a trusted friend. I had no specific qualifications, but I did have some skills. If the housekeeper was away I could cook lunch. If Jenny was away I could accompany him to any event. If something needed doing and I couldn't do it myself, I knew how to find the right person. And I knew Michael well enough to make sure things were done in the way he would want. That, of course, was quite a skill in itself. He was very particular and riddled with what might seem to many to be rather eccentric idiosyncrasies. I think instinctively I always understood how important it was to take those details seriously. Also, I had got to know the staff in the house and liked them all.

Michael wasn't someone to show great interest in other people's lives unless they were more famous or wealthy than him. But when someone who worked in the house was unhappy or going through a difficult time, I would let him know. He and Jenny could concentrate on their work and I would do my best to ensure that the domestic side of things ran smoothly. Michael liked to make the decisions, however small, so often it was simply a case of keeping him informed.

The days frequently involved great drama. This was usually because of his short temper, impatience or simply the shouting and swearing he is famous for.

One morning I heard a bellowing roar from the stairs and, rushing out, I saw Lily cowering in the hall and Michael shouting over the bannisters.

HOW DARE YOU BRING A STRANGER INTO MY HOUSE, HOW DARE YOU, I WILL NOT TOLERATE THIS BEHAVIOUR, IT IS FUCKING OUTRAGEOUS, YOU WILL NOT EVER BRING A MAN IN HERE WITHOUT MY PERMISSION, DO YOU FUCKING UNDERSTAND? I SAID DO YOU UNDERSTAND? IT IS TOTALLY FUCKING UNACCEPTABLE.

Lily looked terrified and was sobbing, 'Sorry, sir, sorry, please sir, sorry, is my fiancé, is my fiancé, we get marry soon, sir, sorry, sir.' Michael stormed back up to his bedroom and slammed the door behind him. He had just had his early morning swim and seen Lily tiptoeing to the front door with Dante, her fiancé. Poor Lily was very shaken and upset, and I got her up to the kitchen and tried to calm her down. She had met Dante only a few days earlier and they had immediately fallen for each other. Dante had proposed and they were married by the end of the week. All turned out well. Michael agreed that Dante could share her rooms at the top of the house. He even told me that he was glad to have another man about. It was good extra security, especially when he was away. And Dante was clearly a kind and good man. He worked as a hotel night porter and Lily would let him in noiselessly in the early hours of each morning. One day Michael presented him with a key to the front door. This was an honour bestowed on very few people and Dante became one of the trusted members of the household. When Michael was away I noticed that he would go and work outside, raking the lawns or clearing leaves from under the terrace. I was surprised when I first saw him doing this and asked him if he had been told to. He said no, he hadn't, and begged me not to say anything. He said he was very grateful to Michael and he just wanted to help in some way. Through the most unlikely scenarios Michael usually managed to have some good and loyal people around him.

One morning the buzzer went and Michael called me up to the office. 'What's this, what's this, what's this?' he was repeating as he waved a newspaper at me. It was a black-and-white photograph of me wearing only a kind of leopard-print loincloth when aged about twenty. I was a bit embarrassed. 'I don't fucking believe it,' he went on, laughing. 'You never let me see your tits but now everyone in the fucking world can stare at them. You are un-fucking-believable.' Michael never struck me as lecherous; it was more like the fascination of a schoolboy. The picture tore as I tried to grab the newspaper from him. It had not occurred to me that he did not know I had occasionally modelled topless. Pictures like this would occasionally appear in a newspaper but it all seemed so long ago. When I was going out with Jim Lane he had bought as many of the prints and negatives as he could find but a few pictures were still around. I hadn't really minded them going out into the world at the time. I just didn't really like people I knew seeing them. Later, I sometimes found them irritating, but, to be honest, that was mainly because I wished that they had been a bit better quality.

* * *

It was 1991 when work began on the television series *Michael Winner's True Crimes*. Michael introduced each episode, which would tell the story of a crime through re-enactment. It might be from the recent past or long ago. He enjoyed being a raconteur and through *True Crimes* had found a place for those skills. I remember he told me it made him feel like he was Alfred Hitchcock and I think he modelled his voice on him too. Jeff Pope was the director, and it was produced by Simon Shaps. Together they had created it, and Michael had great respect for them both. He thoroughly enjoyed working with them, too, and felt that the series had great value. After Michael Grade, then chief executive of Channel 4, criticised it as exploitative, the programme was axed. Michael vehemently disagreed with Michael Grade's opinions and felt it was as a direct result of his comments that the series was stopped. He didn't hide his anger, but there wasn't much choice but to get on with other things. After all, Michael was no stranger to the cut-and-thrust or the capricious nature of the business. But it did seem that he felt he had lost something important that could have run for years and that fitted him so perfectly.

There were many lunches when he and Jeff talked endlessly about the programme. But it wasn't to be saved.

Among everything else, an artist named Peter Edwards would occasionally call at the house. Michael was having his portrait painted. It was huge, of course – I think a little bigger than life size. Well, I suppose it had to be just that bit 'larger than life'. Peter was quite a serious young man and would work on sketches as Michael sat barking orders at Jenny or me to bring more wine or crisps or something. He enjoyed those sittings and I'm certain it made him feel rather grand.

He couldn't resist showing off a little and would bellow and swear even more than usual. I felt sorry for the painter sometimes, as he had work to do and it can't have been made easier with The Michael Winner Show going on around him. Michael would nitpick about how his hair looked or, most often, about the size his feet appeared. But I think that was just an excuse to amuse himself by trying to terrify Peter. In mock outrage he would shout things like,

PETER, I KNOW THAT THERE IS SOMETHING CALLED PERSPECTIVE BUT HOW CAN THIS FOOT BE EIGHTEEN TIMES BIGGER THAN THAT FOOT? IT IS FUCKING HUGE. AND I LIKE THAT YOU'VE PUT IN SOME PIGEON SHIT BUT THE MAIDS SCRUB THIS TERRACE EVERY FUCKING MORNING. PUT IN SOME SHIT BY ALL MEANS, PETER, BUT PLEASE, NOT A WHOLE MOUNTAIN OF FUCKING GUANO.

Michael had a good time and Peter survived. It was comical, but perhaps a little alarming if you did not know him. But Peter had painted Ivor Cutler and some of the Liverpool poets, so I'm sure he had come across eccentricity in various forms before. In the final painting, we see Michael sitting in a teak garden chair on the terrace with his right foot up on his left knee. His hair is unkempt and he has holes in his tatty black moccasins. That is what Michael wanted. And it shows a side of him very well. When finally it was finished it was put up above the main staircase. At twilight in the winter when the trees were bare you could see it from the street as you approached the house. It made me jump a few times when I first noticed it. It was as though he was really there, looking down at me.

By now, I had known Michael for a long time and worked at the house for over a year. Many times I had witnessed him screaming and yelling at some poor soul. He had snapped at me or sworn at me sometimes and we had the occasional small argument but I had not yet been on the receiving end of one of his tirades. One evening I went to meet Diana at Il Portico, a restaurant just round the corner in Kensington High Street. When Michael gave me use of the bedroom at the back of the house, he had made it clear that, except for the nights I visited Diana in hospital, I was to be back by 10.30. Other people might want to sleep, and to return later than that was, he considered, just plain rude. If I went out with friends, they knew about the rule and made fun of my curfew. I had always respected it, but on this occasion Diana's sister was late to pick her up. This was before most people had mobile phones, so I could not leave Diana alone not knowing how she might get home. She was still not yet fully mobile again after her accident. It was 10.45 when I crept into the hall. The house was in darkness except for the swaying shadows of trees cast by the street lamps outside. Not wanting to risk waking anyone, I didn't put a light on but found my way slowly up the first flight of stairs. Just as I passed the landing by Michael's office, the roaring started. I nearly jumped out of my shoes. 'IT IS VERY DANGEROUS, IT IS VERY DANGEROUS, THIS CANNOT HAPPEN, IT IS VERY SERIOUS.'

Michael was shouting from the darkness, his voice low at first and then building in volume. I was terrified and my first thought was that he was warning me that someone had broken into the house or something had happened. I tried to ask what was going on but he did not stop, instead his shouting grew louder and louder. 'THIS IS UTTERLY IMPOSSIBLE, THIS MUST NEVER HAPPEN, DO YOU UNDERSTAND? PEOPLE NEED TO SLEEP, IT IS SO DANGEROUS YOU WILL BE FIRED, YOU CANNOT FUCKING WORK HERE IF YOU FUCKING DO THIS, IT IS VERY, VERY SERIOUS.'

I tried to explain that I had been in an impossible situation, but he would not stop shouting, never mind listen. I backed upstairs to my room and on and on he went screaming and screaming. I was terrified. If I had not seen him like this before I would have run out of the house.

When I got to my bedroom he followed me in and still he was bellowing, 'THIS WILL NEVER HAPPEN AGAIN, YOU MUST UNDERSTAND, DO YOU FUCKING UNDERSTAND? IT IS UN-FUCKING-ACCEPTABLE, IT MUST NOT HAPPEN, YOU WILL BE FIRED, DO YOU UNDERSTAND, FIRED, FIRED, YOU CAN NEVER WORK HERE IF YOU EVER FUCKING DO THIS AGAIN...' I stood there frozen. I was in shock. Tears were now running down my face. I had been so frightened.

Still the shouting went on, probably for about ten minutes, though it seemed much longer. Eventually he turned and walked out of the room. I had started to grow angry as his screaming continued. He may have stopped because he had sensed that. I slammed the door very hard behind him. As the shock and anger subsided I felt very lonely. Everything had been going so well, and suddenly it all seemed ruined. I kept asking myself if I was foolish not to have seen it coming. I felt trapped at the top of what now felt like an icy castle.

From that time on, something changed for me. I realised that at any time there could be a similar explosion. At any time he could throw a hand grenade into a situation. A good day or a happy evening could be blown to smithereens by an outburst like that. The next morning in the kitchen with Lily, the atmosphere was very gloomy. She had heard the outburst and she knew exactly what I was going through. When the buzzer in the kitchen rattled I did not quite know what to expect. 'Good morning, Dinah, could you come up here please.' Michael sounded normal and I went up the stairs to the office. It was as if nothing had happened. In fact, he was chirpier than usual. 'Good morning, dear. Did you have a nice evening? How was Diana?'

There was no mention of his behaviour the night before, but I'm certain he felt the need to be a little bit charming that day. It was a Friday, and soon I was on the train home. I wanted to blank the memory of his vicious rant. It made me shudder when I thought of it. It made me want to never go back. But then I thought of all the good times, and besides, my job was now the only regular income for the family. My thoughts pulled me backwards and forwards.

When I told my mother the story it sounded rather feeble. I realised she couldn't possibly know how earth-shattering and horrible it had been. That made me feel a little lonelier again, but I couldn't blame her. 'Yes, well, we know he has a bit of a temper,' she said. 'But probably not as bad as your stepfather. At least he doesn't throw things or hit you or anything. And it's not as if you're married to him. At the end of the day you can just walk away. Don't let it bother you, it's a good job and you can't let a trifle like that get to you.' I tried not to think about it that weekend, and the children, friends and muddy dogs made that quite easy.

On Monday morning as I stepped into the hall Lily was there grabbing at my coat and pulling it off me before I could even put my bags down. 'Quickly, quickly, he want to see you quickly, madam, quickly, quickly, hupstair, hupstair.'

I was still trying to wake up from the cold and draughty early morning train journey as I ran up to the office. Michael was hopping from foot to foot with excitement. 'I've got a great treat for you tonight, dear, a fabulous treat,' he said, grinning at my blank face. 'We are going to the Guildhall, the Guildhall.'

Now he was dancing about and waving his arms as I stood staring and waiting for the punchline. 'We are going to the Guildhall to have dinner with ... to have dinner with ... Princess Diana, Princess Diana.' He was squeaking with delight. My jaw dropped. Then my face must have lit up. He knew I was a very big fan. He was too.

'What ... Princess Diana, Princess Diana?' It was all I could say at first. Repeating her name was helping it to sink in. Soon we were jumping and skipping round the desk singing 'Princess Diana, Princess Diana, Princess Diana', and giggling like children.

'But what am I going to wear?' I said when the reality of it had struck home.

'Oh, your black trousers and white shirt will be perfect,' he said. We spent the next few hours sorting out *his* clothes. It was the first time I had seen him pay any great attention to his appearance. He wore black silk trousers and jacket and we made sure they were immaculate. Michael had black boots with a bit of a heel which he put on if he wanted to look taller. Michael White, the chauffeur, took us in the Phantom and it was all still quite unreal, gliding almost silently through London. Guildhall is a fantastically beautiful building that dates back to the 1400s. Inside it was like a glittering cathedral. With the red carpet, candles and chandeliers, and all the tables set for dinner, it was breathtaking. My memory of it is as if remembering a dream. Michael did exchange a few words with Her Royal Highness. I smiled at her and was happy she did not ask me anything. I'm sure I would not have been able to speak. At dinner, if I looked to my left she was on the next table and I could see her back and then profile when she turned to talk to her neighbour. I looked to my left a lot that evening. She was wearing red. And what a fine profile. What a nose. I could not stop smiling and Michael stayed as excited as ever too. Before we left, he went off in search of something and in the car home he produced an embossed plate. He gave it to me, saying he thought my mother would like it. If I didn't still have it I might have thought that evening really was a dream. The dinner was for the Royal Marsden Hospital Cancer Appeal. The banquet of the '90s presented by the great cooks of the decade in the presence of Her Royal Highness the Princess of Wales. I was there, I'm sure I was; I've got the plate.

*   *   *

The house had become increasingly busy in the lead-up to Michael shooting his next film, *Dirty Weekend*, adapted from Helen Zahavi's thrilling novel, which centres on a weekend killing spree committed by a former sex worker. There were offices high up in the attic rooms and an editing suite too. Ron Purdie, one of the producers, and also Charles Hubbard, the location manager, were often there, and Michael did the casting from his own office. I never saw Michael ask an actor to perform from a text, improvise or even read for him. He would just talk to them for a while. For a later film he did ask Chris Rea to do a screen test, but that was simply because Chris was a musician and Michael wanted to see what he might be like as an actor.

Sue Wain was to be head of wardrobe and Michael told me that I would do all the hair and make-up. I asked him if he would promise not to shout at me and he said simply, 'Of course, dear, of course I won't shout at you.' The first few weeks of filming took place in London and then we all went to Brighton, where rooms in two hotels were booked. Lia Williams and Rufus Sewell played the main characters, and there was quite a host of other well-known actors, such as David McCallum, Christopher Adamson, Lorraine Doyle, Simone Hyams, Sean Pertwee and many others. Some were very young but on their way to increasing success. Sylvia Syms also had a part and it was lovely seeing her again. Sue and I set up our things in neighbouring rooms.

Before we had started I had said to Michael that I just couldn't see how I could prepare all the actors on my own. He agreed that I could have a friend with me to act as runner. 'Hele' Hunt came down from Heswall. She lived not far from me. She could talk for England and Michael quickly nicknamed her 'Motormouth'. It became a running joke with the crew, as even when she was quiet Michael would often just shout, 'MOTORMOUTH, WHY DON'T YOU JUST SHUT UP.' She gritted her teeth and put up with it, and without her help I would never had got actors ready in time. I would certainly never have had a sandwich or even a cup of coffee. As it was, by the end of the six weeks or so filming, I had lost more than a stone.

During the early weeks of filming I had sensed a bit of

tension growing among the crew. The schedule was pretty frantic and Michael had been screaming and shouting at people quite regularly. They were aware that I knew Michael well and now worked for him. And they had also noticed he had not shouted at me. At best they were wary of me, and as usual I was in a slightly difficult position. But I was kept so frantically busy I did not really give it much more thought. One day, when everyone was gathered on Brighton Pier, Michael asked Sue for a safety pin. She couldn't find one. Michael exploded.

You are the head of wardrobe, you are the head of wardrobe AND YOU HAVEN'T EVEN GOT A FUCKING SAFETY PIN. IT IS UN-FUCKING-BELIEVABLE, YOU FUCKING MORONIC IDIOT, I JUST NEED ONE FUCKING SAFETY PIN. I'M NOT ASKING FOR A HUNDRED FUCKING PINS, JUST ONE FUCKING PIN, IT IS COMPLETELY UN-FUCKING-ACCEPTABLE...

I had a safety pin and ran over to Michael with it. I thought it would stop his tirade. I soon wished I hadn't. It just made it worse.

WHAT? WHAT THE FUCK IS THIS? WHAT IS FUCKING GOING ON? EVEN THE FUCKING STYLIST HAS GOT A PIN. CAN'T YOU BE BOTHERED TO CARRY YOUR OWN FUCKING PIN? YOU ARE THE HEAD OF FUCKING WARDROBE AND YOU DON'T HAVE ONE FUCKING SAFETY PIN, WHAT KIND OF FUCKING MORON ARE YOU? I SHOULDN'T BE HAVING TO ASK AROUND THE WHOLE FUCKING CREW, I SHOULDN'T BE HAVING TO FUCKING WELL ASK

AROUND THE WHOLE FUCKING CREW BECAUSE YOU CAN'T BE FUCKING BOTHERED TO CARRY ONE FUCKING PIN. IN FUTURE WHEN I ASK YOU FOR A PIN YOU WILL HAVE A FUCKING PIN, DO YOU UNDERSTAND? I SAID DO YOU UNDERSTAND...?

It was horrible and went on for quite a while. When the filming was done for the day, Sue came and found me at the hotel. She was furious and began shouting at me for being so unprofessional. I really didn't understand what she meant at first.

She made it very clear that it was not my job to supply safety pins or interfere in someone else's line of work. She was right. That's how it is on a film set. I may have intended to be helpful but all I had done was undermine her. There was not a good atmosphere for a while after that. I heard rumours that the crew were trying to set me up to get an outburst of Michael's temper. Lia Williams was needed for a retake in a red dress, and Michael had given us twenty minutes to get her ready. After quarter of an hour she emerged from Wardrobe. I was never going to do her hair and make-up in five minutes. Her hair needed to be put up in curls and match exactly the earlier takes. I did my best and she was only a little late on set. But there was no yelling from Michael. I was in quite a difficult and lonely position so it was a real godsend to have my friend Hele working with me. But after a day or two Sue and I had put it all behind us and got on well again.

During the weeks of filming I didn't see much of Michael in the evenings. By the time I had prepared everything for the next day, it was too late to sit down for dinner and I just wanted to sleep. He would spend his time with the bigger stars of the cast. David McCallum was perhaps the most famous of the actors. He had been rocketed to fame as agent Illya Kuryakin in the television series *The Man from U.N.C.L.E.* His father, David McCallum senior, had been principal first violinist of the Royal Philharmonic Orchestra, and David nearly took up a musical career playing the oboe and French horn. Instead he went to the Royal Academy of Dramatic Art and was there in the same year as Joan Collins. Michael told me that David had been married to Jill Ireland for ten years. He also said she had been his own girlfriend once, and in 1956 she had proposed but he had not accepted and Jill went on to marry David later that year. He said he had always got on so well with Jill and really loved her but he had been very young and had no idea of how he was going to make his way in life. She was one of his very first girlfriends and one he seemed to genuinely regret losing.

I was very glad when the filming for *Dirty Weekend* was over. I missed home and the children and also felt totally drained. And none of my clothes fitted any more. When I first walked in the door Luke, my youngest, reached up and pulled at my belt and my trousers just fell down. In six weeks I had become a rake. Filming had been all work and worry with not enough time to eat. I've been lucky in not ever having to pay much attention to my weight. That's a mixed blessing, though, as girl friends can be irritated by it. Michael often said that I was a pleasure to take for dinner because I would eat anything put in front of me. After a particularly large meal he would sometimes proudly announce to the waiter something like, 'She would now like to have a large selection of cheeses and berries.' But day-to-day work with him did involve a fair amount of exercise, mostly running up and down stairs or backwards and forwards to Kensington High Street.

Back at Woodland House, things were increasingly busy. Also, from my point of view anyway, they had taken a turn for the worse. Lily and Dante had upped and left. Michael had bombarded Lily with an ever-increasing number of memos and her nerves were in tatters. I saw them recently and they both showed great respect and gratitude towards Michael, and Jenny too. But Lily showed me a folder of Michael's angry notes, all written in felt tip in his shouting capitals. She read some out. 'THESE BAGELS ARE ROTTEN – WHY DO YOU REFUSE TO DO WHAT I ASK – GET THEM ONLY AT HARRODS.' Another read, 'GET BAGELS ONLY AT HARRODS – FOR THE 50TH TIME I ASK.' A few of them had become comical, divorced from whatever event had sparked them: 'THIS IS DISGRACEFUL OF YOU' and 'THIS HAS GOT TO STOP'. After reading each memo she would shriek with delight and I noticed Dante could not help but smile at the memories too.

The kitchen was the heart of the house and Lily had kept it beating happily with her constant cooking and shrill laughter. And we had always looked after each other during any tough times. The table in the kitchen had been my sanctuary during the day but now it felt cold and deserted. While a new housekeeper was being found I agreed to fetch and arrange the flowers and also cook lunches. The one thing I had asked was to be allowed a little leeway in timing. I knew the rage that Michael could fly into if a meal was two minutes late. He agreed not to shout if lunch was not always served dead on one o'clock and he stuck to his word. The house was especially busy, as much of the post-production work for the film was taking place in the various upstairs offices. Michael enjoyed being involved in lots of activity and was thriving on it, but he seemed to be increasingly insensitive, especially towards Jenny. It can't have helped that he had not cast her in the lead role of the film. There was no clear reason why she would not have been ideal. But far more than this, Jenny's mother had died and Michael was not showing much understanding. She was growing quieter and their happiness together seemed to be slipping away. At the end of the working day, Michael had gradually stopped being his usual cheerful self and instead was often difficult and argumentative. Jenny is a strong character, but his behaviour was wearing her down. She and I had discovered that if we could get him to have even half a glass of wine it could make him quite jovial for the evening.

We had also taken to hiding a bottle of vodka upstairs and would often have a couple of shots each at about six o'clock. It would 'take the edge off' if he started shouting and carrying on at either of us.

It was not a good day for me when the new housekeeper arrived. Ping was Chinese and wore a uniform that was white and heavily starched. She was a stern and serious lady and made it clear that she did not want anybody in the kitchen during the day. It distracted her from her duties. I was appointed an office up the stairs from Michael's and he set me the task of indexing his huge collection of newspaper cuttings. With no buzzer, I worked with the door open so that I could hear him bellow when he needed me.

One evening, Michael said to get ready to go for dinner at the Belvedere on the edge of Holland Park. He then pointed out into the garden and told me that 'the Jewish Princess' was coming too. Simone Hyams was on the lawn. I had met her during the filming of *Dirty Weekend*. She went on to become well known for her role in the television series *Grange Hill*.

Jenny was away, I think working on a film, and Michael probably wanted me as a kind of chaperone for appearance's sake. A few weeks later, I went down to the kitchen early one evening to get something to eat and the door from the lounge opened and a startled woman shouted, 'Who the hell are you?' I had my back to her, as I was getting something from the fridge. Michael was yelling for her to close the door but I recognised her as Simone.

I didn't like the situation I now found myself in. We all know how difficult it can be when friends who are a couple are going through a break-up. Sometimes it is clear where your loyalties lie and you are supportive when really needed. But ideally you don't get involved. I was now employed by Michael, but at the same time I had grown to feel that Jenny was a close friend. As his assistant and confidante, I was, in effect, paid to be on his side, even though I was actually much more in sympathy with Jenny. It was sad that Michael was carrying on this kind of secret liaison and I certainly really hated knowing anything about it. When I found a chance I would try to talk to him. I wanted at least to tell him how destructive I thought he was being. He would listen sometimes, but there was no sign of him changing his ways. It was clear that Jenny was not at all happy. Michael had found her in tears shortly after her mother died and shown little patience, let alone sympathy. 'Light and bright' was his new expression. He would announce that he only wanted people around him who were 'light and bright'.

Through his time with Jenny I had watched Michael gradually become more considerate and civilised. Now he seemed to be dropping back into his more selfish and arrogant ways.

Years later he did say that the more he felt himself falling for Jenny the more he felt panicky and would lash out at her. His star sign was Scorpio and he said it seemed like sometimes he stung himself with his own scorpion tail.

Little by little, the atmosphere in Woodland House was souring. I spent miserable days doing filing and other paperwork in my tiny office. Now and then the monotony and loneliness would be broken by an outburst of screaming from Michael. At this time it usually concerned the gluing and layout of the cuttings books. These were like giant scrapbooks – huge volumes bound together by brass bolts. Articles from newspapers and magazines were cut out and pasted onto large white loose-leaf pages. The articles were of course only about, or bearing mention of, Michael Winner. When completed, the sheets would be sent to John Fraser at Farley Court to be bolted into the current volume. Sometimes I would do the cutting and pasting and sometimes a receptionist would be trained up. It was a serious business as there were so many possible ways of getting it wrong. And getting it wrong would mean a very angry Michael. The edges had to be straight and the various cuttings arranged on the page to minimise wasted space. Pritt Stick was the chosen glue but any lumps had to be carefully identified and removed from the back of the sticky newspaper. Then and only then was it safe and ready to be very carefully smoothed onto the page. It was a task that required great skill, concentration and nerves of steel. Even when I felt I had finally mastered the process there could still be a sudden and horrible hoo-ha.

WHAT ARE YOU DOING, YOU FUCKING MORON? WHAT THE FUCK ARE YOU DOING? HOW MANY TIMES DO I HAVE TO FUCKING TELL YOU THIS

IS UN-FUCKING-ACCEPTABLE, YOU ARE COM-
PLETELY FUCKING RUINING EVERYTHING.

While trying to cope with Michael's bellowing my mind would
start racing, searching for the mistake … Are they cut straight?
… The sides are glued parallel … No lumps in the glue …
I'm sure I didn't miss a glue lump … They are well arranged
… What have I done? … What have I done?

YOU ARE FORTY FUCKING YEARS OLD, A CHILD
OF FOUR COULD MAKE A BETTER JOB OF IT, YOU
ARE FORTY FUCKING YEARS OLD FOR FUCK'S
SAKE, CAN'T YOU EVEN GLUE A FUCKING PIECE
OF FUCKING PAPER?

There was no point looking for a glimmer of humour in his
eyes. This was the cuttings book and was never to be regarded
in any way other than with the utmost seriousness. You didn't
need a high degree of intelligence or intuition to know that
any flippancy here could lead to instant dismissal. And he
needed to see that someone was suitably shocked and shaken
by his shouting or he would simply increase the volume. Tentatively I would have to say something like, 'Erm what … what
is wrong … I … err…' That was usually just enough to get
him to pinpoint the problem.

ARE YOU FUCKING SERIOUS? LOOK AT IT, LOOK,
JUST FUCKING LOOK AT IT. IT IS USELESS, IT
IS FUCKING USELESS, WHY DON'T YOU USE THE
FUCKING GLUE, I PAY FOR THE GLUE, IT'S NOT
YOUR FUCKING GLUE SO FUCKING USE IT YOU

STUPID FUCKING MORONIC TWAT, USE THE FUCKING GLUE, LOOK, LOOK THEY ARE HARDLY STUCK AT ALL, THERE IS NO FUCKING GLUE ON IT, WHAT ARE YOU TRYING TO DO? WE DO NOT HAVE A SHORTAGE OF FUCKING GLUE, WHEN I TELL YOU TO GLUE SOMETHING I EXPECT YOU TO GLUE IT NOT JUST PUT A FUCKING SPOT IN THE MIDDLE AND THINK I'M SUCH A FUCKING MORON I WON'T NOTICE. IT IS USELESS, DO YOU UNDERSTAND? I DON'T EVER WANT TO HAVE TO TELL YOU AGAIN, YOU ARE FORTY FOR FUCK'S SAKE, NOW DO WHAT YOU WERE TOLD TO DO AND THIS TIME USE SOME FUCKING GLUE...

While the screaming went on he had pulled at a corner that was not stuck down. Everything had been going so well but I had missed a corner. Maybe I had put the Pritt Stick on it but it had dried too much just on that corner before I pressed it onto the page. Maybe I had spotted some lumps in the Pritt Stick and the time it took to pick them off had allowed that corner to dry. It was not always possible to know exactly what had led to the catastrophe. But what I did know was that I was beginning to feel that I couldn't go on like this for much longer.

One evening, just before the 10.30 curfew, I got back to the house and was met by Jenny and Michael looking rather worried and glum. They had just returned, having been out to dinner, and discovered there had been a robbery.

My room had been ransacked and all my jewellery stolen. The only other thing missing was a small clock belonging to Michael. There was no sign of any break-in and the police concluded that it was an 'inside job'. A few months earlier Jenny had lost the jewellery given to her by her mother. I had not been working that week and heard that a maid was fired although there was no clear evidence that it had been her. The mystery was never solved. It was such a sad blow for Jenny as with the recent loss of her mother they were her most cherished possessions. I only kept my jewellery in the house so I had something when I went for dinner with Michael. There was a pearl necklace, a pair of diamond earrings and my wedding jewellery. When I mentioned insurance, he said I would have to claim from my own as he was not going to. I felt a little let down by his attitude.

At home that weekend I was very unhappy. Gradually my situation with Michael had deteriorated and now I realised I did not want to continue working for him. One by one, things had mounted up. I had recently been told that he did not want me going to any more auditions. He said that even Jenny was struggling, so for me to hope to earn my living as an actress was ridiculous. From the beginning I had worked two weeks on and two weeks off. I was only paid for the days I worked, of course. At the time this was because I was not prepared to only have weekends with the children. It meant we only had just enough to pay the mortgage and survive, but it was enough and I did have a good amount of time at home. Over the past few months I had realised that even if I needed a bigger income I could not think of working full time for Michael. After two weeks I had to get away, or I would have had some kind of a breakdown. Work had become increasingly stressful. To add to everything, Takis had discovered he had problems with blocked arteries and would need one or two operations. That weekend, with Diana, we wrote letters and then threw them into the waste bin. We wrote long polite letters, short rude letters, angry letters and funny letters. Eventually we settled on a short and polite one which simply thanked him but also made it clear that I would not be continuing to work for him.

A day or two later the phone rang. It was Michael. He wanted to know how, as friends, I could think of writing him such a short letter of resignation. I explained that I felt he no longer seemed to be behaving like a friend or even treating me as a valued employee. He apologised for his behaviour and asked if I would come in on Monday so we could at least talk about everything.

On Monday I drove down with Diana. We had agreed that whatever happened that day I would stay with her at her flat in Hammersmith. I did not want to set foot in the office, so Michael and I sat in the lounge. He was at his most charming and insisted that we were good friends and should be able to sort out any problems. As I went through all the things I found difficult or disturbing, he did his best to find a solution. He said that Ping the housekeeper would soon be leaving and so I would be able to use the kitchen again. Of his shouting, he told me that by now I should realise it was just his way and not to take any notice of it. I presume he saw that I was not looking enthusiastic as, after repeating many times that we were friends, he went on to say that he would leave me £500,000 in his will. He knew that waving a large sum of money in front of me, and for a distant and unknowable future, would not carry much weight, so he focused on how my two sons would benefit. I said that was very nice of him but I was having to think of *now* and how to survive. It was then that he offered a wage increase. I was not really expecting that and I had to think fast. Takis was still not working except for occasional gigs and my contacts in the acting world had been fading fast. I was still keen to set up a hair salon, but I knew it would take time and be almost impossible without any savings. I agreed to give work with Michael another chance.

It was 1993 and when Easter came, Jenny had to fly to America to work. Michael did not like evenings alone and certainly did not like to be seen out without a woman at his side. He had no intention of spending Easter on his own at home. He decided on Paris and asked me to go with him. I had been looking forward to being at home with my family but he promised I could be back for Monday. At least I would be there in time for the egg hunt with the children. We flew to Paris and Michael had booked rooms at the Ritz. I grew very uneasy when he hired a Porsche. Fortunately, most car journeys with Michael also included a chauffeur. Even a short journey with Michael driving was always a very frightening one. As far as I'm aware, he never killed anyone. But the experience of most passengers was the feeling that the next few moments would probably be their last. On a Monday morning, the chauffeur would know if Michael had used any of the cars over the weekend. A wing or bumper would be scratched or dented. It was a regular sight at the beginning of the week to see a man in a dark suit make his way from the garage through the garden and up to Michael's office to report the damage. And the chauffeur had to keep a straight face when he said, 'I've found a dent on the left front wing of the Bentley, sir.'

Michael would flap his hand and say, 'Yes, yes, I know, I know, just get it sorted out, will you, get it sorted out, get a quote, get a quote.' Michael always wanted them repaired straight away. It will have added up to a fortune over the years.

As I lay back in the low passenger seat of the Porsche I got no feeling of reassurance from the clunk-click of the safety belt. Flashes of my life were already starting to pass before my eyes. Michael happily crunched into gear and the car jumped off in kangaroo hops. 'I've never really got the hang of a Porsche,' he said. 'They don't handle well at all.' His driving style fitted in with the general honking and sign language of the Parisian approach. And I learnt some new French words; 'connard' and 'merde' were the main ones.

When we found a nice, almost stationary traffic jam I felt a little safer. But then to my horror he mentioned that we were going on a *trip*! My heart pounded. A 'trip' must mean more than a few miles, I thought! My mouth went dry and I sipped water from a bottle before saying something like, 'It seems such a shame to leave Paris, there is so much to explore right here, right on our doorstep. Are we going on a motorway?' I needed to think fast. There might just be a way to get out of it.

'Oh, it's not far.' He said cheerfully. 'Only twenty miles or so, and you will love it, dear, it's an absolutely delightful place I know, and they do an amazing cheese. I know you like cheese, dear; you'll love it.' He was right; I did enjoy cheese. But just at that moment I could only think of my children; how they needed me and how I wanted to be there as they grew up.

We were headed to Barbizon, a little village just south of Paris. Michael was squinting at road signs, looking for names of places he recognised so he could find the way. He had said not to bother with the map. When we got onto the motorway our speed increased and my knuckles whitened as I gripped the sides of my seat. We had not gone far when a fork in the road was fast approaching. The left lane or the right lane? The decision would have to be made quite soon. Michael was not sure. The car rolled from side to side as he tried to make up his mind. He could not remember and he was damned if he was going to go the wrong way. As we hurtled towards the point of the dividing barrier he slammed on the brakes suddenly and we skidded to a halt on a tiny triangle of gravel. The air was thick with dust and there was a constant drone from the horns of passing cars and lorries. The traffic sped past, only inches from either side of us. Beyond the grey steel barrier I could see a thin island of grass. If there had been room to open the door I would have made a dash for safety.

Michael unfolded a map which quickly filled the whole car. The correct road was found but somehow we had to get back into the fast lane from a standing start. I was not much help as by now I was so terrified I was having trouble breathing. I found out one very good thing about a Porsche: it can go from nought to eighty in about a tenth of a second.

Michael had spotted a ten-foot gap between cars and we shot into it. It was a manoeuvre that could only have been pulled off by a very talented driver or a very, very lucky man. For the rest of the journey he told stories which were especially funny and I remember laughing till my sides ached. He was often good with his stories, but I think on this occasion my hysterics were due partly to the euphoria that follows a near-death experience.

Barbizon is an amazingly beautiful place near the forest of Fontainebleau. It was like walking into an Impressionist painting. But it had attracted artists even before their time and in the 1840s it was the bohemian home to painters such as Corot, Millet and Rousseau. There were about twenty artists who became known as the 'Barbizon School'. They had seen an exhibition in Paris of Constable's pictures and were impressed by his kind of realistic painting. It wasn't until a few decades later that their work was noticed by the younger generation, including Monet and Renoir. So this was the spot that joins Constable to the Impressionists. It was fascinating and magical, but the truth is we went straight to the cheese place. The restaurant was in the Hôtellerie du Bas-Bréau. We ate a starter and huge main course before moving on to the cheese that Michael was keen to introduce me to. It was called Fontainebleau. When it arrived, it was the size of a small football and was served in a ceramic pot. The texture and colour and the way it was so beautifully decorated made it appear more like a very large vanilla ice cream.

It was fabulous. And being so mild and light it meant we could eat a huge amount. Now stuffed with cheese, we needed to walk and so we wandered around the narrow streets. Many of the buildings were timber framed and everything was perfectly cared for. The house and studio of Millet and Rousseau had been preserved and were open to the public, but Michael was keener to keep walking. I think he was worried he might not fit into the Porsche. I had made sure to drink as much as I could to give me courage for the return journey. When we got in the car to go back, I reminded him that I had a family and that they loved me and needed me. He admitted that he had been a 'bloody idiot' on the drive out and would go more carefully.

Another highlight of that Easter weekend was a meal at La Tour d'Argent. One of the most famous restaurants in the world and one of the oldest in Paris. It dates back to the 1780s, when it was the Hôtel de la Tour d'Argent. What I remember most was the view. Michael was greeted by an elderly gentleman

My wonderful mother Shelagh enjoying a party moment!

Perks of *Password*. With two Goodies! Bill Oddie and Graham Garden.

The pinnacle of my mother's career as my 'agent'. I am crowned Miss Great Britain.

Honda publicity.
With Dickie Henderson
and Bruce Forsyth at the
Wentworth Golf Tournament,
Virginia Water.

February 1978. Getting hypothermia – a
photo shoot for *Vogue*.

1982, Aintree. One of the most
exhilarating days of my life.

Brookside days. With Dicken Ashworth,
who played Alan Partridge. Leaving the
Mersey and setting off to film on the
Isle of Man.

With Diana Morgan-Hill on
the set of *Deathwish III*, 1985.

With Albert
Finney, Sandy
Lane, Barbados.

John Gielgud and
Peter Ustinov enjoy a
break during filming
of *Appointment with
Death*, Israel, 1987.

Dinner in Israel during
the filming of *Appointment
with Death*. Steven Berkoff,
David Soul and partner,
Hayley Mills, Peter Ustinov,
Lauren Bacall, Piper
Laurie, Clara Fisher.

Jenny on the set of *Appointment with Death*, Israel, 1987.

Michael with his friend Bill Wyman at an opening at the Chris Beetles Gallery, 1988.

Being silly in Whitby during the making of *A Chorus of Disapproval*.

The cast of *Chorus of Disapproval*: Richard Briers, Anthony Hopkins, Prunella Scales, Jeremy Irons, Jenny Seagrove, Gareth Hunt, Lionel Jeffries…

Cocktail happy hour with Jenny Seagrove. Bloody Marys … with a dollop of horseradish sauce!

Sylvia Sims and Lia Williams during filming of *Dirty Weekend*.

Jenny Seagrove, Kenny Everett, Jennifer and Jon Anderson at Woodland House.

Michael with fashion designer Bruce Oldfield, 1992.

The chauffeur Michael
White with the Rolls Royce
Phantom IV.

With Peter Edwards,
the painter of Michael's
favourite portrait.

Dina, my son Luke, and Lily
in the newly refurbished
studio (bedroom) at
Woodland House.

Woodland House and the
banana trees. Michael's
office, and vantage point,
can be seen above the
front door.

Michael with Lara, David and Diana. A happy ending after a five-year battle with British Rail.

With little Ryan – so much a part of the family.

Georgina with Michael on *This is Your Life*, 2001.

Happy days – with Marco Pierre White at Georgina's birthday party in Woodland House.

John Cleese
with the lovely
Georgina, 2001.

With three important
ladies: Zoe, Shirley
and Nicolanne.

Happy times
with Georgina.

whom he called simply 'Tom'. He seemed a lovely man and showed us to a table right by the window. One thing about going to dinner with Michael was that you usually got to sit at the best table. Sometimes he would not be able to book the table he wanted and on arrival would make a big fuss. Mostly I was never very bothered about which table we were at, but he enjoyed making a drama and showing off until he got what he wanted. Now and then he paid for people's meals or champagne in order that they moved. On this occasion I saw that there was definitely a best table and was very glad to be sitting at it. The interior of the restaurant was exquisite but the view was breathtakingly magnificent. You can look up or down the Seine or across the river to the cathedral of Notre Dame. In the early evening light I was hypnotised. I would not really have minded if they had just served me a packet of crisps. I made a mental note to tell my sons when they were older that it was the perfect place to propose to a girl. The atmosphere was timeless and so romantic. I woke from dreaming to see Michael biting into a fat piece of duck. Pressed duck is their speciality and they are reared on the restaurant's own farm. 'Eat, eat, what's wrong with you, dear?' said Michael.

'It's such a beautiful place,' I replied dreamily, still gazing out of the window.

'Yes, I knew you would like it, that's why I brought you here, but eat your fucking duck, it'll get cold and the view's been here for hundreds of years, it's not going anywhere, darling.' Michael was beaming. He really liked seeing people enjoy something he had arranged.

'Wouldn't this be the perfect place to propose to Jenny?' I suggested. The floodlights on Notre Dame had turned it into a fairy-tale castle.

'No, no, I've brought her here already. I'm going to get a ring. I'll get a ring before she gets back from America.' He had occasionally mentioned that he was thinking of asking Jenny to marry him. In the past he had made grand romantic gestures, like the time he had got the entire band of the Coldstream Guards playing on the back lawn for her birthday. That was amazing, but I had begun to feel that his idea of romance was to show off rather than have good insight and imagination.

I worried that he was taking things for granted. 'Well, I'm sure you'll think of something she will really like,' I said. I think I was hoping to plant a seed in his mind.

'I suppose you think I should dress up like a fisherman and do some kind of crazy fucking fish dance. Not everyone's the same, dear, not everyone likes fish.' He roared with laughter. For some reason he always found it hilarious that I had married a Greek man who was not rich. But if I mentioned one of the multimillionaires I knew it would always shut him up.

'He was never a fisherman,' I reminded him. 'Why do you keep saying that? And I never said everyone's the same. Women like romance. That's all I'm trying to say. Women like romance.'

'I make them laugh, darling, I make them laugh and spoil them and they adore me.' Michael was so full of contradictions. He would talk like he was an expert on everything and in the same breath admit that he was a complete idiot.

I made a last attempt to try to put my point over. 'Yes, and that is great for a week or two but I'm telling you: women … like … romance.' Of course I can't remember the exact conversation, but it was over that dinner that we had talked about romance and marriage and I wondered if his recent bad behaviour was to do with his fears. It was obvious he adored Jenny. Michael also liked to be in full control and so his feelings were probably fighting with that. I didn't want to interfere and at the same time, as a friend, I didn't want to stand by if there was some way I could help. And it was horrible seeing Jenny upset. Michael would ask me about all kinds of things. He thought my intuition was good, especially about people's characters. I do trust my intuition most; but I get it wrong sometimes too. He would ask me about all manner of things but when it came to romance he would usually turn it all into a joke.

The next day Michael said he was going to introduce me to a girlfriend of his from the past. We had dinner with a lively and beautiful woman called Geraldine Lynton-Edwards. She had been a dancer and Michael told me she had been his girlfriend for a little while when he was in his twenties and she was still a teenager. They had kept in touch and spent the meal catching up on each other's news.

When I returned to Woodland House, Ping had been replaced by a new housekeeper. The icy winter of the Ping dynasty had drawn to a close and I was introduced to Edith and her warm smile. Edith Sutherland was a cheerful Scottish lady of about forty, and her bright pale-blue eyes and long ponytail of ash-blond hair made a striking impression. Her family had a farm in Scotland and Edith had come to London and left her brother to run it.

There was something about Edith. If someone had told me that she was a duchess or countess I would not have been surprised. She had that kind of grace and confidence, that kind of quality about her. And I was so glad to be out of my lonely office and back at the kitchen table.

On the day Jenny was getting back from America, Michael had asked Mr Cuss, from Henry Hallpike the jeweller's at the bottom of Melbury Road, to bring engagement rings to the house.

He had chosen one and I suggested he meet Jenny at the airport but Michael said he was too busy. I even suggested he drive the Phantom himself. Perhaps even with a chauffeur's hat. He thought that ridiculous. Maybe it wasn't a great idea but sometimes any ideas felt like 'pearls before swine' with Michael. And he would admit he could be a pig at times. At times I fully agreed with him.

All was happy when she arrived and he did propose to her that day. But she told me later that she was bemused by the fact that he could propose to her yet not make the time to meet her at the airport after her six weeks away. I remember we had a few drinks and everything was cheerful, but I can't say I felt Michael had put enough real thought and care into such a special event. Perhaps he really didn't understand something or maybe there was a part of him that would sabotage any attempt he made. Sometimes I did feel sorry for him. He seemed in a kind of trap. Frightened to lose her and scared to get closer. I hoped the atmosphere between them would improve slowly but over the next few weeks it didn't seem to.

Michael called me at home one weekend and told me to get a train to Newcastle instead of London. I was to hire a car and meet him at the airport.

Michael had founded the Police Memorial Trust in 1984 after WPC Yvonne Fletcher had been shot. He had noticed that the men and women of the armed forces frequently have memorials erected in their honour and felt that something similar should be done for police officers. After all, they too could lose their lives in dangerous work and their presence is vital to everybody in the community. On this particular day a plaque was to be unveiled in memory of Sergeant William Forth, who had recently been killed in the line of duty. When we arrived at the site of the ceremony we were greeted by the Member of Parliament for Sedgefield. He was also the shadow Home Secretary – a man called Tony Blair. He was dressed immaculately and Michael became conscious of his own less than perfect appearance. Before sitting down for a cup of tea I tried to tidy him up a bit. His shirt was too small to do up the top button so I made a large knot in his tie to conceal it. He was anxious not to appear disrespectful to the police officer's family. I assured him that they would appreciate his presence there and would be certain to know that he was a slightly eccentric film director.

'Well, I hope you are right, dear,' he said. Tony made a very moving speech and without referring to any notes, which impressed Michael; he told me he thought Mr Blair had a chance of being Prime Minister one day.

Jenny was in a play in the West End and Michael was still busy finishing *Dirty Weekend*. One night shortly after we'd returned from Newcastle, I woke aware of something and got a shock when I opened my eyes. It was about 2 a.m. and Michael was kneeling by my bed in his boxer shorts. He had tears in his eyes and was repeating over and over, 'I've lost her, I've lost her, I've lost Jenny.'

I said, 'What do you mean, what's happened?'

He had phoned the theatre where she was working and then the restaurant she had gone on to. They told him she had left two hours ago.

Michael was in a very upset state so I made him a hot drink

and talked to him until he was a bit calmer. She came in a short while later. But from what I remember that really was the beginning of the very end. Before I left for my few weeks' summer holiday, Jenny told me she did not want to go to Barbados that Christmas. She said she didn't know yet but felt she might not still be at the house when I got back.

In my first week away in Greece I saw an article in the papers about Michael needing a heart operation. I called him and he told me he had had chest pains but wanted to get the film finished and premiered before going into hospital.

He did not mention anything about Jenny. When I got back two weeks later she had gone. He told me that they had argued and she said she was leaving just before he felt ill. When they discovered he needed major surgery she said she would look after him through it. He didn't want her to, but he rarely gave her credit for offering. He would usually make it seem that she left because he was ill, or some other nonsense story. Once she had moved out, he subjected her to a barrage of nastiness. He demanded the return of any jewellery he had given her and even sent a van to pick up furniture. All this had happened before I was back from my summer holiday.

Michael was being dangerously stubborn to delay his operation until after the first screening of *Dirty Weekend*. At 6.00 each evening a doctor would arrive and put him on a drip. This was designed to keep his arteries open and so reduce the risk of a heart attack. Michael would sit watching television and chatting and at ten o'clock the doctor would remove the drip. He needed to have someone near day and night. With some trepidation I offered to work full time until his operation. Fortunately, he had already spoken to Catherine Neilson and she had agreed to stay with him during evenings and weekends.

The final preparations for the premiere were being made and Michael also found time to write foul letters to Jenny. I think what really angered him most was the fact that she had walked out. I'm not sure anyone had done that to him before. From what I could see he had only himself to blame, as his recent behaviour had been terrible. But rather than put his hands up he blamed Jenny for everything. He showed me one letter he wrote. I knew he had it in him to be venomous but this was truly shocking. The language alone was disturbing but the accusations were even more upsetting. He sent me on some errands in the high street and told me to put the letter through the door at Jenny's flat too. I knew that she was finding it a very difficult time and I just couldn't think what to do. I couldn't see how I could put such vitriol through her door, but if I took it back unposted he would explode with anger and post it anyway. Coming back from the shops I bumped into Michael White, the chauffeur. He was walking back from the separate garage where the Rolls-Royce Phantom was kept. He could see I was very upset and I was fighting back tears as I told him what was happening. He took the letter out of my hand and said, 'I'll post that for you, Dinah. Don't you worry about it any more.' With that he took a few steps down the road and posted the envelope down through one of the slots in a street drain. 'That's the place t'post that kind of letter,' he said in his broad Yorkshire accent. I could have kissed him. I knew if any trouble came of it he would take the rap for it too. He respected Jenny and was not frightened of Michael.

I remember one time he strode into the office in a very angry mood. Instead of talking to him during the day, Michael had taken to pushing envelopes under the garage door in the evenings. They were instructions or petty complaints. One day,

Michael the chauffeur had had enough. He marched into the office and dropped an unopened letter on the desk. 'What's that?' he said.

Seeing his anger, Michael replied, a little shakily, 'It's a … well, it's a letter, why don't you open it?'

The chauffeur went on, 'Is it my notice then, Mr Winner?'

Michael seemed quite flustered and as he tore up the letter was saying, 'No, no, of course it's not your notice and it doesn't matter now.'

The chauffeur looked at him and said, 'In future if you've got something to say to me you can say it to my face.'

Michael fidgeted nervously and was going a little pink. 'Yes, yes, OK, OK, but at least working for me, working for me, you know I'm straightforward. You know with me I will always call a spade a spade.'

The chauffeur leant over the desk and said, 'Where I come from we call a spade a shovel,' and then turned and walked out, leaving Michael fidgety and red faced.

Robert Earl, one of the producers of the new film, had recently founded Planet Hollywood, and this was the chosen venue for the screening of *Dirty Weekend*. I thought Michael would be taking Catherine and that she was his official girlfriend, but instead when the day came he told me to get ready. I wondered what I should wear, as I was thinking it would be a grand premiere.

He told me it was just a first screening and any nice dress would be fine. Sure enough, it was quite a low-key event. The film was shown and there were drinks afterwards. I wondered why he had risked his life for it. *Dirty Weekend* was not well received by the critics, so the reviews were probably not very good for his heart either.

The night before he was due in hospital for his triple bypass operation, Catherine arrived at 6.00. Michael had told me he had known her since she was in her teens. Her parents were Polish and moved to London when she was only a few years old. While she was in a play at the Royal Court Theatre in Sloane Square, Michael would go every night and sit in the front row of the audience. Eventually she agreed to have dinner with him. I heard him say on several occasions that she was the most beautiful girl he had ever seen. Her acting work began on the stage and she starred at the National Theatre and also in the West End. She then worked in many television dramas, including *The Ruth Rendell Mysteries* and *Coronation Street*. Her big break in film was as Lady June Carberry in *White Mischief* in 1987. I did not discover until a few years later that she had recently played Irene Saunders in *White Hunter Black Heart*. It was a Clint Eastwood film based on the story of John Huston filming *The African Queen*. Clint Eastwood has always been the only film star whose picture I was happy to have on my wall. He was my pin-up as a teenager and I always hoped that one day we would have a farm together and lots of children. If I had known that Catherine had met him and actually sat at the same table, let alone worked with him, I would have grilled her with questions. Instead she kept doing impersonations of Michael. We were in the kitchen and crying with laughter. I started to get cramps in my stomach. She didn't stop until we noticed Michael's face was turning red and his lips were purple. We got him to sit down and take some deep breaths.

Catherine looked after him well but her humour could be dangerous to anyone with a heart problem.

I liked Catherine, but from the day she arrived to look after

Michael I did sense a growing tension. Just like some other girlfriends, it seemed she was becoming increasingly wary or resentful of me. And I didn't need to be a psychologist to work it out. It had never been a problem with Jenny. She seemed to know from the beginning who I was and why I was there. But often other girlfriends, past, present and future, would see me as some kind of irritation or threat to their position in his life. Also, they knew he confided in me. They knew that I would probably have been told if any kind of arrangement had been made, such as their bills being paid or other incentives offered. Michael would talk to me about all manner of things they very likely would have preferred to remain private. And he would sometimes take pleasure in making them angry or resentful. He would sit back and enjoy the drama. He often told me he enjoyed it. 'It's entertainment, darling, it's just entertainment, don't take it all so seriously.' After all, it was all centred around him. And there were all kinds of ways he could use me to get at them. If they didn't want to do something or go somewhere he could say, 'OK, I will take Dinah then.'

At the very least, they saw me as a thorn in their side. At worst, they saw me as someone they thought could push them off their perch if I chose to. Michael would make it known that he had asked me to marry him several times. They couldn't help but make all kinds of false assumptions based on that. With that kind of snippet of information anyone would assume I was an ex-girlfriend. And *he* wasn't going to correct them. I could understand why they didn't want me around. But in those early years I did not see it quite as clearly as I do now. It's very different when you are going through it, when you are living it. But now I can see it was Michael who made it that way. He liked it that way. He was the one in control and he was enjoying it.

The operation went well and in just over a week he was home. He had agreed to do a shoot for *Hello!* magazine and give the proceeds to Catherine as a thank you. He had only been out of hospital for a day when they turned up.

Michael still had to be careful of his stitches. He walked around with a cushion and if he laughed or coughed he would keep it pressed against his chest. Michael and Catherine were photographed for hours inside the house as well as in the garden and they did various interviews, with Michael saying how their 'renewed love saw him through' his triple bypass surgery. It was a worrying day, as he insisted on carrying on despite it being completely against the doctor's recommendations. I remember running to the shops to get more Lucozade energy tablets.

Michael was making a quick recovery, but for me things had been gradually worsening ever since Jenny had left. One evening Catherine found me and said they were going to dinner and was I coming. I tried to say that maybe it was better if just she and Michael went. I was trying to improve the situation and find a way to end any hostilities, but she took it as a snub. Michael told me later that she had said I was rude and had made it clear that she did not want me having meals with them in future. I was to eat later with Edith. On its own that was fine – I really liked Edith – but it didn't help the general atmosphere.

In the evenings I could go out and keep pretty much invisible, but during the day I had a job to do. It was becoming a bit absurd and I didn't feel comfortable. But Michael and Catherine seemed very good together. I liked her and could see she was a kind person. I could also see why she might not like me around. It was an impossible situation. Times had changed and I felt it was best for me to go. I told Michael that I didn't feel things were working any more and said I thought it best if I started looking for other work. To my surprise, he sat me down and explained that things were not what they might seem. He said that although Catherine didn't like the hot climate she had agreed to go to Barbados with him over Christmas. But after that she would not be living in the house. I was taken aback. I had thought that there was a chance that he might have been heading for an engagement. According to Michael, that was not going to happen. She was quite eccentric and, like him, she enjoyed her freedom. They were friends, but once he was safely through his recovery they would pick up their separate lives again.

Sure enough, when I returned in the New Year it was as he had said. He was looking much better with his suntan from spending three weeks at Sandy Lane in Barbados. And in all the time I had known him this was the first time he had been on his own with no girlfriend. It had become a routine that every Monday evening, if I had been working that day, I would go to dinner with him. He had lots of new plans. One of them was to have the huge studio room in Woodland House rebuilt. The house had been designed by Richard Norman Shaw for the painter Luke Fildes and was completed in 1877. It stands next to the Tower House, built at about the same time by the architect William Burges for himself. This had later been the home of the poet John Betjeman and then the actor Richard Harris. Jimmy Page, the guitarist of Led Zeppelin fame and an admirer of the Pre-Raphaelites, bought the house from Richard Harris in 1972 and was Michael's neighbour from then on. Luke Fildes had begun his career on the staff of an illustrated weekly paper called *The Graphic*. He was dedicated to social reform and believed in the power of pictures to influence public opinion. His black-and-white illustrations were designed to highlight the suffering of the poor and homeless. His work caught the attention of Charles Dickens, and Fildes went on to illustrate *The Mystery of Edwin Drood*. What I found most intriguing was that when Charles Dickens died in 1870, Luke Fildes drew a picture of the writer's empty chair which appeared in publications worldwide. The illustration was called *The Empty Chair, Gad's Hill*. Vincent Van Gogh saw it and went on to paint *The Yellow Chair*. It is quite a tenuous link between the studio in Woodland House and Van Gogh, but I like those kinds of stories.

Michael's plan was to have the studio room restored to its original state. This was going to be a messy and expensive business, as it involved demolishing the offices and bedrooms that had been built into it over the years. Mr Edwards, otherwise known as Eddie, and his sons Stephen and Colin were to tackle the job.

They made a good team as Eddie would mastermind the project and seemed skilled at everything, while Stephen was a first-class joiner and Colin a trained electrician. Since installing the swimming pool, Eddie had agreed to work for Michael until his retirement and so, in effect, Eddie was also part of the household staff. And it was good to have him around, as he always had either a funny story or a word of advice when someone was going through a tough patch. The other characters who were a constant part of 'Winner's World' were Nobby Clark and Sidney Frost. In the first week I worked there I spotted them outside the front gate. 'Oh, it's Nobby and Sid, they're here for the rubbish,' said Michael. 'I'll come down and introduce you.'

Nobby was the brains behind the operation and owned quite a fleet of old trucks and lorries, which he would take to shows. And still does, I'm sure. Usually they appeared in a huge Leyland lorry from the 1960s painted smartly in red and green. Sidney was big. He was over six feet tall and nearly as broad. A human crane. Michael introduced me with his usual, 'This is Dinah, and she was Miss Great Britain, you know.' This time my wince was partly due to Sid's gentle handshake nearly crushing my tiny outstretched palm. We all stood dwarfed by the oily vintage lorry. Nobby and Sid were cheerful souls and I couldn't help feeling they had stepped out of an Ealing comedy. The garden waste, rubble or whatever else would be dragged or wheelbarrowed through the side gate by the garage. When loaded, the lorry would rumble past Michael's office, with Nobby giving a long rude rasping blast on the horn. In the thirty years I worked there, Nobby, Sid and the lorry remained unchanged.

Without Jenny to take care of the garden, Michael had begun to send me out to rake the lawns or get bedding plants to add a bit of colour to the borders.

In cold weather, I think he sometimes set me tasks in the garden expecting me to complain or be silently annoyed. I never let on to him how much I enjoyed it. Cutting the grass, weeding, planting, it didn't matter to me. To be out of the hot, dry, air-conditioned house and in the fresh air was wonderful. They quickly became my favourite times. In those hours I felt calm and free.

Michael had made various attempts to find a gardener after Jenny left. Once he asked Nobby and Sid to prune a small tree. They took a few small branches off but when Michael saw it he said, 'No, no, I meant really fucking well prune it. Prune it harder.' When he went out to look half an hour later, there was just a bare trunk standing on the edge of the lawn like a big upside-down carrot. 'Oh Jesus, I suppose it might live,' was all he could say, and he never asked them to do any gardening again.

Over a few weeks, various people turned up but rarely survived more than a day. A girl from Rassells Nursery managed to last until nearly lunchtime but walked away in disgust in the middle of one of Michael's shouting rants. The others were told to go, or 'fuck off out of my garden', as Michael would put it, because of their 'complete incompetence' or 'fucking impertinence'. That suited me, as I hated the thought of losing my outdoor job. One morning I was raking leaves from the little lawn by the front door when a figure appeared at the gate. A man in his thirties was trying to see which bell to press. I knew Michael had arranged to talk to another gardener and, judging by the brown jacket and mud on his boots, this would be him. My heart sank, but I told him to go to the front door as the bell by the gate was not working. The receptionist scurried off to find Michael and I found myself hoping he was in a bad mood. But he bounced out of the door in good spirits. After quickly shaking the offered hand and saying hello, Michael went on to announce cheerfully that 'all gardeners are c***s'. The new arrival looked a little taken aback and Michael continued, 'Yes, they come here and dig up all my plants and they sell them and then they come to me and say, "Mr Winner, it's looking a bit bald round here, do you want to buy some plants?" I hope you are not that kind of fucking gardener?'

Michael did not wait for a reply but was already off down the path. The new man's eyes widened and he strode off in pursuit. To my annoyance he survived the first day, and the second, and within a few months Matthew Houston, or 'Matthew the gardener' as he was often called, became another regular figure in the household. Michael was always very proud of his garden and liked it to have something of a natural woodland look. He loved the trees and exotic-looking palms most, but also wanted to see as much colour as possible in the beds and borders. Given how fussy he was about dust and tidiness in the house, it was odd that in the garden he liked the moss left on the paths and didn't want lawn edges cut sharp. He wanted it to look cared for, but not overly manicured.

It was not until the early 1990s that Michael had been given his regular newspaper columns. One was for the *News of the World* and another for the *Sunday Times*. It was Andrew Neil, when he was editor of the *Sunday Times*, who first asked him to do a restaurant review. Michael had written a letter to the paper about a Dover sole he was served at Le Pont de la Tour, a Conran restaurant near Tower Bridge. He alleged that the fish was not fresh. Andrew Neil had a good hunch that as a critic Michael would not baulk at writing exactly what he thought. Before long this new column would become 'Winner's Dinners'. I think Michael gradually became as known for his weekly reviews as for the films he made.

Through the *News of the World* he could express his views on anything or anyone that amused or irritated him. The exceptional cases would have the honour of being appointed 'Twit of the Week'. With 'Winner's Dinners' he could focus on one of his favourite subjects. He had always eaten out several nights each week even though he had a housekeeper who would cook whatever he wanted whenever he wanted. He much preferred to take someone for dinner rather than host an evening at home. By his own admission, he knew little about food and virtually nothing about wine. However, he had dined in so many places that he did have a huge experience from which to draw comparisons. And he paid attention to the whole experience, from booking the table to settling the bill.

Michael kept in touch with lots of people he had worked with and was also always eager to meet anyone who interested him. If someone was calling in or he had arranged to go out for dinner, he rarely mentioned it until the last minute. My diary was kept in the kitchen so the housekeeper had some idea of what was going on. I would know in advance when he would be out for lunch or dinner but rarely knew with whom until a few moments before the event. If I was to go with him he would usually tell me just before 6.00. He did not like going out on his own in the evenings unless perhaps to see his closest friends. One afternoon he told me to get ready, as we were going to the Park Lane Hotel and then on to Harry's Bar in Mayfair. He didn't say who we were meeting until I asked. This time it was Robert Mitchum. I knew they had worked together on Michael's remake of *The Big Sleep*. I've often heard people talk about meeting an actor and being surprised by their stature; they are so much smaller or slighter than expected. I know what they mean, and have felt the same sometimes. But it wasn't like that with Robert Mitchum. He was tall and very broad shouldered. A big man and in many ways the archetypal movie star. His distinctive voice and features were exactly as I remembered from his films. I know it's a cliché but it did feel like I had stepped into one of his movies. But talking with him, I could see that he had no interest in stardom or the glamour of Hollywood. I had heard some extraordinary stories of his tearaway youth. Looking at him, I could believe them all. He grew up during the Great Depression of the 1930s, when times must have been especially hard. At one time he had been put to work in a chain gang and escaped and made a living for a while as a boxer. He seemed to have no trace of vanity and talked in such a straightforward way. I had learnt that Michael didn't like anyone else talking too much if he was with someone particularly famous. He liked to do the talking and have their full attention. I did manage to ask Robert something about Marilyn Monroe. He said, 'Yeah, when I first knew her she was Jeane "Dowerdy".' Through his accent I thought he was saying she was 'dowdy', as in she looked rather plain when she was younger.

Michael butted in, 'No, no, dear, he said Dougherty. It was her name. You don't pronounce the "u" or "g" or the "h".' I felt rather foolish but Robert gave me a big patient smile. He had worked in some kind of steel works during the war and the man he worked alongside, Jim Dougherty, had shown him a picture of his wife. The girl in the photo was only about sixteen.

Through different paths, both Robert and the young Jeane, later to become known as Marilyn, found their way into acting, and I think Robert became one of her closest friends. I loved how he talked. He did not seem an old man at all but his experiences stretched far, far back. And anything he talked about he had a way of planting firmly on the ground.

Harry's Bar was a private club and we had a quiet candle-lit corner. I could have listened to him for days. Every time

Robert asked me if I would like another drink I was saying 'yes, please'. Michael started to give me impatient looks. When Robert went off to the gentlemen's room, Michael made it clear that he thought both Robert and I had drunk quite enough.

*　　*　　*

Immediately on his return from Barbados, Michael had placed an advertisement in *The Stage*. It stated that a receptionist was required by a film company and that the position would suit an actress or dancer, as time off would be permitted for attending auditions. Lots of curricula vitae with attached black-and-white photographs began to arrive. Predominantly, of course, they were of young women. Michael wanted a new girlfriend and this was his preferred method of looking for someone. Soon there were several women arriving each day for an interview. A shortlist was drawn up and the first successful candidates began to turn up for work. The amount of time they were employed for was variable. It could be anything from a day to a few weeks and mostly it depended on how amenable they were to his advances.

He would ask them for lunch or dinner and if they said yes and he liked them he would ask them again. I would show them the dos and don'ts of the job knowing that they might well be told not to return the next day. The accounts they gave of his interview technique were quite mind-boggling. Often they were asked to stand by the window. I don't think any were too naive not to realise that this was for him to get some glimpse of their shape under their clothes.

The ones that refused would not, I presume, make the

shortlist. The questions they were asked included 'Which agent are you with?', 'What does your father do?' and 'Do you have a boyfriend?' All this was carried out with politeness and humour, but as some agents became aware of what he was up to and made objections, he began to filter the applicants according to who they were represented by.

One morning Michael called me into the office and introduced me to a very pretty dancer with short, dark hair called Vanessa Perry. Vanessa had been a chorus member in the West End production of the musical *42nd Street*, which launched the career of Catherine Zeta-Jones. When star and understudy were absent, the teenage Catherine Zeta-Jones had stepped into the role of Peggy Sawyer. Vanessa looked about twenty and, unsurprisingly at that age, seemed quite unworldly. Michael asked me to take her into Kensington High Street and help her find new shoes and an outfit or two. She was going on holiday with him to Gstaad in Switzerland. The day before they left I was asked to style her hair and cut her fringe. In the first few weeks and months Vanessa was shy and rather quiet. She cannot possibly have had any experience of a world similar to Michael's.

At that time, the restaurant that Michael went to most regularly was the Canteen. It caused quite a stir when it was opened in 1992 by Claudio Pulze, Michael Caine and Marco Pierre White. Often Michael Caine would appear and Marco would emerge from the kitchen. Michael loved all that kind of attention and activity and Vanessa gradually began to get more used to the new world she found herself in. Most evenings, if Michael was going out, he would invite me too. When Jenny had lived there it had been fine and had evolved naturally. Now that Michael was moving into a new era without her,

I was starting to be less comfortable. I did not feel Vanessa wanted me there so often when she was being introduced to his world. At the Canteen, if Michael Caine or Marco joined us it would become a noisy and entertaining social gathering, which was lovely. If it was just the three of us, I could at least happily look out of the window at the boats in Chelsea Harbour and sometimes keep out of the conversation.

But I did often feel a bit of a gooseberry. At the house, due to the chaos and demolition work going on in order to reinstate the original studio room, I now had a small bedroom next to Edith. I was still living there for two weeks in every month. If Michael said, 'Come on, we're going to so-and-so,' I would need a very good excuse before he would take no as an answer. He knew my circle of friends in London was quite small, so excuses were not easy to find. And he might just as easily say, 'Oh, bring them along too.' After the first months I felt that Vanessa was beginning to be slightly resentful of my frequent presence on their evenings out. I sympathised with her and broached the subject with Michael. His reaction was straightforward. 'Don't be so fucking stupid, of course you're coming, you can't sit in your fucking room all night. Never mind her, of course you're fucking coming with us.'

One afternoon, with the usual short notice, Michael announced, 'We have been invited to a dinner party at Tramp with Joan Collins.'

As we walked into Tramp her guests were being greeted by the owner, Johnny Gold.

The last time I had met him had been years ago with Bernie, so I was flattered that he recognised me. Of course, never forgetting a face must be one of the skills that made him the most legendary private club owner. Joan was with only a small group of her friends. Michael had known her a long time and she ribbed him almost constantly. He didn't always like that from people, but she did it with charm and warmth and he couldn't help but keep chuckling. At some point she asked me how on earth I put up with him. And she didn't mince words. She said she thought him vulgar and uncouth. But her kind and worldly smile could make even a remark like that seem like a compliment. It was a fabulous dinner and very nice for me having Joan Collins, of all people, keeping Michael in his place. I will admit to being more than a little in awe of her. And I couldn't stop marvelling at her complexion. I had wrongly assumed that her youthful look on the screen might have a fair bit to do with lighting and make-up. I knew roughly how old she was but she had a natural-looking beauty that really did make her appear way, way younger than her years.

Shortly after we finished dinner and as the party was becoming more and more lively, Michael began to say his goodbyes. He rarely stayed long after a dinner was over. I heard that some people stopped inviting him to things because that habit of his irritated them. In her perfect diction, Joan called him 'a proper party pooper' and off we went. As we were gliding back to the house in the Phantom, Michael was still smiling from the evening's banter. I told him I thought he was very lucky to have a friend like that. Joan would tell him a few home truths and hold a mirror up to him where it mattered. Only good friends take the trouble to do that. When I got back home to Little Neston everyone I knew was climbing out of the woodwork to hear about Joan Collins. I went over the evening again and again as friends sat wide eyed, like children listening to a fairy tale.

Not long after this, Joan invited Michael to lunch at her

London home in Belgravia. In some conversation around that time, I had talked to Michael about the various cars I had driven in the past. As he was about to set out he suddenly said, 'Come with me, darling, I've got a very special treat for you.' He didn't mean joining him for lunch with Joan but having the privilege of driving his Ferrari … and looking after it while he enjoyed his meal with her! 'You've always said you wanted to drive the fucking car,' he said. 'Well, you can today. It's a special treat.' He turned left down the side path and headed off towards the garage. I was apprehensive but having to concentrate on tiptoeing in heels on the slippery Yorkstone crazy paving.

He had a dark-blue Ferrari which he rarely took out. Much to their annoyance, he had never let any girlfriend drive it either. When I got to the garage, Michael the chauffeur had taken the cover off and the car was gleaming. I found myself in the passenger seat. So I'm not going to be allowed to drive after all, I thought! There was lots of revving and smoke as we reversed out into Ilchester Place. I noticed the chauffeur wince as we missed the side of the garage by a fraction of an inch. He had only recently remade the doors perfectly.

'When we get there you can drop me off and take the car,' Michael informed me. He knew that James Lane had let me drive his Ferrari Daytona around the TT circuit. I think sometimes it got up his nose that I knew people wealthier than him. I only mentioned their names when I felt he was being particularly patronising and unpleasant. He was less of a bully when he realised that I was not totally without connections. Without even knowing it, Jim was a great help to me over the years.

Michael sped along the bus lane and was swearing at a bus

that had stopped to let passengers off. He managed to lurch out suddenly in front of a car in the right-hand lane. 'FUCK-ING IDIOT,' he screamed and I glimpsed the pale face of the woman who had slammed on her brakes to save our lives. I had aged several years when we pulled up outside the Collins residence. I don't think even La Prairie or Crème de la Mer could undo the ageing effect of Michael's driving. I don't sup-pose Joan ever got into a car with him at the wheel. A woman of twenty could look ninety after a few hours of that. If she survived, that is.

'Park it somewhere but be back where I can fucking see you in just over an hour. I shouldn't be much more than that,' he told me. He noticed that I looked very frightened but didn't realise it was largely down to his driving.

'And don't be scared, dear, you've driven all kinds of fuck-ing cars. You'll be fine,' he went on reassuringly.

'Yes, but I knew Jim wouldn't have minded if I had bumped one of his cars,' I said. 'But I think you might be angry.'

Michael laughed. 'No, no, I won't be angry, dear, but it will take you most of your life to fucking pay for it.' Laugh-ing again, he strode off.

It felt a long time ago that I had last driven a car with a lot of power. And I hated driving in London. I managed to get the rumbling and grumbling car into a nearby space and turn off the engine. I daren't go for a spin in case any damage was done. Now I desperately needed to find a loo. A group of amused builders had helped me into the parking place and they promised to guard the car with their lives.

When Michael reappeared he decided it was best if he drove for the return journey too. I don't remember that at all. It may have been so terrifying that my mind has blanked it. Some of Michael's 'special treats' were good, and some were not so good.

*   *   *

Michael continued interviewing for a receptionist, which meant that quite often a receptionist would answer the door to someone who would be saying something like, 'Hello, I am here to see Mr Winner about the post of receptionist.' This, of course, could unsettle the reigning receptionist. She would turn to me in alarm and want to know what was going on. I had been told to say that Michael was interviewing for someone to work as back-up if the receptionist was attending an audition or ill, or if there was a busy spell and he needed two receptionists. Michael had tapped into a rich vein. There was no shortage of actresses or dancers in London. Receptionists would chop and change and disappear and reappear; some doing a few weeks and some just a day or two. The timekeeping rules were strictly applied and no concessions made. Quite often I was told not to admit a late arrival. Michael could see the front gate from his office window above the front door. The buzzer in the kitchen would go and I would hear crackly shouting through the intercom.

'GO AND TELL HER TO FUCK OFF. TELL HER SHE IS FIRED, DO YOU UNDERSTAND? SHE IS FIRED.' In the hallway I would try to gently explain that because they were late Michael had asked me to tell them that they no longer had a job with him. Frequently it was a matter of being late by only a minute or two, and with jaw dropped they would stare at their watch or the time on their phone as they tried to form a sentence. 'But … it … I … it's … I …'

If they took more than a few moments to turn on their heel and go, Michael would appear behind me at the top of the stairs. Then they would hear it from the horse's mouth. 'FUCK OFF, DON'T YOU UNDERSTAND WHAT FUCK OFF MEANS? HOW DARE YOU COME WANDERING IN HERE WHEN YOU FEEL LIKE IT. YOU ARE A FUCKING DIS-GRACE AND YOU ARE FIRED, NOW FUCK OFF...' Michael would ask the surviving receptionists to lunch or dinner. Now he could have a girl on his arm whenever he wanted to go out.

Gradually, it became a routine that Vanessa would appear at the house at about six o'clock on Friday afternoon and stay through until Sunday. If there was a premiere or other high-profile event that Michael was going to, she would make an appearance for that too. After a while she was to become his official girlfriend, but it took a little time. During the week he might have been out to dinner with other girls but of course I was under strict instructions not to talk about any of that. Vanessa may have been young but she wasn't stupid. She would ask me about the week and could tell if I had to be vague. Now that Jenny had gone, it was a problem that was only just starting to appear and I was going to have to get used to it.

CHAPTER FIVE

A PUMPKIN
AND A PALACE

A S TIME WENT ON AND Michael went out with other
women and had other girlfriends, it became one of the
biggest stresses of working for him. And he could take
great pleasure in making it worse sometimes and delighting
in the resentment that was directed at me. He had many ways
of doing that. For instance, if I was having dinner with him
and any woman he was with, he might sometimes only talk to
me, or ridicule anything that the other woman said. I could
try to stand up for her but with his overbearing manner that

137

was not always easy. In the end I just had to accept that as Michael's employee I had no choice but to follow his instructions and then do my best to cope with any bad feeling that was thrown at me as a result. It had not been a problem with Jenny, as I think she always saw that any argument she had was just with Michael.

Since Jenny had left, Michael had pushed me to try to see her whenever possible. I knew he wanted to hear that she would like to return to him. I was very happy to meet up with her and sometimes I would have lunch at her flat or we would go out for an evening. If Michael knew that a theatre tour was bringing her close to my home in the north he would insist I went and took her for dinner. She came to my house occasionally and we would walk the dogs together. But I could never bring Michael the news he wanted. I knew that Jenny was seeing someone else now and there was no possibility of her deciding to return. Eventually Jenny and I agreed that something had to change. I told Michael that she was not really happy seeing me, as she had moved on and I was a reminder of the past. He was crestfallen but accepted it.

*   *   *

In the four years working at the house I had never taken a day off for illness.

But one Monday morning as I got ready to get the five o'clock train I was feeling horribly weak. I had not felt good all weekend but put it down to the stresses of the week before with Michael. On the train, I remember chatting briefly to the lady next to me. The next thing I knew I was looking up at concerned faces. Apparently I had fainted and my neighbour had rushed to get a ticket officer. She helped me to the buffet car and gave me water and a blanket to wrap round myself. When I told Michael about it he didn't show much interest. Fortunately, it was not a difficult week and I took myself off to bed as soon as I could after work each day. I felt very peculiar and had no energy at all. One evening Michael came banging on my door saying that he wanted me to go to dinner with him. I told him I could hardly sit up, never mind go out. His sympathetic reply was something like, 'You've only got to sit there, I'm not expecting you to do a fucking song-and-dance act.' Somehow I managed to get myself ready and at least I had a good dinner. When Friday afternoon came I was counting the minutes. By now I was feeling so strange and drained that I was even quite panicky. I asked Michael if he could lend me some money to get a cab to Euston station as I had run out of cash. 'Of course I am not lending you cash, dear,' he said, laughing gleefully. 'If you were rich or had married me you wouldn't have this problem, would you? It was your choice, dear, so you'll just have to get a fucking bus, won't you? Yes, get a bus or walk or whatever poor people do.' I wobbled out, leaving him dancing about like a wicked goblin. Valerie the secretary gave me some money and I spent my two weeks off in bed with pneumonia.

Another lesson I had learnt about Michael was that, although he could be supportive at times, he could also find it amusing to let you down. It was disturbing when I saw him apparently enjoying seeing someone suffer. And he could be like a small child who breaks everything if they can't get all their own way. The next time I saw him, I insisted that in future I would be paid in cash. Michael knew by my tone that I would probably not be staying unless he agreed. He protested at first and he apologised, saying that he wouldn't do anything like that again, but I was adamant.

By this point I had worked for him for five years and was feeling increasingly insecure and nervous about my situation. Michael had been generous and helpful in some ways but also shown his ability to be cruel and undermining. I told him how I felt. I could speak very plainly to him sometimes but had learnt that the moment had to be chosen carefully. If he was interrupted at the wrong time there would just be an outburst of rage, and no conversation was possible. After work or over dinner was often the best time, but it was not as simple as that. It was important to sense his mood, too. I say 'important'; it was absolutely crucial. Anyway, I did let him know my concerns and I knew he had listened. The subject of my employment cropped up now and then in the following weeks and eventually he came up with what he considered the best solution. He offered me a pension. In short, the agreement stated that on my sixtieth birthday I would receive the sum of £250,000 if I continued to work for him. That was a huge sum in 1995 and I hoped that in nearly twenty years' time it would still be enough for some kind of security. It was agreed and life continued. I felt a little safer.

One evening, out of the blue as usual, Michael announced that we were off to the Belvedere restaurant for a champagne reception hosted by the then owner, Johnny Gold. The Belvedere is in a part of Holland House that was not destroyed in the Blitz. In fact, Michael's house was built on land that at one time had been part of the grounds of Holland House. It was only a few hundred yards away, so we strolled up the road. On arrival, Michael plonked me down at a table so he knew where to find me when he had finished wandering among the celebrities. I was delighted to find that George Best and Bill Wyman were there with their wives. They were people I could feel completely at home with, and it was the first time I had seen George since starting to work for Michael. It was a glittering event but I stayed chatting happily at the table with them. Bill had recently married Suzanne Accosta, a lovely woman and very beautiful too, and I think it was around the time that he was leaving the Rolling Stones. But we didn't talk about that. They were interested to hear about what it was like working for Michael. Chatting with them reminded me of some good times not so long past. Although I'd been very busy rushing from job to job, life had been much simpler and less stressful then.

Michael really liked Sticky Fingers Café, which Bill Wyman opened in 1989. He particularly praised the milkshakes. And, being in Phillimore Gardens, it was just across the park from his house. I went there many times with him. It was a favourite place for me too, as it was friendly and informal and the steaks were always good. Michael would moan about the music being too loud. I did try to point out that it was a place where people went partly because of the music and the connection with rock 'n' roll history. 'I CAN'T HEAR A WORD THAT YOU ARE SAYING, DEAR,' he said loudly, with a smug grin. Bill would make sure that the manager knew to turn the volume down a bit if Michael was around.

Michael did not like late nights. He had an expression that was something like 'sleep is money in the bank'. If midnight approached and he was not close to his bed he could get quite agitated. If he was late getting to sleep he would get up later in the morning whenever possible. He didn't do tiredness.

I very rarely witnessed him head home after midnight. In all the evenings I spent with him, the award for 'Michael's Latest Departure' goes to a restaurant called the Restaurant Marco Pierre White, housed in what was then the Hyde Park Hotel. Michael and I were with Michael Caine and his wife Shakira. One of the undeniable perks of my work was to eat in some of the finest restaurants. And sometimes it would be with some exceptionally remarkable and gifted people. I wouldn't really describe those times with the word 'perk'. 'Privilege' would be a better word. It would be just plain arrogant not to say that at some point, and this is as good a place as any, given the company and who was doing the cooking. At first I had felt a little nervous as I noticed I was wearing the same top as Shakira. I hoped perhaps, by keeping my jacket buttoned up, the fact might remain veiled, so to speak. I was shown to a chair opposite her. Almost immediately she leant towards me, smiling, and said, 'You have very good taste, Dinah. M&S have some good things at the moment, don't they?' We both laughed and I relaxed. The top was black with a heart-shaped mesh front. And I shouldn't have worried; I had met her several times before and knew her to be not only beautiful but warm and kind.

Our table was near a door to the kitchens and Marco emerged, his arms and hair waving theatrically in greeting. As with Michael Caine, I don't imagine that Marco needs any introduction. He must be the original 'celebrity chef'. I had been to Harvey's, his first restaurant in Wandsworth, with Jenny and Michael. The Restaurant Marco Pierre White was his second venture. Throughout the meal he would appear regularly in his blue-and-white striped apron and say something about what we had ordered, tell some anecdote or other, or just pop his head out to see how we were enjoying it. Marco had seemingly inexhaustible energy and enthusiasm for his work. And what amazing work it was, too. Everything I tasted was beautiful and extraordinary.

I love cooking myself and have eaten in many top places, but there was clearly a touch of genius here. Most of the time, the conversation centred on the food. Plates would appear bearing all kinds of extra things for us to try. And I tried everything. Nothing looked over-elaborate or excessively decorative but the textures and flavours were so fabulous and distinct. That was the real beauty.

After the meal we all moved to a seating area by the bar. Michael moaned about how long a walk it was to the toilets. Michael Winner, that is. But it was just friendly banter. He had to find something to criticise. And his friends would know that criticism to Michael was as natural as a wagging tail is to a dog. It was best to enjoy his happiness and just plain mean to try to stop him. Michael Caine had a quick wit and was good with impromptu humour, and when Marco joined us we became quite a raucous party. But by now the restaurant was closed and nearly empty. Michael lit a cigar – Michael Caine, that is. I realise I will have to use surnames in future when the two Michaels are together. I noticed Michael Winner light one too. The first since his heart op, he told us, and said he didn't intend to make a habit of it again. But they weren't quite the size of his old favourites, the Montecristos. I never saw him smoke another one after that night. He was having such a good time I'm sure he just got carried away. And he was very rarely carried away from his set routine. We were all by the bar for some time and Michael, Michael and Marco kept up a constant stream of anecdotes and jokes and occasionally ribbed each other quite mercilessly too.

Suddenly Michael Winner sat bolt upright and stared at me as if in shock. He must have just looked at his watch. 'We must go, we must go,' he was saying, almost in panic.

Michael Caine was chuckling at the spectacle and said something like, 'Relax, Michael, you're already a pumpkin.' We all fell about again but, although he was laughing, Michael didn't lose his sense of urgency. Somehow he just could not break his habits. I'm not sure what the time was. I had lost count of how many glasses of brandy I had drunk, too. It was probably about half past one in the morning and definitely long past Michael's bedtime.

* * *

I was worried when I heard that Edith the housekeeper was leaving. She had found similar work but with someone who travelled the world, and I think the chance to do that appealed to her. Edith was a good cook and I knew also I was losing an ally. Over the years I discovered that one of the downsides of the job was the frequent departure of people on the household staff. If they weren't fired I think they just reached a point where they couldn't take the constant onslaught from Michael any more. The secretaries and housekeepers especially were the ones I gradually built up friendships with, and we would support each other through the ups and downs. Well, the ups were fine, of course; it was the downs that it was nice to have help with. When someone new arrived it took quite a time for them to get to grips with the unique world of Michael Winner. Until they really understood things it could be quite nerve-racking for people around them. There was what became known as the 'honeymoon period', when

Michael would be charming and tolerant of any errors. In that time I'm sure they felt that all the staff were neurotic and delusional in their constant whispered warnings and advice. But it would send shivers down the spine when I heard the newcomer say things like, 'Oh, I'm sure he won't mind that', or 'But he's always really sweet'. In their first innocent weeks of employment they could unwittingly drop any of the staff into deep trouble.

Fortunately, Lily and Dante agreed to return. They had been working for Flavio Briatore, the managing director of the Benetton Formula One team. Their time with him between 1992 and 1995 coincided remarkably exactly with the team's period of historic wins. Perhaps Lily's good cooking and exuberant character were in some part responsible for the extraordinary run of trophies. Of course, Michael Schumacher must still take some share of the credit.

Meanwhile, receptionists were still coming and going. Michael had kept in touch with the actor Dermot Walsh, and his daughter Elisabeth worked at the house for a few weeks. Her mother was the actress Elisabeth Scott. She was only in her late teens and quite shy but a lovely girl. I liked listening to how she spoke, too. My accent has always hinted at the fact that I grew up near the Mersey, whereas hers suggested that she might have grown up at Balmoral. I persuaded her to give me elocution lessons now and then, in between one of us being sent on an errand or shouted at by Michael. I also discovered by accident that she had a crystal-clear and magical singing voice, too. One baking-hot day she had been sent out to water the flowers. This was the best task to be set as it simply involved holding a running hose and moving slowly along the flower beds, enjoying the sunshine and some peace and quiet. When I carried some bags of rubbish out to the tip at the end of the garden I overheard someone singing what I think was an operatic aria and soon spotted the slender figure of Elisabeth tiptoeing among the flowers.

Another receptionist who appeared at that time was Paola Lombard. She had trained as an actress and also had several hit singles in Italy, where she spent the latter part of her childhood. Paola was sacked several times, usually for being a minute or two late, but each time Michael had relented and given her another chance. It was quite comical as she would not be rattled or shocked by his bellowing but would simply shrug her shoulders and say polite goodbyes to everyone before picking up her bag and heading off. I'm sure he liked the fact that she was not impressed or particularly affected by his outbursts. And when she wasn't being sacked they got on very well. She worked at the house quite a lot over the course of a few months, and I went to dinner with her and Michael a few times. Then she got a good job with Cinesite, a production company in Soho, and disappeared for a while, although I heard that Michael still spoke to her regularly. Recently Paola showed me a letter he had written her at about that time. I had not realised quite how early on he had declared his feelings to her. But she knew he had recently started seeing somebody and said she just didn't trust him. This was about the same time that Georgina Hristova had arrived for an interview. She was neither an actress nor a dancer but worked as a receptionist in a hotel.

Being Bulgarian, and recently arrived in London to study, she knew nothing about Michael or how well known he was. In the interview she had assumed that Michael was a secretary working for the film company she was applying to. Michael found her naivety and way of talking very funny but he could also tell that she was a bright and no-nonsense kind of girl. He didn't offer her a job but a couple of weeks later he did call her and ask her to lunch.

After that they would go to dinner occasionally. I went with them several times and it was always great fun. Georgina saw nothing of his celebrity and had no agenda so would talk absolutely plainly. It was refreshing and often hilarious. Then one day she was at the house with him when Vanessa appeared at the front gate. Michael frantically pleaded with her to leave quickly by the French windows and promised that he would explain everything later. She did and he called her that evening and confessed that he had lied about being single and unattached. Georgina really didn't like that deception and it was quite a while before she would speak to him again after that.

Gradually, Vanessa had become his steady partner. Knowing how overbearing and controlling Michael was, I had not been very comfortable seeing him with someone so much younger. It seemed a bit unfair. But I soon realised that Vanessa was quickly rising to the challenge. I remember one Monday morning when I asked him how his weekend had been, he said, 'Well, I spent most of the time running round the house while Vanessa threw eggs at me. And when she ran out of eggs she found other things.' I had heard the story from the maids as soon as I had arrived, but was still not entirely successful at keeping a straight face as he recounted it himself. 'Oh, you think it's really fucking funny, I suppose, but we will be finding bits of eggshell for the next fifty fucking years.' Sure enough, over the following weeks I would occasionally come across the maids giggling when they discovered another piece of shell. Michael and Vanessa may have had their arguments, but slowly he became increasingly kind to her.

*　　*　　*

There was great excitement in the house when Michael told everyone that we were off to meet the Queen. When I heard more of the details, it turned out that I was to accompany him to a charity event in St James's Palace where the Queen would also be present. We were not going to be formally introduced to Her Majesty. That was fine with me; I was over the moon to be there at all. On arrival we made our way into a huge and very grand room filled with a bustling throng of people. Michael noticed a double door leading into a long room where people were beginning to form two lines. He moved towards it and was peering in excitedly. 'That must be where she walks through and greets all those people,' he said. Suddenly, unable to contain himself any longer, he whispered, 'Quick, quick, let's go and have a look, I think we've just got time.'

He strode off, up a few steps and into the room, and I kept close on his heels. Spotting Julia Morley, he made a beeline for her and we got into conversation. Her husband Eric I knew through the Miss United Kingdom events although I didn't see him on that occasion. He had created the Miss World pageant in 1951. The Miss Great Britain contest was a little older and was first held just after the war in 1945. Anyway, as we were talking Michael turned to see that the big double doors we had come through were now closed. He was suddenly quite panicky and, nodding and apologising, he squeezed us into the line of people. There was a bit of a kerfuffle as the last six or eight people had to shuffle sideways to make space for us. Now there were two neat lines of people, one on either side of the room. 'Just say you are a director of the Police Memorial Trust,' Michael hissed in my ear. I had hardly had time to fully grasp this new situation before the Queen and Prince Philip entered at the far end of the gallery. The Queen turned and walked down one line. We got Prince Philip.

I didn't know whether to be relieved or disappointed. He reached me before Michael and I managed to say my line about the Police Memorial Trust. As he beamed his broad smile and shook my hand he said, 'Ah yes, of course, very good work, very good work.' When he saw Michael he recognised him.

'Guards, seize this man, he is an impostor,' he shouted.

No, of course he didn't, but by Michael's red face I think he half expected it. Pausing, His Royal Highness congratulated Michael and they talked very briefly before he moved on. Together the Queen and Prince Philip then headed for the now reopened doors. As soon as was reasonably dignified, we hurried behind them. We both wanted to get as close to the Queen as we could. And we did get very close. As she moved through the room and talked to people, Michael was pushing me to follow her.

'Go on, go on,' he kept saying. Soon I was right behind her, marvelling at her perfectly curled hair and flawless skin. It was so exciting and extraordinary to be so close. For a few minutes I was gazing at the exquisite earrings and the colour and texture of her silk jacket. But I think Michael was still rather jittery from our accidental intrusion and we didn't stay very long. Perhaps he was still picturing himself hanging upside down in chains at the Tower of London. There were to be times in the future when I was to find that image quite therapeutic.

As soon as we were back in the car we both burst into almost hysterical laughter. We were acting like children who had been up to some serious mischief and got away with it by the skin of their teeth. I liked Michael best when he was behaving like an overexcited schoolboy. He had booked a table at Wiltons, as it was so close, and soon we were seated in one of their booths.

In those days one side of the restaurant was divided up, so it was a bit like having dinner on a train. I had ordered lobster, the perfect topping to a very memorable day. I've always loved seafood and lobster is my favourite. Well, a very close second to langoustine. Michael had turned to talking about colours. It's hopeless trying to describe them with words like 'yellowy orangey pink', so we were pointing to parts of nearby paintings. Already he was thinking about how to decorate the studio room, although there was still a lot more to be done. Fairly cold pinks seemed to be what he was settling on.

I was suggesting something warmer. My lobster arrived right on cue. 'There, look, how about something like that?' I suggested. He glanced at me quickly to check that I was serious. 'Well, I'm not sure I want to wake up thinking I'm inside some fucking sea monster,' he said. Perhaps it wasn't the ideal way of showing a colour sample. In the end he settled on cold pinks but I think the mottled paint effect he went for owed something to the lobster.

Building work in the house was continuing apace. Eddie would warn any newcomers of Michael's idiosyncrasies. One was that they must never be seen chatting or drinking tea.

There were official break times when they would leave the house and go to a café. Holding a cup of tea and talking to a colleague was rarely excusable. It was an offence which could inspire Michael to perform a high-volume tirade. He once poured away the tea that a maid had given to two scaffolders who had just started work. As he did so he was shouting, 'WHAT THE FUCK ARE YOU DOING? I AM NOT FUCKING PAYING YOU TO COME ROUND TO MY HOUSE TO DRINK FUCKING TEA.' For a moment I thought they might decide to hoist his head up on one of their poles. They looked physically somewhat stronger than Michael.

Instead, they took down their scaffolding and left. Eddie often had to find new people because they either walked away or were fired by Michael halfway through a job. Despite the danger, Lily or one of the maids continued to smuggle tea or coffee out to the workmen. During the winter they had particular sympathy for Matthew the gardener. Buckets or flower pots would be tucked under a bush, gently steaming with their hidden treasure of hot coffee and biscuits. Then there would be frantic hissing and whispering until Matthew emerged from the shrubbery and the hiding place was pointed out.

Eddie had nicknamed him the Scarlet Pimpernel as, if you walked round the garden paths, you couldn't often see him through the trees and shrubs. Michael's method was simple. He would open the front door and bellow 'MAAAAAATHEWWWWW'. Within a few seconds the gardener would appear.

I remember John Fraser giving me a garden magazine to pass on to Matthew. In turn I passed it to Eddie to give to him. Looking at the cover, Eddie read out one of the headings: 'A good gardener is hard to find.' Quick as a flash, he continued,

'Well, Matthew must be a bloody excellent gardener 'cos he's almost impossible to find.' Having Eddie around was good for general morale. He was respectful towards Michael but not afraid to speak his mind when he had to. They had all kinds of arguments over many years, and it would cheer the other staff up when they heard Eddie confronting him with statements like, 'It's one thing when you get out of your pram, Mr Winner, but it's quite another when you start throwing your toys around.' There were some major fall-outs, but they were usually quickly resolved. I'm sure it helped that Eddie had worked for Michael's father, George. Eddie had a lot of ways to describe Michael, but of his father George he would simply say, 'He was an absolute gentleman.'

Eddie had organised the small unused room at the offices in Farley Court to be redecorated as a bedroom for me. I had suggested to Michael that it might be better as there was so much building work and upheaval in Woodland House. It was only a two-minute run if I was needed. I was happily surprised when he agreed. Quite often he would react to a request by doing the very opposite, so it was a nerve-racking business. My main motive was to put a bit more distance between myself and his private life. It would also mean that my 10.30 curfew would no longer be relevant. That was a lesser concern, as most evenings I spent on the phone to family and friends. But at Farley Court I felt at least I would have an evening to unwind a bit away from 'Winner's world'. The room was small but Eddie built in a wardrobe and dressing table and there was just space for a single bed too. At first it was rather quiet and lonely but I was soon enjoying the feeling of being a little freer. If I was out with Michael in the evening, he would drop me at the door and wait in the car until I waved from the window. He laughed at my fear of the dark but he didn't dismiss it. My day-to-day work remained unchanged, and before John Fraser or the accountant arrived in the morning I would be hotfooting it up Melbury Road to Woodland House.

CHAPTER SIX

SIXTY AND ONWARDS

RECENTLY, I SAW A PHOTOGRAPH I had taken of Michael with the film director John Landis. He had a small part in the film *Burke and Hare*, a black comedy involving grave robbers. Michael was in Victorian dress with long grey mutton-chop sideburns and a top hat. He seemed to look very much himself.

In fact, he was quite annoyed as he had hung around waiting in the make-up department, but when they got to him he was told he looked just fine as he was. I was not surprised that he so suited the Victorian garb, as it had occurred to me before that he would have been quite at home in those times.

155

He could not have been a film director, of course, but could have used his legal mind or business head for something. A judge or mill owner, perhaps. As it was, he did manage to live with one foot in a Victorian way of life. For almost all his years, he lived in a grand Victorian house with maids and a housekeeper, chauffeur and other staff.

They always addressed him as 'Sir' or 'Mr Winner' and usually, if he passed them in the house or garden, he would ignore them. If they offered a 'good morning, sir', he might reply or just grunt or ignore them again. He was comfortable with his place of power and importance in a way that sometimes struck me as rather old fashioned. He could have lived pretty much any way he wanted, so I don't think it any accident that he lived as he did. When it came to choosing a venue for his sixtieth birthday party, he settled on Leighton House, the nearby large Victorian former studio and home of the painter Frederic, Lord Leighton. For a theme he chose the Victorian era. Michael had not requested that everyone dress up but on arrival guests were greeted by something of a film set. Street sellers were roasting chestnuts, and doormen stood resplendent in top hat and tails. Just as I was walking up the road with Takis, we heard the clop-clop-clop of horses' hooves and Michael and Vanessa passed us in an open carriage. We caught them up as Vanessa stepped elegantly down to the pavement, looking very beautiful in a black velvet dress. We were able to wander around the house for a while drinking champagne before making our way upstairs for lunch. Girls in exotic and colourful dance costumes mingled with the guests in the magnificent Arab Hall with its glistening mosaic walls.

Looking out into the gardens, women in lace bustles and long ornate dresses were pushing perambulators to and fro

across the lawn. Those details were lovely and, together with
the incredibly decorative interior of Leighton House, made
for a magical step back into the grandest of Victorian times.
The main dining table was not large enough to seat everybody, so another group of smaller tables had been made ready
in an adjacent room, separated only by an arch. Takis and I
were seated with Ruby Wax and Nigel Havers and their partners. For the starter, a huge plate of ice was put on the table,
topped with a small mountain of caviar. I had never seen so
much in my life. It was Vanessa's favourite, Beluga caviar,
and Michael had ordered plenty. I quickly discovered that
no one on our table liked caviar except me. I could not bear
the thought of it being wasted, so felt obliged to work my way
through it. Ruby Wax was being Ruby Wax and I found that
you can get quite a stitch through laughing and eating at the
same time. Speeches were made at the main table, and it was
good to hear Michael refer to John Fraser as his 'oldest and
most trusted friend'. And it was nice that John had actually
been invited and was there to hear it. He took quite a daily
ear bashing, so it felt only right that occasionally it was made
clear that he was appreciated.

*   *   *

I didn't know it at the time, but it was an important day for
me when I first met Zoe Vigus. She had come all the way
from Torpoint near Plymouth to be interviewed for the post
of receptionist. A minute or so after I had showed her up
to Michael's office, she reappeared in the kitchen. Although
only twenty-one she was wearing a lot of make-up and he had
sent her out to take it off. I passed her endless tissues as she

dabbed it all away before running back upstairs. A few days later Michael told me that Zoe would be working part time. I liked her immediately, and she was always bouncing with energy and enthusiasm, a kind of female Tigger from *Winnie the Pooh*. I could see that she was also rather wide-eyed and excited by fame and celebrity. She was young and eager to find success as an actress and had just completed a diploma from Laine Theatre Arts in Epsom, Surrey. Zoe was soon introduced to Michael's office manner. One of her first faux pas was when she opened the door to see an actress she recognised from the television series *The Good Life*.

She asked her politely to wait in the hall and ran up to the kitchen to notify Michael on the intercom. 'Mr Winner, Penelope Keith is here to see you,' she said, cheerily.

His reply came quickly, 'IT'S NOT PENELOPE KEITH, YOU FUCKING MORON, IT'S FELICITY KENDAL.'

The blushing Zoe showed Felicity up to Michael's office. When she had left, Michael gave Zoe a short lecture on how some people had worked very hard to reach the top of their profession and did not appreciate being confused with one another by 'moronic idiots'. She survived her first few weeks and went on to become the ruling receptionist. Although regularly upset by Michael's frequent outbursts, she showed resilience. An ability to withstand the high winds of his temper was one of the main attributes required for the job, and Michael appreciated the people who could bounce back and get on with their work. Other receptionists would come and go but Zoe became a regular member of staff.

As she lived near Shepherds Bush, she would often walk to Farley Court with me at the end of a day and we would have a glass of wine with John Fraser before he left. It was a good way to shrug off any of the day's traumas. I found in Zoe a friend and ally and in some ways we became key to each other's survival.

Not long after Zoe had settled into place, tragedy struck at Woodland House.

Michael White, the chauffeur, was killed on his motorbike. The mood in the house was wretched. It was such a loss to everyone. He had just always been there in the background. And the earthy good sense and humour of the Yorkshireman had been an essential part of the balance in the household. Everyone got on with things as usual, but for Valerie the secretary it seemed to be the final straw. During the rearrangement of the house she had been moved to a small room next to Michael's office. This meant that she could be constantly barked at by Michael without him even having to leave his desk. John had been moved out to Farley Court and now she had lost her only other long-serving colleague. One morning she telephoned to say that she could not come to work any more. It was a sad day, but I knew she was doing the right thing. I could see that she had been suffering and her nerves seemed in tatters.

It cheered me up a little when I heard from James Lane again. He was rarely in London now, as he had moved to Jersey. I met him for dinner at Maxims, a restaurant in Palace Gate House at the end of Kensington High Street. The coat of arms above the door made it look medieval, although the house was built in the 1860s. Inside was very grand and the wood panelling gave it the welcoming warmth of an old country house. I knew Jim from my days of modelling and acting, and talking with him sparked good memories of what was already beginning to feel like a previous life.

Michael had always had some kind of fixation with Jim's wealth. Jim had inherited his father's substantial business when he was very young, so he had had to grow up fast. He showed great skill at management but, unlike Michael, he always avoided publicity as much as possible. That afternoon Michael had given me the names of a few fine wines that I had drunk with him at the house. They were all several hundred pounds for a half-bottle at wholesale. He wanted me to order one to see Jim's reaction – the one he particularly told me to order was Château Latour 1961! He knew it would be thousands of pounds for a whole bottle in a restaurant. It was an absurd competition that only existed in the mind of Michael. He didn't seem to realise that no one else was playing the game. Jim had no mean streak and was no show-off either. Jim and I laughed about how, when he first knew me, I was very happy drinking Blue Nun. And quite large quantities, too, sometimes. I remembered that in Belfast with Bernie Winters the hotel gave us an award for being the biggest drinkers.

A dubious honour, perhaps, but quite something to achieve in Ireland. We had sat at the bar right through the night and apparently got through a dozen bottles of Blue Nun. His brother Mike was furious when he found us still up and singing songs in the morning. I might have been a bit tipsy but I wasn't good at singing in tune anyway, even when I was sober. We had to do a show for the troops early that day. As we drove to the barracks in an armoured car, Mike sat there scowling at us like we were misbehaved children. Mike was the businessman of the duo and did all the worrying. But the show went off all right.

Anyway, to get back to the wine, when I mentioned the one I had in mind Jim threw back his head and roared with laughter. 'That will set me back a couple of grand, why don't we settle for vintage Dom Pérignon,' was his response, and I was certainly happy to go with that! Jim was with other friends and as we talked I heard about how he had entirely relocated to outside the UK. I had a strong feeling that Michael was worried that I might be offered a job. It hadn't really occurred to me as a possibility until he started to give me a little lecture on how lucky I was to have a pension and be able to be with my family at weekends. As it turned out, Jim did offer me work. He owned hotels in various parts of the world, so it would have involved almost constant travel. At the time I just couldn't agree to that as it would have increased the time away from my family. I already found it difficult enough as it was with my working week spent away from home.

Daniel, my eldest son, was now seventeen and had passed his driving test. In two weeks he had had two minor accidents and had lost confidence in his driving ability. I didn't want to encourage him back onto the road if he was nervous, but it was sad to see him so rattled at the thought of getting back behind the wheel. I told Michael about it and he said he would give him a call and try to build his confidence. I was not in the room when Michael phoned him.

If I had been I might have snatched the receiver away. Daniel told me later that Michael had been very encouraging and said it was like riding a horse; if you fall off you have to get straight back on. That was understandable, but he went on to say that when he was about Daniel's age he had driven his Sunbeam through the wall of a house and into someone's lounge. Apparently Michael joked that he could have watched television with the family if the power had not gone off. It made my hair stand on end but it seemed to do the trick for

Dan and he got back in the car again. I found Michael's driving terrifying at times, even when he was just talking about it.

A short while after this, Daniel was involved in a rather horrible football accident. There was a playing field in Ness, a little village near Neston, and he and Luke and his friends were kicking a ball about. As his brother Luke and the others were only about ten, Daniel was being the goalkeeper. Jumping up to make a save, he caught his arm on a metal net hook behind the bar and tore his forearm badly. One of the boys fainted when they saw it, and Luke and the others ran off to get help. The first I heard about it was when my mother called from the hospital. She described it as a 'nasty cut', to stop me from getting upset or panicky, but said it would be good if I could come home.

The boys later told me it looked like 'the Terminator', as they could see all the muscle and bone exposed. It was a Wednesday, and I asked Michael if I could leave early and also have the next day off. He told me to calm down and get on with my work. To be fair, at the time we had no idea how severe the damage was. I was annoyed with Michael and very worried, but then another drama unfolded. The new secretary, a young woman found to replace Val, gave Zoe a handful of letters to post. In the bundle of envelopes the secretary had included a letter to be sent by courier and had not mentioned it to Zoe. To save her own skin, the new girl told Michael that she had pointed it out. Zoe had pushed the whole lot into the postbox and hurried back to the house only to be greeted by a very angry Michael. 'YOU FUCKING MORONIC C***, YOU HAVE JUST POSTED A FUCKING IMPORTANT PIECE OF PAPER THAT WAS MEANT FOR A FUCKING COURIER...' It was a dreadful tirade of the foulest language and it went on and on and on.

Zoe was standing outside his office, looking down at the carpet and sobbing.

Michael was in the doorway, blue in the face and bellowing at the top of his voice. In the dressing down he told her over and over that she must go to the central sorting office and retrieve the letter or she need not return to work as she would be fired. 'DO YOU UNDERSTAND ME, YOU C***, YOU MORONIC FUCKING C***, YOU WILL BE FIRED, FIRED, FUCKING FIRED, NOW FUCK OFF, FUCK OFF.' I was at the foot of the stairs and knew if I interrupted we might both be sacked immediately. When Michael disappeared, Zoe came into the kitchen. She was trembling and crying uncontrollably. I had made her a cup of coffee with brandy in it, which I gave her and sat her down at the table. I went up to Michael's office and asked if I could go with her to help get the letter back. 'YOU BETTER GET THAT FUCK-ING LETTER OR SHE WILL BE FUCKING FIRED, DO YOU UNDERSTAND? DO YOU FUCKING UNDERSTAND? SHE WILL BE FIRED.'

I took that as a 'yes, you may go too', and got Zoe out of the house as quickly as I could. First we stopped at Farley Court to tidy her make-up and let her calm down a bit. John was still in his office and, after making a few calls, managed to discover that letters from Kensington High Street were first sorted in Paddington. Zoe then called the sorting office and was told that there was no point coming before eight that evening and that she was to come on her own.

I found that a very peculiar and rather sinister instruction so I felt I should go with her. John wrote a note to authorise Zoe Vigus to pick up the unstamped letter on Michael's behalf, and off we went to the Tube station. The sorting office was vast but we had a number for the man that Zoe had spoken to, and when she called him he directed her to a side door. When he saw me with her he said straight away that he had told her to come on her own. I said that I also worked for Mr Winner and had been sent too. We went into a huge aircraft hangar of a place and he showed us the letters running through gigantic sorting machines. Then he told me to wait while he took Zoe to look for the courier letter. His manner and the whole situation were growing more and more disturbing, and I made sure I did not let her out of my sight. He saw that I was following at a distance and eventually picked the letter up from under a counter. It was clear to me that he knew exactly where it was all along. I shuddered to think what was going through his mind, but Zoe and I had more urgent things to worry about. It was about 10.30 when I pressed the bell at Woodland House. Zoe was still too frightened to see Michael on her own, and after a minute or two we heard him bellow 'WHO IS IT?' from above us. He had come out onto the little balcony by his office.

Stepping back, we looked up and I held out the letter that we had retrieved. 'It doesn't matter, it doesn't matter, I had a copy anyway,' he said laughing down at us.

'What? I can't believe you would do that,' I said, and I knew he could hear from my tone of voice how disgusted I was.

'Just go and get some sleep, get some sleep, both of you,' Michael was muttering as he turned and went back through the long glass door. Late that night I heard the full extent of Daniel's arm injury. Thirteen staples had been put in to hold the wound together and he was kept in hospital overnight. I got to work early that morning to tell Michael that I really had to go. He agreed immediately and also said I should go to the playing field as fast as possible and take some photographs of whatever had done the damage.

Daniel had just returned home when I got there, and as soon as I could I drove out to the scene of the accident. The steel hook was gruesome as there was still skin hanging on it. Just as I was taking some photographs, a council van arrived and two men began to remove all the net hooks. Michael's advice had been good, and he had also snapped into action and hired an accident lawyer. Dan's arm healed up slowly but with no lasting problems, and eventually he was awarded £11,000 in damages. He was able to buy a car and pay off a lot of his university fees too.

* * *

As the time to start filming *Parting Shots* approached, the house became a hive of activity. Nick Mead was in the attic rooms working on the screenplay, and Eddie and his sons were put to work making props. The main characters were played by Michael's actor friends, people he had worked with before or other actors he particularly admired and wanted to work with. There was Felicity Kendal, John Cleese, Bob Hoskins, Diana Rigg, Ben Kingsley, Joanna Lumley, Oliver Reed, Gareth Hunt, Peter Davison, Chris Rea and more. It was certainly a star-studded cast. Auditions were held for the smaller roles. Ruby Snape, a tall blonde actress in her thirties, was seen for the part of Melissa. I heard afterwards that, as usual, there was no reading or demonstration of ability required in the audition. Michael said, 'Stand by the window, my dear, so I can see you better.' Ruby did as asked and was then told, 'Now stand and face me, my dear.'

Feeling she was being ogled at, she then swung round putting her back to him and said, 'And do you want to see my arse as well?' Michael laughed and Ruby said later that she was pretty sure that was why she got the part.

Chris Rea was to play the leading part of Harry Sterndale, a man told he has only six weeks to live and so decides to kill the people who have adversely affected his life. For Chris, a well-known singer-songwriter with many albums and hits to his credit such as 'Fool (If You Think It's Over)', this was his first major role as an actor. Zoe and I had a bit of a brainstorming session with Michael when he was still trying to decide on who might be best for the role.

In the end we all settled on Neil Morrissey or Martin Clunes. I'm not sure if they were even approached, as Michael then met Chris Rea on the beach at Sandy Lane, Barbados. He felt he would be perfect, so that was that. I liked him too and found him very good humoured and easy to get along with. He and Michael became firm friends, and I never heard a cross word throughout the making of the film. That in itself was quite an achievement for Michael.

Michael had known Oliver Reed for a very long time. He had stared in *Hannibal Brooks* in 1969, considered by many to be Michael's best film. He certainly knew that Ollie liked a drink now and then. By 'now and then', I mean now and then throughout the day. Filming had to be delayed once or twice while Ollie sobered up. Michael could lose his temper even with friends, and a few days later when he saw Ollie waving a flask about and taking the odd gulp he suddenly blew a gasket. Ollie stood frowning and looking at his toes as Michael called him 'un-fucking-professional', among various other adjectives. When there was a lull, Ollie smiled and offered the flask to Michael to taste. He had filled it with cold tea and enjoyed luring Michael into his trap.

I don't think Peter Davison enjoyed himself very much. I remember chatting to him a few times between takes and he said he wasn't going to rise to Michael's nonsense. Michael would bellow insults at him in the manner he usually reserved for the extras. I'm not sure that he knew quite what a big name Peter was. He may not even have known that he had played Doctor Who.

It was toe-curlingly embarrassing really, but the more Peter kept his cool the more ridiculous Michael looked. I'm sure he was not very impressed by the Michael Winner method of directing, and it certainly showed that it takes more than a ranting Michael to ruffle a Time Lord.

One of the tasks given me on the film was the hair and make-up of most of the extras. This meant I needed to start work around five, and we worked six days a week, too. I was also the hair stylist for Felicity Kendal and Joanna Lumley.

Michael said he wanted me to do Diana Rigg's hair as well. I was looking forward to that, but in the end it was not possible with all the other things I had been scheduled to do. She had always been an idol of mine, ever since I saw her in the 1960s television series *The Avengers*. As a teenager I really wanted to be an 'action girl' like Mrs Emma Peel, the character she played.

Michael seemed very unfriendly towards Felicity, and she told me she felt uncomfortable working with him, as he was constantly brusque and unhelpful.

You could never tell with Michael how he was going to behave or what petty irritations or misunderstandings were affecting his mood. I was glad to be able to tell her what he was like, or she could have been forgiven for taking his behaviour quite personally. Anyway, her attitude was impressive and she rose above it all and just got on with the job. On a film set, where work is often very intense, people can quickly become like close friends, or family, even. But then, when it's finished, everyone goes their own way and may never meet again. I was very glad to have spent a short time working with Felicity. I remember she gave me a lovely perfume afterwards, too.

My memories of a film project are usually a kaleidoscope of incidents and snippets of conversation. Bob Hoskins I remember talking to quite often as he waited for his next scene. He was just as I imagined: feet on the ground, and often very funny too. Ben Kingsley came to the house to rehearse his caricature chef and was breaking plates, swearing and banging saucepans around in Michael's kitchen. Seeing an actor like him working on a character was fascinating. Not the most subtle role he had taken on, perhaps, but fascinating all the same. It was moments like that which made me feel very lucky to have the job I had.

And then Michael stepped in to give an example of the kind of mad chef he was looking for. He began waving his arms about and shouting, 'Watch me, watch me, be crazy, be crazy, I'm fucking crazy, look at me, look, I'm crazy, I'm crazy, like this, look, a really fucking crazy chef.' I know my jaw dropped. I couldn't believe what I was seeing.

Thankfully Ben was laughing because I really needed to, but didn't want to be the first.

Joanna Lumley arrived at five one morning looking radiant. Without a dab of make-up her skin looked flawless. Her hair was amazingly thick and healthy and I had the laborious task of crimping it for the hippie character she was to play in

the film. It took about two hours and in between me applying the hot irons, she put on her various foundations and
shaders. I don't think she *needed* any make-up at all, but she
knew exactly how to make herself look right for the camera.
Michael had asked Daniel and his girlfriend Nicolanne Cox
to come down to London to be extras in a pub scene. They
were eighteen and seventeen at the time and got talking to
Joanna during the filming. To my embarrassment, I discovered they had told her that occasionally at parties a friend
and I would dress up like her and Jennifer Saunders in *Ab
Fab*. But Joanna had a gift for making everyone around her
happy and comfortable and seemed naturally very warm and
kind. When Michael told her that her scenes were complete
she immediately came and asked me to gather the girls from
Make-up and Wardrobe. We all squeezed into her caravan and
she thanked us with lashings of champagne.

The day after filming was completed, Michael seemed a
little melancholy. He said it would probably be his last film
as he felt he was getting a bit old for it.

With *Parting Shots* as a title I had assumed he had made a
clear resolution that this would be the close of his movie-making
days. In talking to him, I felt that it was not quite such a conscious decision. He did say that working with Chris Rea had
been a real pleasure and that he had enjoyed making *Parting
Shots* more than any other film. He had made almost a film
a year for three decades, and where possible he had always
gathered the same crew together. They knew how he liked
things done and he knew that they worked hard and would
put up with his frequent outbursts of shouting. It was the
end of a chapter for them too, as Michael had been such a
regular employer.

Just after the filming of *Parting Shots*, the Inland Revenue began to take a closer interest in Michael's financial affairs. Michael blamed Lily. He said it was her fault for becoming pregnant. Yes, on the face of it that might sound a bit mad, so I will try to explain his reasoning. Lily used to cook lunch for Michael at one o'clock and then serve the staff a meal at 1.30. Not all the staff, but Maria and Dina, the maids, and also Zoe and me. As her pregnancy advanced Lily asked if her workload could be decreased a little. It was decided that she be excused from cooking lunch for us and Michael agreed that £5 each a day would be given as compensation for our lost meal.

Everyone was happy. Well, everyone except the taxman, apparently.

Michael always insisted that it was this little lunchtime cash bonus that was first picked up on. Investigations began. Over two years the tension grew and grew. It gradually became about bigger things than sandwiches. I had my suspicions that he had brought money into the country to fund *Parting Shots* and somehow forgotten to make this absolutely clear to the appropriate authorities. A special investigation was made by the people who do these kinds of special investigations. I'm not sure what they are called. Anyway, the climax came one day when men from the Ministry of Very Naughty Money-Moving Matters made an appointment to visit Michael. Michael was a very worried man. At 2.30, just before the meeting was due to start, he asked me to tell all staff that they could have the afternoon off. Everyone had got wind of what was happening, of course, and his instructions only served to fan the flames of their imagination. It encouraged an image of Michael being handcuffed and dragged to a waiting police car. I stayed to help him make preparations and perhaps be something of a calming influence.

Doug Stoker, his accountant, was the first to arrive. Michael was at his desk. His cheeks were red and he was trying to find a way to stop his hands from shaking. As men in dark suits rang the bell I showed them into the arena, one by one. There were three or four of them in all. Although not required for the meeting, I occasionally took in tea, coffee and biscuits. I was glad of an excuse to pop in now and then as it was nice to see Michael getting a bit of a roasting for a change. He had told me that the best-case scenario would be that he was required to pay a large penalty on top of any tax demand that was made. In the worst case, he could face a term in prison. That never really seemed to me to be a likely outcome, but he was certainly genuinely frightened.

Just the thought of prison meals must have worried him more than a little.

By the time everyone had left, Michael was a nervous wreck. He played me the recording he had made of the meeting. I think he needed to hear his sentence again so it would start to feel more real. Although he had been excused prison, he had to pay about £1 million immediately and another £2 million in instalments. He was miserable, but at the same time hugely relieved. And through the worry of it he had shed half a stone in a few days.

The really sad part of the story was that Lily and Dante lost their baby. They had discovered that he had Edwards' syndrome and only a very small chance of survival. Being devout Christians, they asked Michael if they could have time off to fly to Massabielle, the sacred place near Lourdes in the foothills of the Pyrenees, to pray for the unborn child. In the 1850s a local peasant girl had a series of visions of the Virgin Mary and in one of them was shown to a spring in the grotto of Massabielle. Since then the water has been thought by many to have miraculous healing qualities. Michael agreed their request and even paid for the flights. When they returned, Lily told me that they had spoken to two nuns about their situation. The nuns had said that their baby would not live, but would become an angel. They found comfort in this when little Emmanuel was born on 20 May and lived just a few hours.

Lily stopped work at Woodland House a few months before the baby was due. Once again we all missed her laughter and good heart.

With *Parting Shots* now finished, Michael's working weeks were back to a less hectic routine. While filming he had to squeeze his writing time into evenings and weekends, but now his columns could have more of his focus once again.

He was always on the lookout for new restaurants or places he had not yet discovered. I would pass on any leads I had and sometimes get on the phone to friends if Michael was scratching about trying to find an interesting eatery to sample. In the early days, people would excitedly put forward their favourite places or some new restaurant where they liked the owner or manager or chef. But this would often backfire when they rushed to buy the *Sunday Times* only to have a brutal review sour their Sunday morning coffee.

It worked the other way too. John May told me about Assaggi, his local favourite place, just off Westbourne Grove, when it opened in 1997. Michael wrote a glowing report and from then on John found it very difficult to get a table. People soon learnt to keep quiet.

Various housekeepers came and went before Donata Iscala

arrived. She was a cheerful but stoic lady, also from the Philippines, and quickly learnt to cope with Michael's detailed demands and frequent loss of temper. The maids were soon to change too and Lalaine Meneses and Cirila Dantes Villar, always known as Shirley, took up their posts. The three of them would talk in Filipino together. On a hot day, hearing their chatter and shrill laughter and with the tall palms outside swaying in the breeze, there were moments when I felt I could be in a tropical island paradise. Those moments were never long lived, however, as the shout of 'DINAH, DINAH' would soon bring me back to my senses.

After the tragic loss of the chauffeur Michael White, an adequate replacement for him was not proving at all easy to find. Some managed to last a few months before they had had enough or were sent packing. The piles of magazines next to their chair in the garage would speak of their interests.

With Michael White it had been motorbikes, both classic and modern cutting edge. Of the new chauffeurs, I noticed one was a very enthusiastic carp fisherman, another was especially interested in naked ladies and a third showed an equal fascination for breeding canaries. I think the canary breeder was only with us for a few weeks. Driving Michael was not an easy task and definitely not a job for someone easily angered. He would bellow directions and instructions from the back seat and mix in some insults too. A chauffeur could be brought to a state of boiling road rage before he had turned out of Melbury Road or even seen another car. Michael's instructions could also lead to dilemmas such as 'Do I carry out my employer's orders or do I follow the Highway Code?' For example, 'FASTER, YOU FUCKING MORON, AND USE THE BUS LANE OR WE'LL BE HERE ALL FUCKING DAY.'

One new driver climbed out of the Rolls-Royce Phantom in Piccadilly and disappeared into the crowds, leaving Michael to make his own way home.

Eventually Jim Sharkey, a policeman who had taken early retirement, appeared one day. He had been the driver for Lew Grade, who had just died at the age of ninety-one. Lord Grade had had an extraordinary career as a media impresario. Early on he had been a talent scout in partnership with Joe Collins, father of Joan and Jackie Collins, and among their clients were the jazz group Quintet of the Hot Club of France, founded in 1934 by guitarist Django Reinhardt and violinist Stéphane Grappelli. Later he was instrumental in bringing many television series to our screens, such as *The Saint*, *The Prisoner* and *The Muppet Show*. Jim said he was always a very thoughtful, considerate and quietly spoken gentleman. The contrast between his previous employer and Michael was clearly quite considerable and was going to take some getting used to. His attitude was to just take one day at a time. It seemed to work and the days became weeks and the weeks became months. When satellite navigation screens became commonplace, other chauffeurs often asked why he didn't have any navigational aid. Jim's response was always, 'I do; he sits in the back of the car.'

There were changes afoot in Michael's love life too. He and Vanessa began to agree an amicable split. She wanted children, but that was not part of Michael's plan for the future. He knew that he had been heavily criticised for his meanness towards Jenny and didn't want to be accused of repeating that ever again. He ensured that Vanessa was well looked after and also announced it to everyone so it couldn't go unnoticed. They remained friends, but went their separate ways. Michael did not like to have to spend evenings or weekends alone and so he was quickly on the lookout for a new girlfriend.

There was a pool of receptionists and actresses he knew that he could call on for evenings out, but what he really needed was someone to go with him on his frequent holidays away. Paola agreed to see him again. He often told me how much he adored her, but I could see that she also presented him with something of a paradox. Although he enjoyed the way she spoke her mind and would thwart his schemes to control her, it also drove him crazy.

He just could not let go of the reins or let someone else share them, except for just a few moments now and then. In Paola it seemed he had found someone who could push him off his horse and although it thrilled him, it was frightening too, of course. Over several years, through her work as receptionist and through numerous evenings out, I had got to know her well. One Friday, Michael surprised me with the news that she had agreed to move in. He was in a state of great excitement and was running around making sure that everything was perfect and that bottles of Cristal champagne were being chilled. Friends had invited her to see Luciano Pavarotti that evening, but Michael was certain she would abandon that idea under the circumstances.

Sure enough, at five o'clock a black cab pulled up and out stepped Paola. She had brought just one suitcase. Well, it was more of a trunk than a suitcase and was huge and incredibly heavy. The cabbie was a big man and with a bit of grunting and groaning he managed to drag it out of his cab and leave it lying on its side on the pavement. The word was quickly put out and the maids and builders gathered around it like ants. With Michael directing, the absurdly heavy object was inched slowly in through the gate and up the steps towards the front door. Over the next half-hour or so the shrill laughter of the Filipinos faded as the trunk was moved slowly into the heart of the house. I drank champagne with the happily chattering couple until leaving them at six to catch my train home. My friend Jackie always picked me up from the station and would stay for a while as we caught up on any news. This time, as I walked through the door the phone was ringing. It was Michael. 'She's gone. Pava-fucking-rotti. She's fucking gone, dear. I don't fucking believe it. She fucking went. I threw her out. Can you believe that? Fucking typical. So fucking typical. Italians! Fucking Italians. They just fuck off. She just fucking fucked off.'

Slowly the story emerged from his anger and upset. Paola had made it clear that she would move in that evening, but did not want to miss Pavarotti. Michael had expected her to abandon her plans and go out to dinner with him. They argued and Michael said if she went to see Pavarotti he would not let her back in the house. She said, 'OK then,' and left. God knows how they got her suitcase out. I suppose it was a bit easier going down the stairs. It wasn't long before they were on speaking terms again, but it is a good example of the Paola-with-Michael problem.

At about this time Michael decided he needed a gun. I don't know where he got it and I didn't care. I just hated it. It was an air rifle, but nothing like the flimsy toy-like ones I had seen as a child. The heavy wooden look of it was more like something from a Second World War film. When Jenny was living in the house, Michael had had a dovecote installed in the centre of the big back lawn. It was a white-painted wooden structure and looked a bit like a little block of flats on a post. For doves, I suppose that's exactly what it was. I felt it was a lovely addition to the garden, but the reality was not quite as simple as that. Firstly, the doves that were introduced, and kept confined for a while, did not return quite as much as would have been nice. Secondly, they were not actually doves but 'white pigeons', so were very happy to spend most of their time with their local grey cousins. Gradually, a small colony of white and grey birds began to use the dovecote as a nesting place and it was good to see them bobbing and cooing on the little wooden roof.

When Edith was housekeeper she made sure they were well fed with seed and grain and scraps from the table. But pigeons from miles around soon heard about Edith and her food parcels. When she made her way down the garden path with the basket of food, the skies would darken with a thousand flapping wings. It soon did get a little out of hand and the paths needed to be hosed down after each feeding frenzy just to get rid of the day's droppings. A year or so after Jenny left, Michael ordered Edith to stop feeding the birds. She continued to smuggle food to them as often as she could when he was out or on holiday, but their numbers were falling away. When Edith left there were still quite a few pigeons that regarded the garden as home, but Michael had gone off the whole pigeon thing. He had become more and more excited about having an increasingly colourful garden and the pigeons were not helping. The dovecote was demolished and replaced by a stone birdbath, and that's when Michael got the gun.

I noticed it one day by the French windows, half hidden by the curtains. When I confronted him about it he tried to laugh it off, 'Oh, you know, it's good to have just in case, you know, in case animals or something, or an intruder, yes, in case of an intruder, that's all, dear, just in case.' I talked to Eddie about it and he said not to worry as Michael was such a poor shot he wouldn't hurt anything. Apparently they had nicknamed him 'the Great White Hunter'. Michael had appeared one day on the wooden terrace holding the heavy rifle just as Matthew was crossing the lawn with a wheelbarrow.

Eddie shouted from the garage door, 'Run for your lives, it's the Great White Hunter'.

His son Stephen yelled, 'It's all right, if you stay in front of him you're perfectly safe.' Michael had then taken a shot at a pigeon and it had flapped off unscathed. If I was at the house the gun remained hidden, but when I was not around I knew the pigeons were an occasional target. And then I discovered he had it in for the squirrels too. Matthew would plant hundreds of bulbs in the morning and the squirrels would dig them up and eat them in the afternoon. They especially liked tulips. Attempts were made to make the bulbs taste unpleasant, such as dipping them in hot mustard before planting them. That had no effect. Everything was tried, including chilli paste, but the squirrels still dug them up and would sit in the trees nibbling at them happily. It seemed they really liked tulip curry. Michael's answer was to shoot them. When he found they would not stay still long enough he decided to trap them and then shoot them. Matthew told him it was not going to work as there would always be plenty of local squirrels to take up their territory. He put cones of mesh over the newly planted bulbs to protect them until they were sprouting and that worked well. But Michael knew best. I got wind of the fact that he had bought about a dozen squirrel traps. One poor creature was caught eventually and a little bird told me that he stood over the wire cage and shot the helpless animal repeatedly.

For many years it was part of the daily routine that I would have a glass of wine with Michael at six o'clock. If I was not in his office the buzzer would go at about 5.30. 'Open a bottle of wine, dear, oh, and first will you bring up a cup of coffee.' In the summer I often opened the doors onto the terrace and walked round the garden for a few minutes before Michael came down. I enjoyed it and also it meant I could have a cigarette and a moment's peace. During a working day I knew I had to measure my opinions and comments quite carefully, but in the evenings I could be quite candid. If there was nobody else present, and my intuition gave me the thumbs-up, I could be absolutely blunt. Michael had discovered that after a glass of wine I would, in his words, 'come straight out with it'. I'm far from being an intellectual or eloquent speaker, but Michael understood my ramshackle way of talking. It's almost irritating to admit, but I know he enjoyed it too. But then I think that was one of the main reasons we managed to get on for so many years.

Usually he would be trying not to smile as I delivered my little sermon. There were very few occasions when I raised my voice to Michael, but his attitude towards the squirrels had really got my goat. I told him I had heard about the traps and he sheepishly tried to assure me that any squirrel caught would be taken to the park or somewhere and released. But he knew I wasn't falling for that one. 'What is the point of having such a beautiful garden if you just go shooting and trapping and killing everything? You've got woodpeckers, foxes, hedgehogs, squirrels and even parakeets. It's fantastic. If you don't like them you may as well go and live in a brick house.'

'But I do live in a brick house,' he corrected me and was trying not to laugh.

YOU KNOW WHAT I MEAN, I MEAN A CONCRETE
BOX. WHY DON'T YOU JUST CONCRETE ALL OVER
EVERYTHING, JUST CONCRETE IT ALL OVER AND
YOU WON'T HAVE TO WORRY AND WASTE YOUR
TIME. CONCRETE IT, JUST CONCRETE IT ALL
IF YOU THINK IT'S SUCH A SHAMBLES, WITH
PIGEONS CRAPPING ON THE TERRACE, LEAVES
BLOCKING THE GUTTERS AND SQUIRRELS EATING
THINGS AND WOODPECKERS TRYING TO MAKE
HOLES IN THE ROOF. JUST CUT THE TREES DOWN
AND MAKE IT A NICE TIDY CAR PARK. IS THAT
WHAT YOU WANT, A LOVELY CAR PARK? IT'S NOT
FUNNY, MICHAEL, IT'S HORRIBLE, IT'S HORRIBLE
WHAT YOU'RE DOING.

His face had gone a bit red, but only from the strain of trying not to laugh. But I could tell that something had gone in.
'Yes, yes, I know what you mean, calm down, dear, we will
try not to kill things in future. It's a good bottle, this, don't
you think? Petrus, 1964.' In the days I was not working he
did sometimes ask for the traps to be put out, but Eddie or
Matthew would make sure that they were not properly set,
or would release any squirrel before the Great White Hunter
could discover it jumping with terror in the tiny cage. Soon
they were forgotten and the traps gradually thrown away.
With Michael, a slight nudge was often the best you could
hope for.

When Christmas approached Michael needed someone
to accompany him on his habitual trip to Sandy Lane. He
had kept in touch with Georgina through frequent phone
calls and dinners out and he invited her to spend the holiday

with him. Since their first meeting nearly five years earlier, she now had a little boy called Ryan. By her own account, her relationship with the father had been short and had not ended well. Georgina accepted Michael's invitation, but was then told that he was not intending to take Ryan. I know now that he had assured her that I would be delighted to have Ryan for a few weeks. The first I heard of it was when, out of the blue, Michael started laughing and said something like, 'You'll be having a jolly Christmas this year, with Ryan as well, that'll be fun, won't it? Hahaha, you'll have a lovely time.'

I was quite stunned and was stuttering, 'Wha … wha … what? Is that some kind of joke? You must be having a laugh! That is a joke? You can't be serious?'

He had sowed the seed and then quickly changed the subject. 'It'll be fine, it'll be fine. Anyway, have you got the Christmas card list?' Over the next week or so he would bring it up now and then to slowly make it more real. That was his technique. I used to take Jenny's dog Tasha home when they went away, but this was very different: this was a baby still in nappies. When he mentioned it again and saw the same look of disbelief he just waved his arms around, trying to dismiss my shock. 'You love children, everyone knows you do. You've got two, another won't make any difference, you'll enjoy it. It'll be fine, and Georgina will be happy if she knows he's with you.'

It did slowly become a reality. Michael had already booked everything and I knew there would have been a terrible rumpus if I had point-blank refused. But also, by then I had spent some time with Ryan and realised it would be fine. There was another side to this story too. My mother had died in April and left a huge hole in everyone's lives at home. I'm sure I was quietly dreading the first Christmas without her lively spirit. She had somehow always been the centre of every gathering at home and I was nowhere near coming to terms with her loss. It was not something that occurred to me at the time, but it did turn out that having little Ryan was actually to be a blessing in disguise.

When the time came, Ryan and I sat on the train north blinking at each other. He was two and only just beginning to talk. Over Christmas he became part of the family and Daniel and Luke focused their attention on him, coaxing him into saying new words. Luke was twelve and had just got past the Santa Claus stage. For Ryan's sake I started it up again and included my boys, even though Daniel was now twenty. They were very happy. Christmas was 'full on' again. Now there were three Christmas stockings. And that's how it was for the next few years, while Ryan was coming to stay.

The new millennium brought with it the reminder that the world might be becoming a more dangerous place. Michael would have to tighten up his security. There were two incidents which prompted this. The first involved a cup of hot chocolate and the second a bunch of flowers. Every Thursday, Ron Cooper, the accountant, would pick up cash for wages from the bank in Kensington High Street. He would then walk back to his office in Farley Court to sort it into envelopes for the staff. One day, as he turned into Melbury Road on his return journey someone stopped him to ask the time. As he looked down at his watch a second man appeared suddenly and threw a cup of hot chocolate at him. In the split second of shock his briefcase was snatched and the thieves ran off. He was shaken, but fortunately not burnt. From that day on, Michael instructed the chauffeur to always accompany the accountant to the bank on the Thursday wages trip. If the chauffeur was away, another member of staff would go in his place.

The second incident concerned Michael's stalker. A middle-aged woman had been phoning him regularly to declare her undying love and admiration for him. In the evenings he would just put the phone down on her, but during the day the calls were always put through to the offices in Farley Court. John was under strict instructions to write down everything she said. He did exactly that. In the early days she found it rather confusing, but she soon accepted that she could dictate her messages and they would be passed to the great man himself. It was all rather polite and dignified. The handwritten sheets in John's perfect copperplate script would be sent up to the house – at least one a week and sometimes several a day. But not before John had read them out to Zoe if she was working in his office on the cuttings book. In a dry monotone John would read, 'I love you, I need you, I want you.' He would pause and raise an eyebrow sometimes before continuing. 'Kiss … Kiss … Kiss … You know you love me. You know I am the only woman for you.' Zoe would soon have slid to the floor crying and clutching her sides, but still John would go on… 'How long must we be apart? We can't go on like this any longer. I am the only woman for you. You know I am the only woman you have ever really loved … Oh Michael…'

When on reception duty at the house, Zoe had been clearly told not to let any visitor in until she had reported their arrival and got Michael's approval. One day she answered the door to a middle-aged lady carrying a floral display. Having heard the name Zoe felt sure she recognised it, but couldn't place it immediately. Then, just as she was in the process of politely asking her to wait, the woman suddenly pushed past her into the hall and made a bolt for the stairs. I was by the kitchen doorway when I heard Zoe screaming, 'NO, EXCUSE ME, STOP.' Michael must have heard the kerfuffle, as he appeared at the top of the stairs. She had stopped when she saw me, and Zoe already had her arm round her, trying to encourage her to turn and leave.

Michael's voice sounded petrified as he shouted, 'GET HER OUT, GET HER OUT, QUICKLY, SHE MAY HAVE A GUN, SHE MAY HAVE A GUN IN THE FLOWERS, QUICKLY, GET HER OUT.'

Zoe and I swept her swiftly out of the door and closed it. We never did discover if she had a gun hidden in the flowers or if Michael was overreacting a little. But all three of us were left shaking. From then on the black iron front gate was kept locked until any visitor had been vetted and approved.

The new millennium also brought Michael kicking and screaming into the computer age. Until then he had made do with a typewriter and a Dictaphone. And a secretary, of course. His new secretary was Margaret Watson. She had worked for Stanley Kubrick on *A Clockwork Orange*, *Barry Lyndon*, *The Shining* and *Full Metal Jacket* and was production manager on *Eyes Wide Shut* when Stanley died unexpectedly in 1999. Margaret had also worked on many of Michael's films as far back as the early 1980s. When he heard of Stanley Kubrick's death, Michael called Margaret and assured her he would look after her. But she knew it was not going to be easy work, even though she had seen it all before and had long since got the measure of Michael. I think what tipped the balance was that it was regular employment and if she could stick it for a few years it would take her to retirement age.

Margaret was very sweet to talk of Michael's kindness in employing her. It was clear to me that he had found someone at the top of their field and I also happened to know how thrilled to bits he was with the 'Kubrick connection'.

She must have grown a little tired of him saying, 'This is Margaret. She used to work for Stanley Kubrick.' Since Val had left, the secretaries had been coming and going and I had never found an ally. When Margaret arrived I soon realised I had found a friend. The job had become known as the 'hot seat', as the little office was next to Michael's and well within shouting range. One thing Margaret did enjoy about Michael was his sense of humour, and most of the time she managed to keep hers too. There were a few notable exceptions when she lost it. Several times she threw things at him to stem the flow of one of his absurd or foul tirades. I would not normally condone throwing things at people, but in Margaret's case I approved absolutely. I just wished the things to hand had been larger and more squishy. There was a very good reason for Michael not having a bowl of fruit in his office. The most worrying time was when she threw her notebook and pen to the floor and stormed back to her office, gathering her things to leave. Michael begged me to go after her and tell her he was sorry. I managed to persuade her to stay in the kitchen while I made coffee and he came down and made a proper apology. I should make it clear that Margaret was not a volatile character at all, but a calm person occasionally pushed beyond the limits of human endurance.

When a man arrived with Michael's first laptop computer, we knew things were going to get noisy. The first thing that Michael established was that the computer man was a moron, Margaret and I were morons and the laptop was utterly and historically useless. Once he had got that clearly stated, he could get on with the difficult business of learning how to write an email while surrounded by idiots. It was quite a struggle and Michael only had the idiot Margaret or the moronic computer man to call on for help. I agreed with him that I was a completely moronic idiot when it came to computers so fortunately he learnt not to waste his time talking to me about it. Despite all the nitwits, Michael managed to progress and within only a few months he could send an email, visit a website and even open a new Word document.

And he made quite a deep impression on anyone who witnessed him acquiring these new skills.

*　　*　　*

Michael was selected to be surprised by Michael Aspel and the big red book on the very popular television show *This Is Your Life*. It was John Fraser who took the call. He was asked to help in the making of the secret arrangements. The problem was that John knew that the secret arrangements could only be made if Michael knew about them.

To put it more clearly, he knew that the only way that the secret arrangements could stand a chance of meeting with Michael's approval would be if Michael arranged them himself. This would somehow have to be done very carefully. John secretly told Michael about the secret and Michael secretly agreed that he was happy with the secret programme as long as he was controlling things. Secretly, of course. It was as simple as that. With Michael secretly instructing him, John set to work. Michael was well aware that it was a cast-iron rule of the show that the chosen victim had to be kept totally in the dark so they were truly surprised on camera. He knew that the programme's producers would have dropped him like a stone if they had had any inkling of what was going on. Everything had to be done very, very carefully. Friends and associates from the long or recent past were called and asked if they could take part. The whole thing was touch and go for a while when John reported that neither Michael Caine nor Roger Moore could make it to the show. Michael naturally wanted it to be as star-studded as possible. The situation was saved when Michael Caine agreed to film a brief interview about Michael to be shown during the programme. As the big day approached he became nervous of his ability to appear sufficiently surprised when the time came. I tested him once by walking into his office holding the Yellow Pages for central London wrapped in a red scarf. When I looked him in the eye and said, 'Michael Winner, this is your life,' he nearly fell off his chair. But that was through laughing rather than surprise. The rehearsal wasn't very helpful, but when the moment came I think he pulled it off OK. And anyway, the actual reality of seeing so many people from his life gathered together *was* a genuine surprise and delight for him.

Michael Aspel, the show's presenter, made his 'surprise' appearance and 'Michael Winner, this is your life' announcement as Michael dined out with Georgina, Marco Pierre White and his wife Mati. Once this had happened, and Michael had been given time to recover, he was then rushed to the TV studios where friends and colleagues and people whose lives had crossed with Michael's at some point were waiting. He carried it off perfectly and nobody suspected a thing. The actor Dermot Walsh was there in the studio, whom Michael had first met when he interviewed him for a newspaper article aged only fifteen, and also John Fraser, of course, whom Michael had known since schooldays. The composer and lyricist Leslie Bricusse and his wife Yvonne Romain were there too. Michael and Leslie had been friends ever since they first met at Cambridge. Leslie said he had always liked Michael because he was someone who 'always speaks his mind', but also 'like Stephen King, he likes frightening people'. Andrew Neil spoke of that side of him too, saying that his reason for giving him the *Sunday Times* column was because he was looking for someone 'independent, honest and downright rude'. It was Michael Caine who called Michael a 'fraud' and said that he didn't recognise descriptions of him in the press. He described him as 'very kind and very generous'. This side of Michael's chameleon character was reinforced when Sir John Stevens, the Metropolitan Police Commissioner, and also Yvonne Fletcher's parents, Tim and Queenie, gave him a glowing tribute for his work in founding the Police Memorial Trust. Michael was very nearly in tears as he hugged them both. Since the beginnings of the Trust Michael had spoken to them regularly and I often saw them at the unveiling of new memorials. They were such kind-hearted and gentle people and in many ways I felt they had come to be as much the figureheads of the Trust as Michael himself. And I knew he adored them.

* * *

After Mum died I had a bit of money that she had left me. Takis thought it a good idea to use it to have a conservatory built. I wanted to either pay off some of our mortgage or keep it as savings. Over the years I had learnt that there were times with Michael when it was horrible to feel trapped in the job.

Also, I had no contract and he could have fired me, or decided I was not needed, at the drop of a hat. I had no real security. I knew that the windows in the house needed replacing, so that was agreed. There was just enough of Mum's money to build a conservatory too and in the end I let Takis have his way.

One Saturday when I was making tea for the builders, one of them sidled over looking a bit sheepish. He said, 'I thought you ought to know, miss, that your husband just put your mum's ashes into the cement mixer. I hope you knew!' I didn't know, of course. Takis said she had gone now so something had to be done. I had imagined scattering her ashes and saying a few words with both my sons present. As it was, my mother was now included in the concrete floor. From then on when friends walked into the conservatory they would say, 'Hello, Shelagh'. Although I was angered by how it had happened I was happy that she was still, in some way, part of the house.

As a special treat, Michael said he would take me to the Hospital. I had grown wary of his treats over the years, especially when they involved him driving.

On this occasion all turned out well. In fact, it was fabulous. The Hospital was Michael's name for Restaurant Gordon Ramsay in Royal Hospital Road, Chelsea and, to my relief, the chauffeur took us. It opened in 1998 and by 2001 had three Michelin stars. Michael knew that Gordon himself was cooking that evening. We arrived early and Gordon showed us the kitchens. Everything was spotless and gleaming and seemed to be run with military precision. Gordon introduced us to everybody and gave a short speech insisting that everything must be absolutely perfect that evening. The chefs stood at their stations and saluted Michael while Gordon continued to gently take the mickey out of him. We went for the tasting menu and were served sixteen fabulous courses. We were very happy, very impressed and quite full too.

A few months later I found myself in a more traditional kind of hospital: Murrayfield Hospital on the Wirral. That was not so pleasant and the food nowhere near as good. They didn't have any Michelin stars at all.

But I wasn't going to be able to enjoy eating for a while anyway as I was there to have a blockage in my digestive tract sorted out. It had taken five years to diagnose the problem. I think the first time the symptoms appeared was after a gig with Paul Usher's band. Just as I was getting into the Ford Transit I fainted and was sick. People who didn't know me assumed I was very drunk.

The same thing happened about twice a year for the next five years. Once it was after going out to dinner with Michael. We had been to Thomas Goode, just off Park Lane in Mayfair, and I thought it must have been the seafood. Michael got on to them the next day and they immediately sent me six beautiful china coffee cups and saucers in harlequin design and edged with gold. I loved them so much that I asked Michael to see if I could buy the coffee pot, milk jug and sugar bowl. That Christmas, a huge box arrived for me at Woodland House. They had sent them all as a gift. I should really have offered to return them once I discovered the real problem, but I'm afraid that the extraordinary beauty of the chinaware had whittled away at my moral fibre. My illness was finally addressed when I made quite a spectacle of myself at the Yacht Inn near Chester. It had become a favourite lunch place for local ladies and Jackie and another friend, Debbie Welsh, had taken me. Before the meal was over I had stood up, fainted and been

sick as I lay on the floor. The local ladies were no doubt horrified at the sight of what must have seemed like horrible
drunkenness, but in fact I had not even had a glass of wine.

The doctor said it was food poisoning again, but after two
days I was still not well. I went through gruelling tests, but
to cut the story short it was decided that I needed an operation to remove a blockage. On the NHS it meant a wait of
several months and I would have to eat only liquidised food.
Takis had called Michael, who told him I should go privately
and he would pay for anything that was needed. So there I
was in Murrayfield Hospital. A few days and £4,000 later
I was out, but with strict instructions to rest and not lift anything for ten weeks. The first thing I heard when I got home
was that little Ryan was coming for a week. Michael and Georgina were going away and I soon realised that a deal must have
been struck with Takis. Daniel and Nicolanne picked Ryan
up in London and brought him north. Takis went off to play
a gig. It was the beginning of the time in which I was starting
to feel a little used and unsupported. When Mum had been
only down the road she was always there and ready to help.
It was very different without her.

After a few weeks' convalescence, Michael insisted I return
to work. He had been phoning every day, so it was never
going to feel like much of a break, and I agreed. I asked if
Jim the chauffeur could pick me up from the station to save
me lifting any bags. Jim had a little run-around we called 'the
Noddy car' that he used for giving lifts or running errands.
Michael made it clear that it was an absurd and ridiculous
request and that if I was worried I only need bring a couple
of T-shirts in my pocket. I felt that was a bit mean, and then
on Friday when I got paid he took £20 from me too. He had

decided that I should pay back half the medical costs. From then on, every time I was paid, he would take back £20 or £30 and note it down in his diary. It was two or three years before we were square again.

Over her second Christmas at Sandy Lane, Georgina had met Simon Cowell. He was there with his mother Julie and brother Nicholas. This, of course, was before *The X Factor* had made him so famous.

It was Simon who first suggested that Michael throw a big party at his house for Georgina's thirtieth birthday. I had never known Michael have more than a small dinner party at home before. There was one grand dinner with Arnold Schwarzenegger, Robert Earl and other friends, but I was on holiday and only saw the photographs. Michael always maintained that he didn't like people wandering around and damaging things. I just would not have imagined him agreeing to any kind of house party. But he could be unpredictable and, sure enough, he set about making it happen.

His dining room and lounge were two large connecting rooms and much of the furniture was moved so that lots of tables could be set up. Extra ovens were brought into the kitchen, and other rooms were made ready for drinks to be served.

The Admirable Crichton, party planners extraordinaire, had been called upon to take care of everything and they certainly had. The whole house looked beautiful. Zoe and I began the evening downstairs helping to pour the champagne and joined the party as dinner was about to be served. Georgina had friends there that I had not met before, but there were also many of Michael's friends I had got to know a little over the years. There were Don and Shirley Black, Stephen Berkoff and

Clara Fisher, Marco Pierre White and Mati, Terry O'Neill and Laraine Ashton, Cherie Lunghi, Gerard and Rachel De Thame, the film maker and the presenter, Johnny Gold, Adam Kenwright the theatre producer, David Ross, the co-founder of Carphone Warehouse, and many other people. I sat near Simon Cowell; his brother Nicholas and Nicholas's wife Katie were at the party too. This was the evening I first heard mention of *Pop Idol*. Simon was describing the new show he was appearing on as a judge and wondering if it might be a success. 'YES, YES, OF COURSE IT WILL, OF COURSE IT WILL, MARVELLOUS IDEA,' Michael was shouting enthusiastically, always a great supporter of his friends' endeavours and a believer in a good positive attitude too. On that occasion Michael was absolutely 100 per cent right.

After dinner, coffee was served downstairs, for those who wanted it, in what used to be Michael's bedroom but then became a huge lounge known as the 'TV room'. I sat and chatted with Don and Shirley Black. They were always such friendly people and, as they lived close to Michael, I quite often saw them in the high street. They would always stop and chat and knew Michael's character well enough to give me a sympathetic smile when I was rushing off on a mission. I had heard that Don had been a comedian in his early days, before he became a world-famous lyricist, and that was no real surprise, as he and Shirley always seemed to have a glint of humour in their eyes. The scope of his talent is extraordinary. It was especially good seeing Don and Shirley at Georgina's birthday, as there were periods when I think possibly they avoided Michael, and I wouldn't see them in his company for a while. It's quite likely that there were times when his brashness may have grated on them a bit. Michael could be so gracious and charming, and then the very opposite – and with no warning. He often fell out with people, of course, and sometimes that was with some very good friends. In the earlier days I sometimes asked him quite directly, when he was stirring up an argument with someone, why he was being so horrible. He would either just laugh gleefully or fidget about awkwardly and look embarrassed. He never gave a clear answer. It seemed often quite childish, as though he was enjoying pushing the boundaries to see how much people would put up with.

Rebekah Wade, now Rebekah Brooks, was not one of Michael's favourite people. I think they had got on well in earlier times, but while she was editor of the *News of the World* she reduced the size of his contribution and then cut it out altogether. He was very upset. His newspaper columns were very important to him and Michael particularly enjoyed having the power to write about someone as 'Twit of the Week'. When faced with this loss he was not to be outdone and soon found ways of including anyone who really irritated him in his 'Winner's Dinners' article for the *Sunday Times*. And he liked the kind of letters and conversations that only his writing could involve him in. Besides, it meant there was no time for him to be bored and I think he feared that more than anything.

Michael clearly revelled in being a well-known figure, too. You could almost say he was addicted to it. He was always happy to be invited onto any television show and, having helped him choose clothes, I would usually go with him. Once he had gone through make-up I would either join the audience or wait in the green room or at the side of the set. Apart from *Question Time* the programmes usually had a leaning towards comedy, such as Clive Anderson's show, *Mrs Merton, Bang,*

Bang, It's Reeves and Mortimer, Clarkson et cetera. Michael usually got on well with the hosts and certainly respected their talents. On some shows he knew he could be quite vulnerable. *Have I Got News for You* boasted some of the finest wits, and sometimes people that he knew disliked him. They were the only times I saw him a little nervous before going on, but he was not overly bothered by criticism or jokes at his expense. Now and then, on the journey back, I would sense that he was feeling a little bruised. On those occasions I would try to pick out the highlights where he had come across well or got a laugh.

But the television show that most concerned him was *Celebrity Sleepover*, where a celebrity would spend the evening, and the night, with a family they did not know. Michael only liked to sleep in hotels or his own home. A good night's sleep was of utmost importance to him and he was fully expecting to be miserable. He took some powerful sleeping pills with him, just in case, but as it turned out he liked the family and enjoyed himself.

The atmosphere in Woodland House changed when Michael went away.

Everyone relaxed. I'm sure that many offices change when the managing director leaves the room. The staff can throw paper aeroplanes if they feel like it. We didn't throw many paper aeroplanes, but over the years I did catch most of the household asleep at one time or other. Jim the chauffeur asleep in his chair in the garage, the maids asleep on a sofa or even on the stairs, Zoe asleep in the bathroom at Farley Court, Matthew asleep in the shed and, one cold day, on the lounge floor by the French windows. The receptionists sometimes slept slumped over the kitchen table. I needed to be able to hear the phone, so my favourite place to get forty winks was the sofa in the adjoining room to Michael's office. When we weren't sleeping we would be in the kitchen having a hot lunch cooked up by the housekeeper.

When Michael went to Sandy Lane he usually left about ten days before Christmas. He would call the office regularly and if he wanted to talk to me he would call the phone in the kitchen. There might be several people around and they would keep silent while I chatted. Sometimes it was work related or it could just be general chatter. He seemed to like to call when he was standing in the sea, up to his knees in water. 'Can you hear the water, darling, can you hear? It's very warm, can you hear it, can you hear it? I'm doing the waves, you must be able to hear it now.' He would be moving his hand across the surface to make a rippling and splashing sound. If he was doing it to make me jealous, it always worked. I could not move far from the telephone base station without losing reception, so if anyone needed to cough they had to run out. If the call seemed set to be a long one, people would wander off and go back to their work or another nap.

To be fair, it wasn't quite as relaxed a picture as I may be painting here. There were still things to be done, but the usual urgency had evaporated. Apart from the secretary, who was often kept on her toes by frequent telephone calls and faxes needing attention, the rest of us could take things a bit more easily. But a few days before Michael's scheduled return it was a very different scene. The house would become a hive of activity. The housekeeper and maids knew that there was little point in cleaning everything needlessly when it would have to be done again a week later. Instead they would work crazily over the last few days. And so would everyone else.

While they were cleaning ovens and silverware, Jim would be polishing all the cars and Matthew replanting the front and back borders with cyclamen, primula and anything else that was particularly colourful at that time of year. One thing I had to do was make sure that Michael's pills were ready. He took between twenty and forty a day at various times in his life. Most were vitamins or for his heart and had to be carefully sorted into little bags. He liked to have a supply ready that stretched several months into the future.

*   *   *

When Peter Wood told Michael that he would like him to write, direct and star in the next Esure commercials he made him a very happy man. A *very* happy man. I don't think I had ever seen him so excited. He told me he was the luckiest man in Britain. Not only would he be paid a small fortune, but he knew he would be seen in every front room across the country. Michael had been struggling to come to terms with the fact that he would not be making any more films. Through the television commercials he needn't feel left out in the cold any longer. And when the time came he called upon people he liked or trusted or had worked with before. He could have his family around him again.

It all started over lunch with Peter Wood. Michael had great respect for Peter and for the way in which he had transformed the insurance industry. He was also a good enough friend to be able to tell him quite frankly that he thought the commercials for Esure, his new company, were dreadful.

Michael then outlined what he thought would work better. Peter immediately said he liked the ideas and within a few weeks the ball was rolling. Soon, the house was once again a hive of activity. Ron Purdie was back as co-producer and when it came to filming and post-production some of the old crew were called in. I was doing hair, but it was not nearly as time consuming as it was on the films, of course. Michael found a new job for me. When everything was ready my task was to keep within a yard or two of him, holding a packet of Strepsils and a jar of honey. This was for his voice. I wondered if Pavarotti had a 'honey holder'. Well, actually I wasn't just the honey and Strepsils holder, I had other responsibilities too: I held his coat, compact camera and script.

Michael had asked Julia Foster to appear with him in the first commercial. He had known her since his earliest days as a film maker and she was in *The System* in 1963. But she was best known for starring alongside Tommy Steele in *Half a Sixpence*, a film directed by George Sidney in 1967. A bit before that she had appeared in *Alfie* with Michael Caine and a film called *The Bargee* alongside the likes of Ronnie Barker, Harry H. Corbett and Eric Sykes. Later, in 1974, she played Mrs McGonagall in *The Great McGonagall* with Spike Milligan and Peter Sellers.

The simple storyline shows us a bad driver who keeps bumping into other cars. As he goes down Ilchester Place we see Vanessa, Zoe and a part-time receptionist called Anika standing on the pavement. An irate lady, Julia Foster, runs over to protest and is told, 'Calm down, dear, it's only a commercial.' Michael cast himself as the bad driver who claims to be a good driver driving badly for the purposes of advertising. For anyone who had been a passenger with Michael that could sound a bit of a pork pie to say the least, but I think he did regard himself as perfectly competent behind the wheel. It was all the idiots getting in his way that he saw as the real problem.

Over the years I had witnessed the evolution of what was to become Michael's catchphrase. If he had irritated a man and knew he might have his facts wrong he would say something like, 'Yes, yes, calm down, calm down, I'm sure there is a perfectly reasonable explanation for it.' If it was someone he knew very well, or a woman, and they were rising to their own defence, he would say, 'Calm down, calm down, dear, you're probably right, there's no need to get so excited.' This was usually accompanied by the flapping hands, the gesture that became almost as famous as the catchphrase. When I hear it now, it sometimes reminds me of his friend Kenny Everett. There is something of Kenny's comic campness about it and I'm sure he would have loved it.

CHAPTER SEVEN

CHANGES, ACHIEVEMENTS AND COMMERCIALS

IT WAS A SUNNY DAY and I was at a local fair with little Ryan when I got the angry phone call. Over several years Ryan had become part of the family, staying with me whenever Michael and Georgina went away for a week or two, which they did regularly. He was always with us for the Christmas and Easter holidays too, and Daniel and Luke had treated him as a little brother. But unbeknownst to me, towards the end of their current trip to Italy, Michael and Georgina had begun to argue. Little Ryan seemed to be the bone of contention. Now that he was older she felt that Michael should include him in their trips away and had asked if he could go on the next Christmas trip to Barbados. Michael said it would be far too expensive. He had always booked flights on Concorde and Georgina had suggested that Ryan, now five, could fly out on a cheaper option. She recently showed me the piece of paper on which Michael had written out a list of the extra expenses he would have to pay.

Underneath he wrote a note saying that he felt bullied into it. That was the final straw for Georgina. She told him she would spare him having to feel that way as he was fired. There was a big row and Michael booked return flights a day earlier than originally intended.

Meanwhile Luke, Ryan and I were having a good time at the funfair and Ladies Day celebrations in Neston. Ladies Day was the annual event organised by the first friendly society for women. Friendly societies originated from Napoleonic times as a way of local communities paying into their own savings fund. It offered some kind of safeguard against hard times or ill health. In many ways it was an early form of co-operative bank and insurance company. In the north of England, a high proportion of women were employed and in 1814 Neston was the first place to form a friendly society purely for women. Ladies Day and the annual colourful walk was a way to remind all local people of its important role. And, because it was the first of its kind, the people of Neston like to maintain the tradition. The streets were packed with people and a marching band was playing as the procession of women and girls in colourful dresses were making their way down the high street. They all carried white staves garlanded with flowers and ribbons and at the front their banner read 'Bear Ye One

Another's Burdens'. I was holding little Ryan up to see over people's heads when the phone rang.

'GET HIM BACK HERE IMMEDIATELY. PUT HIM ON A TRAIN TOMORROW. GET HIM BACK HERE. GET HIM BACK HERE TOMORROW. GEORGINA AND I ARE FINISHED. DO YOU UNDERSTAND? IT IS OVER. OVER. GET HIM BACK HERE.'

That was all I heard and then the phone was put down. Michael was not shouting to make himself heard over the brass band. In that mood I knew there could be no pleading with him. It was a sudden end to a very happy day and, more than that, as a family we were going to miss little Ryan.

I called Michael that evening in the hope it had been just a moment's fit of anger. It hadn't. I began to say that Ryan was only small and it didn't feel fair to let him be caught up in any argument, and maybe they would work things out in a few weeks ... Well, I don't think I got that far before Michael interrupted. 'I'M NOT GOING TO BE TOLD WHAT I HAVE TO FUCKING DO WITH MY LIFE. DO YOU UNDERSTAND, IT IS FUCKING OVER...' I caught the train to London with Ryan the next day as requested.

A few weeks later Michael and Georgina were on speaking terms again and from then on they spoke regularly, as friends. Luckily she had a flat near Michael so I continued to see her and Ryan quite often too.

Over the next few weeks, Michael's life remained centred around Esure and work on the commercials. I spent most of each day running errands or standing near his desk while he went through details or bounced ideas off me.

There was a spare chair, but I had long since given up thoughts of sitting on it.

I had tried in the past, but then would immediately be asked to fetch a file, pick up something he had dropped or go and make coffee. Michael saw the chair as another handy place for him to put books and papers. I was very glad when I had time off and could sit down now and then. Michael made an effort not to phone me during the day when I was not in work, but if there was something he felt was important he would not hesitate. Sometimes I would return from walking the dogs to find a string of answerphone messages. They would start in Michael's talking voice, 'Where are you? Call me back.'

Gradually his impatience would build and by the last one or two he would often be highly irritated. 'WHAT'S THE POINT OF HAVING A FUCKING PHONE IF YOU NEVER FUCKING ANSWER IT?' I had to accept that it was an unavoidable part of working for Michael, but I also sympathised with Takis and the boys when it interrupted whatever we were doing. If Michael wanted to talk about something it was not usually an option for me to say, 'Yes, OK, how about Tuesday at 4.00?'

His telephone calls were a background to family life. One Sunday I was serving up a big roast dinner and Nicolanne, Daniel's girlfriend, was there too. The phone went and before I could say 'don't answer it', Nicolanne had picked it up.

When she came to the table she said it was Michael Winner and she had asked him to call back later. That sounded an unlikely scenario for Michael, and Nicolanne was looking a little uncomfortable. Gradually it emerged that he had asked to speak to me and as she was saying 'I'm sorry, Mr Winner, she is having dinner, please call back later', he had slammed the phone down on her.

I had learnt that when Michael was in a particularly impatient mood it was better just to drop everything and deal with it. Any delay and a molehill could quickly become a mountain, and in the long run that would be far worse for me. There were the usual sighs and groans from the family when I got up to go to the phone. Once Michael had finished ranting on about the 'fucking idiot' who had dared to tell him to call back he told me he had invited Geraldine to stay for the weekend. He said if they got on he would ask her to move in. I knew he meant Geraldine Lynton-Edwards. I had met her in the 1990s in Paris and also once in London when she had called at Woodland House. She had two grown-up sons, one called Fabrice with Jean Moussy, and another called Julien from her second marriage to Edouard Weiss. She was a few years younger than him and I felt it might be good for Michael to have a girlfriend of similar age for a change. But I certainly didn't say that to him. Once he had updated me on his latest plans I got back to my reheated Sunday dinner.

When I returned to work at Woodland House, sure enough, Geraldine had moved in. She had nipped back to Paris to put some things together and Margaret had arranged for them to be brought over. There was a room known as the Blue Room near the front door, which Michael had used as a dressing room when his bedroom was on the ground floor. Geraldine set up her computer there and it was a place she could be during the working day. Each month she would go to Paris for a few days to see her family and friends there.

Michael was still jubilant over his Esure success. He prided himself on paying people quickly for work done and told me that Peter Wood was even faster than him. I don't think Michael had ever earned so much so quickly.

As Christmas approached once again, he revealed that he had a special treat for me. As a fiftieth birthday present and to mark my twenty-fifth wedding anniversary he said he would arrange for Takis and me to have eight days in Barbados. And he did just that. It was fabulous. On 2 January we landed and stayed at the Almond Beach Club next to Sandy Lane, where Michael and Geraldine were staying. Michael knew I liked to spend as much time as possible in water and had made sure our room was only a few yards from the sea. He said there was no need for us to have dinner every night with them and insisted we did what we wanted and had a proper holiday. He was as charming as I had ever seen him. That was a little annoying as Takis had never seen the other side of him. If I went home shaken and upset or with tales of woe, he would treat me as though I was neurotic and oversensitive. Then Michael would talk to him on the phone and say things like, 'Oh, you know what she's like, I may have raised my voice a little, but there's nothing to make a drama out of...' Over the holiday week we did get together for dinner a few times, but with Michael, dinners were usually short, especially if there was no one he considered highly important at the table. One evening Geraldine's sister and her husband were there too and Michael mostly talked to me over dinner. When he had finished eating he leant over and told me he was off as he couldn't stay trying to make conversation with 'normal' people, as he called them. He did that on a number of occasions over the time I knew him. In that way he could be very rude. But all in all it was a fabulous holiday and a perfect way to break up the long English winter. What was strange was that I didn't see a single celebrity or famous person. Well, no one that I recognised. They may have flown away straight after the New Year, or perhaps it was because I spent almost all the daylight hours in the sea.

Returning to work and cold grey London was not easy after that week. The house was always kept very warm, but Michael's office was stiflingly hot as he liked to sit at his desk in shorts. If the phone went and the conversation seemed to be going on a while I would try to drift out to the secretary's office next door to cool off. Sometimes Michael would flap his hand frantically for me to stay. That would mean that it was someone that he considered of monumental importance, such as Jill Ireland or Marlon Brando.

Marlon called quite regularly and he and Michael would talk for half an hour or so. Michael would hold the phone so I could hear the distinctive voice, but in the last few years their talk often involved a lot of sadness and tales of poor health. Michael would do his best to cheer him up. I think he liked me there partly to share his excitement at hearing from a huge star and possibly he was showing off a little too. But more than that, I think there were some people he had the greatest respect for and had known through many, many years and I was the nearest person he had to share that side of his life with. By then I had been there for more than ten years and known him for twenty. It was after those kinds of calls that Michael was at his most thoughtful and reflective, and we would mull over whatever they had talked about.

I wasn't looking forward to Margaret's sixtieth birthday because I knew that meant she would be off. She had survived three years in the hot seat and was going to be missed; certainly by Michael, but just as much, if not more, I think, by me. She was not a tall woman, but what she lacked in height she made up for in strength and she had shown little fear of standing up to Michael when it was a matter of principle. The hot seat was taken by Sue Roberts, who had worked for twenty years with the travel agents Michael always used. She was a lovely person and a perfectly good secretary, but Michael's picking and shouting quickly wore her down. I felt very sorry for her as she could not have known quite what she was in for. After six weeks her nerves were too rattled and she left. The only good thing that came out of all this was that I met Pat Wooll. She had been PA to Brian Brolly at the time that he set up Paul and Linda McCartney's MPL Communications and Andrew Lloyd Webber's Really Useful Theatre Company. Everyone took to Pat immediately as she was so clearly such a calm and kind person. Once the honeymoon period was over and she got a whiff of Michael's shouting she bit her lip and kept her head down. In order to survive, everyone had to find their own way of coping with him and we were all glad to see she was managing it.

For Michael, this reshuffle was very much in the background. He had much more important things to think about, such as wands, wigs and white dresses.

There were other Esure commercials to be made and Michael had cast himself as a fairy. I discovered he really liked dressing up, and fitting him into the fairy outfit was a bit like getting a small child ready for the school pantomime. It involved quite a lot of laughter too, as you might imagine.

My son Daniel and his girlfriend Nicolanne Cox had split up, but managed to stay good friends. Now twenty-three, she was working as an audience coordinator on the television show *Kilroy* and often asked me if there was any job available with Michael. I had got her involved in *Parting Shots* as an extra, but I was loath to introduce her to more of his world in case she was shouted at. Also, like some other people back home, she seemed to be under the impression that my life was all champagne and helicopter rides and I worried that her illusions might be too brutally shattered. But I had known her since she was fourteen and watched her grow into an energetic and strong character. I put her name forward and she got the job of runner. We were filming in a cul-de-sac and the first responsibility Michael gave her was to stop any car that might approach. With his usual, almost menacing, clarity he gave her instructions. 'If you see any fucking car or van or fucking cyclist I want you to stop them and ask them to wait. Do you understand? Can you do that, my dear? And I mean any fucking car or moving thing. You will stop them and ask them to wait. That is all you have to do, my dear, do you understand? Well, don't just fucking stand there, you idiot, you might be in shot, get in the fucking bush.'

Nicolanne disappeared into a privet hedge and the branches closed behind her. She managed to stay safely inconspicuous and avoid any drama during the few days' filming and, when the Kilroy show ended, began to fill in as receptionist at the house. Michael had remembered Ruby Snape from *Parting Shots* and included her in two of the commercials. As an actor she was of course sometimes 'resting' so Ruby also found a place on the receptionist rota.

Another face that appeared from the recent past was Paola. After an unpleasant break-up with her boyfriend she was living nearby on Kensington High Street and looking for a job. She and Michael had quickly patched up any hurt feelings after her very brief stay at Woodland House and she also began part-time work on reception. Zoe was expecting a baby with her long-time boyfriend Shaun Huggins and would soon have to leave. I was lucky that other friends had sprung up around me before losing her from my working week. Michael was sorry to lose her too. Over the years she had been shaken by some of his fearsome tirades and always managed to survive and bounce back. Her good spirits were almost irrepressible and I knew I was going to miss her terribly.

In the summer of 2004 Greece was to host the Olympic Games. Since marrying Takis, our family summer holidays had always been on the coast near Athens. Because of the Games, various friends were going to come and stay so they could go to some of the events. It would be wonderful and I was already imagining myself swimming in the cool, clear water. That year, more than any other, I was counting the days to my flight out. The atmosphere in the house was becoming difficult. All the staff knew about Michael's history with Paola and were keeping their heads down. I had seen it all before and did not appreciate being implicated. Michael was very jolly. He had everything as he liked it. I also knew he was not going to listen to any sermon from me about good behaviour or respect for people. The house was already a place where most of the staff whispered so as not to draw attention to themselves should Michael be near. Now there was little talk at all. If Paola or Geraldine asked them anything, they knew that even a seemingly innocuous remark could set off an explosion. And I was in the worst position. Once in Greece I started to relax a little, but it wasn't long before my phone was ringing regularly. Michael would be recounting with glee how much anger and upset his latest games had caused. Somehow I managed to gently get through to him that I didn't share his sense of humour over that, and his calls grew less frequent. Then Nicolanne started calling.

She was new to Michael's world and was having to wake up

fast. He had tricked her once already. Seeing her one morning sitting patiently at the kitchen table by the intercom buzzer he had said, 'Why don't you read a book, my dear, or bring something to do? Surely you're not just going to sit there like an idiot all day.'

A few days later he stepped into the kitchen and she was mending a skirt with needle and thread. 'Good morning, Mr Winner,' she said innocently. Michael glared at her for a moment.

What are you doing? What are you fucking doing? HOW DARE YOU? HOW DARE YOU? I HAVE NOT TOLD YOU TO DO FUCKING SEWING, IF YOU HAVE SEWING TO DO YOU WILL DO IT IN YOUR OWN FUCKING TIME, YOU FUCKING C***ING MORON. IT IS DISGRACE-FUL, IF YOU WEREN'T A FRIEND OF DINAH'S YOU WOULD BE FIRED, DO YOU UNDERSTAND, FUCK-ING FIRED, YOU FUCKING MORONIC C***.

His outburst was quite a long one and Nicolanne was under-standably shocked and shaken, and she called me in tears.

As she was working as receptionist, some of her days would be spent with Paola, who was also working. When Paola was not there, Geraldine might be in the kitchen. Nicolanne quickly learnt that taking sides, or even talking openly, was not an option. The only person who was enjoying any of this tension, of course, was Michael. After all, it was centred around *him*.

I was dreading going back to work and sure enough noth-ing had improved.

Often Paola would be given things to do in Farley Court, which helped the atmosphere a little. There were some dramas over the next few months, but Christmas came and went without a major explosion. But we all knew that it was a tinderbox and any day a spark could set the whole thing off. Sure enough, one Monday morning Michael greeted me with the news that Geraldine would not be returning from Paris. I was very glad to have been away when that decision was being made. I was sent off with Jim the chauffeur to get lots of plastic boxes. Donata and the maids and I were instructed to pack her things, and everyone was mystified as to what exactly was going on. On a grey, drizzly day a large van arrived and everyone was called upon to carry out boxes and armfuls of clothes.

Michael seemed to have tuned into the puzzlement among the staff and came and announced clearly to everyone that Paola would soon be living at the house. She, on the other hand, was cautious and kept repeating to Michael that, having only recently emerged from a bad relationship, she wanted to take things slowly. But Michael as always was impatient and said that he had already waited ten years since first meeting her. He wanted her to move in immediately and told me that he was constantly asking her to marry him.

Then there was a rumpus in the papers as Geraldine claimed Michael had ditched her without a care. Michael was furious, saying he had given her a lump sum and a monthly allowance. But soon the noise of the explosion had faded and everyone got back to day-to-day life in Woodland House.

When Gae Exton was looking for work, she telephoned Michael to see if he had anything that she could usefully be employed to do. She knew his friend the photographer Terry O'Neill and had worked with his wife Laraine Ashton in the setting up of her model agency. She came for an interview. 'You are far too posh to work for us, dear, far too posh,'

Michael told her. I think by that he meant that he knew she was well connected and was part of an impressive social circle. She had two children, Matthew and Alexandra, with Christopher Reeve, her partner of some twenty years, but had separated from him in 1987. Anyway, that seemed to be that, but a few days later Michael and Paola were strolling in Holland Park and saw Gae walking Archie, her Scottish terrier. When Michael found she was still looking for work he told her that she could come in the next day. He then went on to explain that he would not be there until after lunch as he was meeting the Queen in the morning. It might have been simply coincidence, but I'm sure Michael used the timing to squeeze out the maximum in 'snob value'. Gae arrived at 9.30 sharp on 26 April 2005.

The house was almost deserted. She said afterwards it felt rather uncanny, like the *Mary Celeste*. Donata was there to offer her coffee, but Pat the secretary had no idea what she was expected to do. Michael, Paola, John Fraser and I had rushed off to The Mall for the unveiling of the National Police Memorial by Her Majesty the Queen.

John was using a wheelchair as he was still not fully recovered from a recent knee operation. Michael joined Tony Blair and the other platform guests to await the arrival of Her Majesty, while John, Paola and I found our places in the seated audience.

This was a hugely important event for Michael, which I knew had involved more than ten years of planning. The final design was by Norman Foster and the Danish designer Per Arnoldi.

Although I was glad to be present at the event, I think all our excitement was sobered by the reality of what the memorial was actually about. The ceremony was very dignified and moving. Afterwards Paola and I had instructions to quickly get John through all the assembled people and into the nearby tent. This was where the Queen would meet the families of the policemen and women the memorial was commemorating. Michael came in with Her Majesty and I knew him well enough to see that he was very proud, but also incredibly nervous. John, Paola and I were introduced first. That morning, as we were getting ready, Michael had insisted Paola and I practise our curtseys. Doing that had sparked vivid memories of when I was seven and the royal yacht *Britannia* was moored off Holyhead Harbour. I had been almost hysterical with excitement as I waited with my gran and brother Stuart for the Queen to come ashore in a launch. As she walked by and waved at us I shrank back horrified and burst into tears. She was dressed in a pale green suit with a hat that looked to me like a tea cosy. There was no golden crown or long white dress and, for a little girl, it felt like some terrible trick was being played. But now, fortunately, my expectations had changed. As she took my hand and I bobbed my practised curtsey I was happy to feel that she reminded me of my grandmother. The kind and protective side of my gran, that is, without the knobbly stick.

As photographs were being taken and Michael began introducing the waiting families, his nerves gave way to pure excitement. I distinctly heard him say to Her Majesty, 'This way, lovey,' and a little later, 'Come over here, lovey.' Afterwards, Michael maintained he said 'darling', but my memory is still certain it was 'lovey'. Anyway, it was not out of any lack of respect, but simply how he always was when overwhelmed with excitement. An aide approached and quietly reminded him of the expected code of conduct. I think Michael thought that Her Majesty would be whisked away after a few minutes, and so was also in a hurry to make sure that everyone got a chance to meet her. He need not have worried. She talked at length with everybody she met and showed sincere sympathy and interest in their experiences. I think she stayed talking to people for an hour or more.

Tim and Queenie, parents of PC Yvonne Fletcher, were there, of course. The tragic loss of their daughter had been the catalyst for what was now a permanent reminder of the importance of our police service. It was a very impressive and dignified occasion and Michael could be justly proud.

It had been a long road, but he had achieved a great deal on behalf of an indisputably worthy cause. In the car home Michael was euphoric. We all were. When we got to the house Paola put the music up and soon corks were popping. Gae was startled out of her eerily quiet day and now found herself in the middle of a champagne party. It was the first time I had met her. She was very tall and had the grace and poise of a dancer. With her ready laugh, she was easy to get along with and we were soon to be firm friends. Knowing her skills, Michael set her onto the long and rather painful task of cataloguing his enormous stash of black-and-white publicity photographs. There was a comic aftermath to the memorial unveiling story, when pictures appeared in the paper the next day of Michael seeming to be hogging the Queen's umbrella while she stood unprotected in the rain!

In fact, Michael's relationship with royalty sometimes took a bumpy turn, particularly when he was offered an OBE and famously refused it, saying it was the kind of award that should go to the cleaners on a railway station. It was a peculiar statement and not surprisingly, there was quite an uproar. However, as a result, Michael invited a Jamaican cleaner from King's Cross station and her daughter to come to tea at his home. Then, on discovering that her daughter had never actually been to Jamaica, he paid for them both to go there on a two-week holiday. Michael's generosity often moved in mysterious ways. From then on Michael always had typed at the bottom of his letters, under his signature, 'Michael Winner (MA Cantab), OBE (offered, but rejected)'.

Once again I was lucky to be part of a team of good people. There was Pat, Nicolanne, Gae and sometimes Ruby. Also, the actress Joanna Kanska appeared now and then when not involved in other work. Michael had known her a long time and she was a welcome addition to the circle of receptionists. I remembered her as Greta from the television comedy *A Very Peculiar Practice* with Peter Davison. It was very good to now be surrounded by bright and cheerful souls who had a canny understanding of how Michael's world operated. Lunches became the highlight of the day and whoever could get there first would save a table at one of the local eateries and put all our orders in. With Michael there was no room for being even a few seconds late back, so lunches had to be set up with military-style planning. Gae lived only round the corner in Kensington High Street so, on the days she wasn't working, would often put lunch together for us. And she understood the 'need for speed' more than some of the local waiting staff. They were good and happy times.

The atmosphere in the house had become almost worryingly cheerful, too. Michael had pinned a fluffy pink sign on the bedroom door which read 'Please Do Not Disturb the Princess'. It was a good-humoured warning to the maids not to go in until Paola had emerged. He also began to say 'hello' and 'good morning' to the staff as he passed them on the stairs, landings or corridors. They found that quite startling at first. Paola had been gently leaning on him to treat people with a little more courtesy, but anyway he seemed genuinely happier and more human than I had seen him in a very long time. If I was out with Paola I noticed Michael would phone her constantly. She told me that she had to get used to that and he would do it even when she was in the house. It became a running joke and she would call him to say she was just going to the lavatory. A few minutes later he would call her back to ask when she was likely to be out. Having worked as a receptionist, Paola knew all the staff very well and would be in and out of the kitchen during the day.

Singing was still a big passion of hers and at six o'clock the music would begin. The whole house became her stage and Michael enjoyed the exuberant displays as she sang and danced down the broad staircases or whirled her way from room to room. Often I would stay for a drink at the end of the day and, once or twice a week, go for dinner with them too. It was always a worry that Michael's controlling nature would clash with Paola's dislike of being told what was and was not acceptable. So far they were managing to laugh at any conflicts and their lively banter and comical squabbles were a constant part of being in their company. He would want her to do or not do something and she would enjoy pushing to do things her way. Once, we were having dinner at the Ivy and she was sitting on locker seats and wanted Michael to shift up so she could get out to go to the loo. He kept insisting she wait politely until the end of the meal. Moments later he looked to his left and she had disappeared, only to emerge a little later from under the tablecloths at the far end of the table. They were little things, but I think it fair to say that there was a constant, gentle power struggle going on. I heard how it had taken him quite a while to persuade her to move into the house and now he was constantly asking her to marry him. I'm sure she was looking for evidence that he could survive and be happy without always having to get his own way. Michael admitted to me that he could see she found living with him a bit intense or stifling at times.

He bought her a small terraced house in Hertfordshire that she could retreat to for a few days now and then. Paola had told him she wanted time to write and they had decided on Hertfordshire so she would be close to her mother when she was there.

Michael had booked a week's holiday at La Réserve de Beaulieu, a famous luxury hotel on the French Riviera. Paola then discovered she needed a small operation a short while before they were due to leave. All went well, but as the departure day approached she did not feel recovered enough to go. Michael was very disappointed, but her suggestion was that I go in her place so he would have company. That was agreed and off we went. It was the most extraordinarily beautiful and sumptuous place and looked out over an azure-blue sea. Even the climate was perfect: pleasantly warm during the day with just a light cooling breeze. I knew Michael's routine well and at nine we would meet for breakfast. Much of the morning I would spend in the sea and after lunch I would occasionally persuade Michael to have a dip in the pool.

Sometimes we would walk along the coast for a mile or two. The views were magical. A week was not going to be too long to simply gaze happily around me. Michael knew some of the other guests and spent time with them during the day, if I was lucky, and I could get back into the water for a while.

* * *

Michael's seventieth birthday party was fast approaching and Paola was doing most of the organising. The venue was to be Harry's Bar in Venice; Michael had very quickly decided on that. Paola was also busy working on the details of the evening and I remember going with her to find favours to put on the dinner table. We also both went out to choose her dress for the occasion and she had persuaded Michael to let me get something too. Friends from home seemed to be under the impression that clothes and gifts were lavished upon me regularly, but that really wasn't how it worked. In the years I had known Michael, this was the third outfit he had bought me. The first was on the trip with him to Los Angeles and the other time was when I went with him to a party at Ronnie and Anne Corbett's house. I think Michael had been very chuffed to get the invitation, as they were outside his usual social circle. It was towards the end of filming *Dirty Weekend* and Sue Wain, the head of wardrobe, helped me pick out something to wear, which Michael paid for. Ronnie and Anne were as lovely a couple as you could ever wish to meet, and an inspiration too, as you could feel how much they adored each other. And I loved the kind of infectious happiness and charm that Ronnie seemed blessed with. It was a lunch party and a perfect and beautiful day. The sun was shining and tables had been set up in the garden. I remember there was a fortune teller there, but being with Michael usually meant having to stick pretty much at his side so I didn't get to talk to the lady with the tarot cards.

For Michael's party Paola had found a silk Armani dress she thought fabulous for me. I agreed, but the price was rather fabulous too. She always had a very good eye for clothes and for finding the right colours and styles to suit different people. Phone calls to Michael began. I wandered off for a while to await the verdict.

I still have the dress. In fact I wore it many times for evenings out with Michael.

A few days later all the activity and excitement came to a sudden stop. Paola had been for a routine check-up and was called back. Michael went with her for another examination and the doctors said she had some form of cancer and they would need to do further tests. Michael felt she should wait until they returned from his birthday party and then they could give her health their full attention. Paola said that the worry of waiting was already unbearable and it was possibly also dangerous to delay things. They could not agree and in the middle of one conversation she picked up her handbag and walked out.

Before the Venice trip there were two parties that Michael had been invited to, and as he and Paola were not yet speaking again, I knew I would have to go.

The first was Roger Moore's birthday dinner. Earlier that day I had been to see Paola and she was dreadfully upset. She had just learnt that she had a form of breast cancer and an immediate operation was recommended. I explained it to Michael, but he was acting as though it was all some kind of exaggerated drama. I was not sure if he really thought that or was just not allowing the frightening reality to sink in. Anyway, he was intent on going to the dinner and I went with him. Earlier I had said that I just didn't think I could do it, knowing what Paola was going through. 'You have to come, dear, just put on a smile,' had been his response. Roger Moore saw straight away that I was struggling and not my usual self. He took me to the bar and I told him what had been going on. I don't know how he did it, but somehow he helped me get myself together. Luckily, Michael and I had Joan Collins and her husband Percy on our table. I was next to Percy and he was kind and understanding of the situation too. I could see that it was a really beautiful party and it was such a shame that all I was really doing was trying to get through it.

Everyone was asking where Paola was, of course, and Michael's response was that she was having tests and there was a worry she might have breast cancer.

By now I felt certain that he just couldn't face any bad news that would shake his world. Paola had sent Michael some very angry texts and now she was not answering any calls. It was a horrible time and there didn't seem anything I could actually do to change things. Simon Cowell had invited Michael and Paola to his mother Julie's eightieth birthday party at the Savoy. It was just a few days later and I went with Michael to that too. It was a huge and glittering event. Julie Cowell was extraordinarily youthful for her age and after dinner a dance band played and it was Julie herself who started the dancing. She had been a ballet dancer and looked fabulously graceful and elegant, as well as radiantly happy. It was on that evening that Philip Green gently prompted Michael to dance with me. Dancing wasn't something that Michael enjoyed, but he managed for a little while and put on quite a brave face, too. Once again it was a fabulous evening, but there was still the cloud of shock and worry hanging over everything.

The next day it became clear just how much there was still to be done to complete the arrangements for Michael's party in Venice. It was to be on a Saturday and Sunday, with dinner at Harry's Bar on the Saturday, everyone staying the night at the Hotel Cipriani, and lunch on the Sunday before flying back. Harry's Bar had been booked, and also a private plane for all the guests. But Michael had not yet found an ideal place for everyone to have lunch on Sunday. Just before I left work that afternoon he told me to be back at the house by eight the next morning as we would be flying to Venice. He felt the best thing was to go there and sort everything out on the spot. Michael had booked a small plane and we were to fly out in the morning and return the following night, staying at the Hotel Cipriani. He called it a 'reconnaissance trip'. As we were about to leave I heard that the forecast was not good. Michael said there was no time to run down the road to Farley Court and instead gave me a black cashmere coat to take. I was very glad of it, as arriving in Venice the heavens opened and the rain poured down.

In fact, the heavens stayed open throughout our whole visit except for a few minutes now and then. Luckily the air was still and not cold. Michael hired a launch for the day and we set off to Harry's Bar for lunch.

Harry's Bar, I discovered, has quite a history. Its founder, Giuseppe Cipriani, had been a bartender who dreamt of opening his own bar for high society. He lent some money to Harry Pickering, a friend in difficult circumstances and, just when he was giving up hope of ever seeing him again, Harry reappeared suddenly and repaid him fourfold. Now with sufficient money in his pocket, Giuseppe opened the new bar in 1931 in a rope warehouse that his wife had found. It was an

My 50th birthday treat. At the Lone Star restaurant, Barbados, with Geraldine, Takis, and Geraldine's sister Wendy and brother-in-law Ben.

Calm down, dear, it's only an Esure commercial – with Michael as a fairy. Vanessa far left and Nicolanne far right.

Working with Michael on the Police Memorial site on the Mall, 2005.

Perhaps Michael's greatest day: the unveiling of the memorial on the Mall, the pinnacle of his achievement for the Police Memorial Trust. Meeting Her Majesty with Paola and John.

At the unveiling of the police memorial on the Mall, with Paola and Cherie Blair.

Private jet to Venice – Michael's 70th birthday begins. Sir Andrew Lloyd Webber, Henry Wyndham, Lady Kristina Moore, Takis, Sir Roger Moore.

With Michael's oldest friend. Leslie and Evie Bricusse, Johnny Gold and I arrive in Venice for the 70th birthday celebrations.

Simon Cowell and Paola, 2005.

Good friends in Venice. Terry O'Neill, Johnny Gold, Sir Roger Moore, Sir Michael Caine.

A walk in Venice during Michael's 70th birthday weekend. Just before Sunday lunch – with Henry Wyndham and Sir Andrew Lloyd Webber.

A slightly late ending to a fabulous weekend. Sir Roger Moore and Lady Katrina heading back to the airport.

A woman Michael
absolutely adored.
With Julie Cowell on
her birthday.

Michael's
pride and joy.
The garden
at Woodland
House, 2005.

Beginning the staff Christmas
party, 2006. Left to right, back
row: Anna Sharkey, Donata,
Lani and boyfriend, Keda,
Shirley and Fred with Jim
Sharkey behind, Pat, Mandy,
Pippa and Matthew. Front row:
Zoe, Geraldine and Nicolanne.

Paola's birthday at
Cecconi's with her
daughter and my
son Daniel.

A Michael Winner book launch at the Belvedere. Geraldine, Sheila Gee and Cilla Black.

Book launch at the Belvedere with Simon Cowell.

Looking a little like *Downton Abbey*. Birthday lunch for John Fraser. Michael, me, Alice, John, Ampi, Sheila and Ruby.

One of Michael's first trips out after fighting through his terrible illness. Scott's restaurant with Ampi.

Michael with his
friend Barry McKay
at La Reserve De
Beaulieu, 2008.

At the pie and mash shop
during filming of *Michael
Winner's Dining Stars*.

During filming of
*MichaelWinner's Dining
Stars* with Joan Hills,
outside the Ritz, 2010.

In Bruges with Justine
Forrest, the winner of *Michael
Winner's Dining Stars*.

With Michael: the calm before the storm, just before guests arrive at the Belvedere for a book launch.

Book launch – Ruby, Natalie, Geraldine.

My magical haven – even more lights than Woodland House. The barge in St Katharine Docks, London.

Happy on the water with two fresh bass. Silversmith Ray Walton and engineer Brendon Honey – seen here eager with filleting knife – caught these beauties. Skipper Nick Eade looking on.

Michael in Victorian garb – with friend and director John Landis (*Blues Brothers*, *Animal House* etc.) on the set of *Burke & Hare*.

Confetti time – Mr & Mrs Winner outside the Chelsea Town Hall with Lady Shakira and Sir Michael Caine.

immediate success and became the favourite watering hole of the likes of Ernest Hemingway, Charlie Chaplin, Orson Welles, Peggy Guggenheim, Noel Coward … the list goes on and on. Giuseppe also invented the Bellini cocktail and, following his interest in painting, named it after a Venetian artist. Using white peach purée and Prosecco, its colour was reminiscent of the robes in one of his pictures.

Giuseppe's son Arrigo was now running the bar. Michael talked to him about his mission to find the perfect lunch spot and was recommended to look at Locanda Cipriani on the island of Torcello, which was run by the same family. Off we went back to the launch and the rain. As we set off I nipped inside under cover and tried to peer out of the misty and rain-splashed windows. Michael had a coat, but no hood or umbrella. Even so, he was braving it outside. I had not been to Venice before and Michael knew how much I had always wanted to see it. He poked his dripping head into the cabin where I was kneeling on a seat and trying to look out. 'You won't see anything from in there, dear, you're missing everything, come out here.' I put my collar up and Michael was my tour guide, pointing constantly to the ornate buildings on the exquisite waterfront that was gliding past us. First I saw the island of Murano, famous for its glass and glass blowing, and then we headed on to Burano, known for the unique beauty of the lace that is made there. With Michael's animated commentary I hardly noticed the water trickling down my neck, or my hair, which was now feeling like a sodden rag draped over my head. He had told me he wanted to show me all his favourite places in Venice and although he had invited Takis and me for his seventieth birthday weekend he knew there would be no time then. I liked the explorer in him. Michael was certainly no Shackleton or Scott, but he did like to search out remarkable places and be the first to announce their existence to his friends and readership. I always found his enthusiasm very contagious and there was nothing that excited him more than seeing a face light up in wonder or amazement at one of his discoveries.

The launch pulled up to a little wooden quay where there was a restaurant that Michael wanted to give the once-over. A kind waiter came out and offered me an umbrella. 'Does she look like a fucking umbrella will be any use to her?' snapped Michael. 'She is way past that. She's on a whole other fucking level.' He was not wrong. By now I was completely soaked through.

Standing still was not too bad, but when I walked there were strange squelching noises from my sodden clothes. The restaurant was beautiful, but a little small, so on we went again. Michael was getting a bit nervous as time was marching by and we were onto the last place on our list. Fortunately, he needn't have worried: it was absolutely perfect. Torcello was a magical island and the gardens around the Locanda were festooned with colour.

Giuseppe had opened it only a few years after Harry's Bar and ran it with Gabriella, his wife's sister. It began as a wine and oil shop, but was soon a small inn and restaurant. Once again they had perfected all the ingredients to make the ideal secluded oasis and over its eighty-year history Locanda Cipriani had been visited by generations of artists, film stars and royalty. Winston Churchill painted it, Man Ray visited and Marc Chagall made a lipstick drawing there. It was as dripping with history as I was dripping with soft Venetian rainwater. And Michael was over the moon to have found such an idyllic place to complete his birthday itinerary. We took various detours as we headed back. Michael insisted he would show me as much of Venice as was possible in one day. Once at the Hotel Cipriani, a staggeringly beautiful hotel situated on a small island overlooking the Venice lagoon and facing the Doge's Palace, I was able to put on dry clothes and Michael and I went through all the rooms, allocating them according to the likes and needs of his guests. That done, he was excited to carry on with the tour. It was dinner time and he wanted to show me a restaurant called Trattoria alla Madonna. He said it was not far, just near the Rialto Bridge, and a cosy little eatery with lots of small rooms, their walls covered in paintings. It was also known for amazingly good seafood. It sounded like just my kind of place. We went back out to the launch and headed off into the rain.

CHAPTER EIGHT

SEVENTY AND ONWARDS

O N OUR RETURN FROM THE whistle-stop tour of Venice, Michael was not his usual self. When I walked into
his office I often found him staring blankly at his desk or
gazing out of the tall window by his chair. He had arranged a
magnificent party with all his closest friends, but his excited
anticipation had evaporated and left him looking very low.
There had been so much to organise and keep his mind occu-
pied, but now everything was set. There was time to ponder,
but still no news of Paola. Michael had made it clear over the
years that he didn't have any time for illness. He was never
ill himself and if someone else was he regarded it as a feeble

excuse for malingering. He would tolerate it for a while yet remain largely detached. But I had not known him to be melancholy either, or to display any kind of prolonged sadness. I felt sorry for him, but made sure I seemed cheerful and reminded him how much everyone was looking forward to the weekend. Michael called Geraldine and invited her. There was some apologising to do and I would think he had quite a large helping of humble pie to eat as well. She was in Milan with her sister and it was agreed that she would fly directly to Venice.

The extravaganza began at 9.30 sharp on Saturday morning at Woodland House. Gae and Donata served coffee and biscuits as people arrived. There were nearly thirty guests and the house was buzzing. In all the time I knew Michael, this was the most spectacular party I had seen him arrange. A few friends had not been able to accept the invitation because of other engagements, but the core of Michael's close circle were all gathered together.

Simon Cowell could not make it, but his mother Julie and also his brother Nicholas and his wife Katie were there. So were Michael and Shakira Caine, Roger Moore and his wife Kristina, Joan Collins and her husband Percy Gibson, Chris and Joan Rea, Johnny and Jan Gold, Andrew Lloyd Webber … the party had already begun as we boarded the coach in Melbury Road that would take us to Farnborough, where a private jet awaited. Champagne and canapés were served before everyone found their seats on the plane. I could happily have got quite used to that way of travelling.

Before we knew it we were stepping onto elegant varnished wooden motor launches which took us on the scenic route along the Grand Canal and then across to the Hotel Cipriani.

I had loved Venice in the rain and it was even more beautiful in the brilliant autumn sunshine we had that day. There was time for people to go for a stroll and Michael and I nipped off to put the favours on the tables that Paola had chosen and to make any final arrangements for the big dinner. There was more champagne served before the launches brought everyone to Harry's Bar. I don't think Michael could really relax until they were finally seated at the tables in the upstairs part of the bar. Everything had been thought of and all had gone smoothly. The dinner of course was magnificent and the laughter and chatter were hushed just long enough for a few short speeches to be made, including a witty one from Michael Caine, who enjoyed the opportunity to tease Michael.

I wandered out to look at the water and the passing gondolas with yet another Bellini in my hand. There was no chance of finding one better made than at its birthplace and some of us had stuck to them through the meal. We all boarded the boats again to return to the hotel and a few of us found the bar for a completely unnecessary nightcap.

But it was a magical evening and I was happy to eke it out a little longer.

The following morning there was time to look around before we all set off to the island of Torcello and the Locanda. Lunch was long and leisurely and afterwards some of us went for a walk and looked around the sixteenth-century church of San Sebastiano. We regrouped gradually in the comfort of the little lounge next to the dining room, and conversation and cocktails began to flow once more. Michael began to gather people together a little earlier than was necessary for the return journey, but his timekeeping neurosis could not make exceptions. It applied to his friends too. Gently he coaxed groups of friends onto the waiting launches and one by one they set off towards the airport.

Takis and I were talking to Roger Moore and Kristina, and Michael looked quite flustered when he noticed that Joan Collins had just been served a fresh drink. He had rolled his eyes at me in a certain way so I followed him outside. 'I've told them they must hurry or they will hold up the plane,' he said with exasperation. 'I'm getting on this boat so you will have to go and get them all out. Get them all out and onto that launch there or they'll be late, do you understand, get them out now. Go on, quickly, you have to insist they come now.'

It was not for me to insist that Joan Collins and Percy or Roger and Kristina do anything, but I did announce to them that Michael had just left and was worried about the time. But all my little speech did was provoke a ripple of knowing laughter and various comments like 'Oh I know, dear, he's been worried about time for many years' and 'Come and sit here, Dinah, there's another drink for you'. Everyone was enjoying the golden afternoon sunlight much too much to go rushing about and, as Joan pointed out, we would only have to sit for ages in the airport lounge. It was more than half an hour before we ambled over to the waiting boat and set off. Michael had been pacing up and down at the airport and was huffing and puffing with anxiety when we arrived. He pointed out all the things that might have gone wrong and caused a terrible delay. Fortunately Joan was there to remind him that all was well and calm him down. Takis and I had seats next to Roger and Kristina for the return flight and Roger kept up a stream of jokes and funny stories, as was his wont. Time flashed by. It seemed we had only just taken off and already we were banking round to the runway at Farnborough. Looking down there was a line of what I think were Range Rovers with their headlights on and a chauffeur standing by each one holding a name board. It did look extraordinary. The kind of spectacle that even the very rich might not often see.

I have to say, I felt more than a little proud of Michael for arranging such a beautiful weekend. I knew his friends were fully appreciative and it had been an act of generosity and thoughtfulness and had taken a lot of his own time to plan. After such an extraordinary time, it felt a bit strange walking into the house for work the next morning. The buzzer went straight away and Michael called me up to the office. It would not have been a surprise to find that it was 'business as usual', and in a way it was, but first Michael wanted to hear what I thought of the weekend. I had already told him how fabulous I thought it was, but what he really wanted to know was how much I thought everyone else had enjoyed it. He was beaming with happiness when I told him what people had said, how they had all remarked on how wonderfully orchestrated it all was, how beautiful it all looked, the line of launches passing under the Rialto Bridge with everyone waving and calling out to each other, like a scene from a film. Michael Caine said what a brilliant idea it was to go to Venice where even moving from place to place was such a pleasure, given the fabulous varnished wooden launches and the magic of the city. He called it a seamlessly wonderful experience.

I told Michael everything I had heard as closely as I could remember. 'Did they, did they? What else, what else did people say?' Michael was desperate to know that his friends had thoroughly enjoyed themselves. I noticed that he was always like that, even after a simple lunch or dinner. It wasn't about getting endless thanks, he just wanted to be sure that he had found the right place or done the right thing and that people had been very happy. I could assure him they were and he was soon chuckling with pleasure.

The other concern that day was of course Paola. Had anyone heard anything?

Michael knew that she had got to know most of the staff quite well so he sent me off to see if anyone had managed to contact her. I heard that she had been in hospital for an operation, but as yet there was no proper news. I had been sending her a text every few days, but was still getting no reply. My friend Jackie had been diagnosed with cancer a few years earlier and was going through various unpleasant treatments. She urged me to keep sending texts.

She explained that Paola might not feel like talking to anyone, but it might at least be some small comfort to know that people were thinking of her.

Michael placed another advert in *The Stage*. There was not such a flood of applicants this time. I think most agents had grown wise to his methods and realised that an audition was unlikely to lead to a film role. One young actress he interviewed made the grade and was appointed as receptionist. She was only in her early twenties and seemed particularly naive. Within a week Michael had taken her for dinner a few times and invited her to go to Barbados with him for the Christmas holiday, which was fast approaching.

She seemed to be under the impression that he was going to make her a big star and began looking for reassurance from Pat and me that he was not expecting anything more. 'It's funny,' she would say, with big innocent eyes, 'but sometimes he holds my hand or talks to me as though I am his girlfriend or something.' At the same time Michael was telling me he really liked her and that she seemed happy to go away with him. Pat and I were in a quandary as we didn't want to be seen as responsible for driving her away, but neither did we like the thought of her coming down to earth with too big a crash. And I could see that the longer this went on the greater the drop would be. Somehow we managed to gently suggest that the suite in Sandy Lane, Barbados was probably shared. The young actress was a little jittery for the rest of the day and scurried off at six o'clock sharp. We didn't see her again.

Michael's priority was to find a new girlfriend, but, as he often said, he could not look in the usual way by socialising and going out with friends. His world did not work that way. He decided that internet dating might be an answer.

After a bit of research he talked to Mary Balfour, who ran an introduction agency called Drawing Down the Moon. Mary came to the house to talk to Michael and the next day he went to her agency to look through the photographs and details of the women she had put forward. He had agreed that it was more realistic to consider people closer in age to him. He also insisted that I went with him. I found it all quite interesting, but when appointments were made for him to meet the chosen few he wanted me there for that too. I suggested it might seem a little odd, but he told me he did not feel very confident that he might meet someone this way so we might as well enjoy the experience. I think he was a bit shy too. The first women we talked to were at the agency offices off Kensington High Street. Later it was agreed that they would come to the house to meet him. I would show them up to his office and when they left we would mull over his thoughts and first impressions. Only one woman got the thumbs up and he took her out for dinner a few times. Michael was undecided about her, and so began to approach women he had been out with in the past. He asked Georgina if she would accompany him to Barbados, but did not offer to take little Ryan. Once again she gave him a very clear 'no'.

In the run-up to Christmas all the staff had seasonal things to think about. In the early days, the people who knew each other well would exchange cards and presents in the usual way. As the years rolled on, the family feeling among everyone seemed to grow stronger and all of us began buying cards and presents for each other. In the last few days at work there was a lot of sneaking off to the high street for last-minute shopping and racking of brains as to what someone might or might not like. I think it was Shirley the maid who came up with the idea of putting everyone's name in a hat. Each of us would draw out a little piece of paper and unfolding it we would get something for the person whose name we found. This certainly made things simpler and more fun. When Lily and Dante were at the house, a few of us who lived nearby had begun to get together about two weeks before Christmas and have dinner out. The first time was with Lily and Dante, Eddie and his wife Beryl, Michael White, Zoe and me. We went to a Chinese restaurant in Holland Park Avenue and Lily and Dante had insisted on paying for everyone. By the third or fourth year it fell to Zoe and me to choose the place and pick up the tab. I had mentioned it to Michael, hoping he knew somewhere nearby that was good, but not incredibly expensive. 'Oh don't be so stupid, my dear, you can't possibly pay for all of them, just the fucking drinks bill will be more than your month's wages.'

I'm not sure where he got the idea that we drank so much! Possibly he assumed that, working for him, we needed to!

Anyway, he went on to suggest the Belvedere in Holland Park. 'Yes, very nice,' I said, 'but it will take Zoe and me all year to pay for that.'

Michael stepped in again. 'Why don't you shut up and fucking listen? I've just told you that you can't afford it. I'll pay for it. You tell everyone, get everyone, you can organise it all, they can all come to the house first and have canapés and champagne, yes, they can all have canapés here first.'

I was happy. It wasn't always good when Michael took over, but in this instance it seemed straightforward and generous. I set about letting everyone know what had been decided. At 6.30 we were all to gather at the house and then cars would take us to the Belvedere for eight.

They had a dining area on a kind of gallery upstairs which Michael had booked and I privately thought it would be ideal in case things got a little rowdy. Michael's only fear about the evening's arrangements was that he might be on his own having to greet the staff when they arrived at the house.

'You must make sure you don't go anywhere at six,' he said. 'I won't have a fucking clue what to say to the idiots when they get here so for Christ's sake make sure you don't go off and leave me on my own with them.' He was being honest. I had often noticed that he showed most shyness when he was with 'ordinary' people. Talking to them on a daily basis about work was fine, but put the same people together in a social situation and he would be very nervous.

When the day came everything went smoothly. There was plenty of Cristal and vintage Dom Pérignon, and canapés arrived from the Belvedere. When Michael got agitated from having to talk to people he would pick up a plate of canapés or a bowl of crisps and wander around offering them. Then he produced his camera and encouraged everybody to pose together in front of the fireplace. With the camera on a tripod he set the timer and ran to his seat before the flash went. It was a simple act and caused quite a lot of hilarity as he insisted on doing it at least half a dozen times 'in case some fucking idiot was picking their nose or sneezing'. The group photograph was to become an annual ritual in the years ahead. Another ritual was Michael's Christmas card. It was no traditional card, and certainly never reflected any kind of religious or spiritual sentiment. Generally it featured a picture of himself, or the cover of his latest book, with the back crammed with quotes from the reviews of previous books and featuring the most famous names he could muster. Michael rarely cared about what people thought and was not going to let tradition or good taste thwart his enthusiasm for self-publicity. The cards were sent out far and wide and very, very early. They would be received by most people before November was out.

The Belvedere was fabulous and the next year Michael suggested Cibo. Being so close, it was an obvious choice and over the years I had been there many times with Michael. And he had filmed part of *Dirty Weekend* there. It is an Italian restaurant tucked away in Russell Gardens near Olympia, and Gino Taddei, the owner, was a delightful man. Michael always got on very well with him, and his wife Sally too when she was working. From the early days when Jenny was with Michael it had hardly changed and the food and service were always excellent. And they usually had langoustine on the menu! If I was there with Zoe or Nicolanne we were always greeted by Gino and he would often take the wine or dessert off the bill. He knew our budgets were not quite the same as Michael's. There were fourteen of us for the Christmas party that year and our ages ranged from Zoe in her early twenties to John in his late sixties. Most of us had worked for Michael for several years or more and the ties of friendship and loyalty between us all were quite strong. And one bizarre thing we all had in common was to have been called 'a fucking moronic idiot' by Michael. Only those who have been on the receiving end of one of Michael's tirades can really know what that was like. The Christmas dinner at Cibo was great fun and not too riotous. Eddie would always encourage Zoe to take to the stage after desserts had been served and perform a few musical requests.

Most restaurants don't have a stage so Zoe would make do with prancing gingerly up and down the table. We would move our glasses as necessary and it was all very entertaining and civilised. After Zoe left, Michael continued to invite her for the Christmas dinner. He also always paid for cars to take people home or for a room at the Kensington Hilton for anyone who lived some distance outside London and preferred to stay nearby. Michael could be effortlessly generous in some ways, but when it came to Christmas presents for the staff he would usually select things from the American Express catalogue. As you might imagine, he gathered quite a few points over a year and so people would get bottles of wine of dubious quality or a television that they did not really need. Because the number of people invited to the Christmas party kept growing, the next place we tried was the Bombay Brasserie, a rather grand Indian restaurant in Kensington, just off the Cromwell Road. I had been many times with Michael and enjoyed both the food and the friendly service. When the group of nearly twenty staff descended on the place, Adi Modi and Arun Harnal greeted us all with the same graciousness with which they always welcomed Michael.

After dinner most of us asked for a Cobra coffee, which was something of a speciality at the Bombay Brasserie. We were shown to the sofas and chairs in the lounge area and grouped around a low table. A waiter arrived with a golden trolley and began the intricate process of preparing the drinks. Firstly, sugar was heated until it caramelised. By pouring this thick, syrupy goo onto a warm glass and rotating it slowly, the caramel formed a snake-like decoration around the outside. An orange was then peeled in one long curling strip which, when held at one end, looked like a tropical snake. The dramatic moment came when the orange peel was dipped into kirsch and whisky and ignited. The blue flames flickered up the orange-peel snake as it was held over a pan of hot coffee. Once a glass was filled with coffee, whisky, kirsch and a little cream it looked beautifully exotic. And, like a cobra, it had quite a powerful nip to it, too.

An impressive amount of wine had already been consumed and John Fraser's stories were also flowing nicely. John was an extraordinarily knowledgeable historian, with a remarkable memory as well. Michael often used him as a talking reference library. His special subjects included the two world wars and the Indian rebellion of 1857. All of us who knew him well were used to his historical anecdotes or accounts of his childhood, which he told slowly and with equal attention to detail. Sometimes, and with no change in delivery, he would wander into areas that were a little more risqué. But with his dry Scots way of talking I was never really sure if he knew the surprise that some of his stories could have on people. Zoe knew and would sometimes encourage him down any path that entertained her. Most of the assembled company were already listening to John when Zoe chipped in, 'What about when you were really young, what are your earliest memories?'

John was off and describing the house he lived in and the nanny who looked after him and his brothers. He took everyone back in time to when he was a toddler, just before the war. He described his family, their Edwardian house and then the bathroom and even the potty he was on. He could have stopped there, but he didn't, he went on. 'I remember sitting and looking up and the nanny was leaning over and cleaning the bath. As I gazed up from my seat on the potty I found I was looking up her pale-blue smock. All I saw was a mass of pubic hair. I think that's my absolute earliest memory. Yes. Just a mass of pubic hair.'

Some of the newcomers were coughing and spluttering into their Cobra coffees and Zoe stepped in with her dulcet tones. 'Ah, isn't that lovely. Such an amazing memory. Is anyone waiting for a drink? So was that before the war then, John?' she said, egging him on again.

Gradually, people formed groups according to where they lived and tottered out to find one of the waiting cars.

The last of us left as the restaurant was closing, and Adi Modi and Arun Harnal were still patiently smiling as cheerfully as when we had arrived.

After each Christmas party Michael was always eager to hear how it had gone.

The following day I would recount the evening in as much detail as I could remember, even down to what everybody had ordered and liked or disliked.

For the first year or two I had worried about the amount of wine we seemed able to drink. Michael was never a great drinker and would rarely have more than one glass with his meal. But he never once baulked at the bill and all the staff had the grace and good sense not to order anything absurdly expensive.

Michael simply wanted to be certain that we had enjoyed ourselves and, as we always did, he was always very happy.

When he flew off to Barbados, the house relaxed as usual. He had asked Geraldine to accompany him and everything seemed more settled again. In the times that Michael did not have a girlfriend I would often spend an hour or two with him after work and go out to dinner with him much more often.

That could be perfectly enjoyable, but it meant I had precious little time of my own during the week. A few days before he left I had finally heard from Paola, but she had insisted that I not breathe a word about her to Michael. On the specialist's recommendation she had undergone several operations and wanted some time to rest and recuperate. She was wary of further contact with Michael as she still felt angry and let down and imagined any conversation might lead to arguments. Even though she knew he would have her best interests at heart, she also thought he would try to control things and didn't feel up to coping with that. I was just glad to know that her doctors were confident that they had caught it in time and, however awful things were, she was gradually getting through.

Jackie had been right to tell me not to stop sending her text messages. I had felt I might have appeared to be a rather odd kind of stalker or something, but Paola assured me they had been welcome pearls of comfort from a world she had needed to withdraw from. Michael was still asking me every day if I had heard any news and eventually she agreed that I could tell him. He was very shocked, but also relieved that the time of not knowing was over and said he would help her in any way he could. In the New Year she agreed to see me after one of her appointments in London. We met at a café in Kensington High Street. Despite what she had been through, she still had her remarkable fighting spirit and Michael's offer of support was going to be a help. Whatever her misgivings, his concern meant something and by the end of January they would speak occasionally on the telephone. I understood why she had been wary of that before. They were both characters who preferred to be firmly in the driving seat of their own lives, which in the past had often led to conflicts, and Paola needed to keep all her energy to build her strength in those first months. There was certainly nothing she could spare for arguments. As her strength returned, Michael began driving out to Hertfordshire to see her at weekends and would take her out for lunch.

* * *

My work had been going unusually smoothly for a while, but it turned out to be too good to last. When I returned to work after Christmas I noticed that Pat was looking more exhausted than I felt was healthy. The secretaries always had the least time to recuperate, as Michael would often be lambasting them every day on the phone. I was in the kitchen one day when I heard a volcano erupting upstairs. Michael was bellowing and swearing and when I went to the landing I saw Pat emerge from her office. I could see she was upset and managed to steer her into the kitchen. A hot coffee with brandy was the 'last-chance saloon' of Woodland House and had prevented several of Michael's employees from marching out. On this occasion Donata was intent on washing the floor and did not seem to realise quite what was going on. Before I could try to calm her a bit, Pat stood up and said she just couldn't stay any longer and was gone. I could see that she meant it and any persuasion on my part would simply have been for my own reasons; for not wanting to lose the close friend I had at work.

Michael gave the job to the woman he had met through the introduction agency. He still seemed interested in her and had been taking her out for dinner now and then. A few months after losing Pat, Gae walked out too. John had needed a convalescent home to stay in while he recovered from a hip operation and Michael gave Gae the task of finding a good place. She noted down the various best options but, horror of horrors, there was a misspelling. Michael erupted. Gae had put up with a certain amount of that kind of behaviour from him, but enough was enough. She told him clearly that his language was worse than she had heard from 'hoodie' teenagers. No amount of brandy was going to get her to stay, either.

One of the downsides to working for Michael was that colleagues whom I had gradually got to know could disappear in an instant. Anyone who worked for him had to get used to the sword of Damocles which hung over us all. John had decided to leave as well. His hip operation meant that he would not be fully mobile again for quite some time and I think he had had quite enough of being yelled at, too. It was common knowledge that John had always been in Michael's will, to the tune of £500,000, but very soon after leaving he told me he had taken him out. It was a sobering reminder of how fickle Michael could sometimes be, especially considering he cited John as one of his oldest friends. Luckily for me, Ruby Snape had become an increasingly regular figure on reception. I was glad she was around as, with Zoe, Gae, John and Pat gone, I was feeling increasingly isolated. Michael liked Ruby too, as she was plain spoken and not easily fazed by his temper. Without a regular girlfriend to accompany him on his evenings out, he began to take Ruby now and then. It started when he had called her one weekend and asked her if she knew what a 'walker' was. Ruby said she understood the term referred to someone who would go out on the arm of a celebrity simply as a companion for the evening. 'Yes, yes, that's right, dear,' said Michael. 'Just an evening out, darling, no bedroom business. So are you free this evening for dinner? No blowjobs involved.' With that level of directness, life was at least straightforward. And Michael seemed most at home with absolute frankness. It was never really any surprise to me, as generally he seemed to like things bold and bright and instant. Too much subtlety or pontificating or tiptoeing around people's feelings quickly irritated him. By nature he was, after all, primarily blunt and impatient.

CHAPTER NINE

CALAMITY AND COMEBACK

IN THE SUMMER OF 2006 Michael told me that Geraldine was returning. It was agreed that she would find a flat nearby. Geraldine would stay at the house now and then, and I went with her on numerous flat-finding missions. It took a few months, but eventually she settled on something in a new block not many minutes' walk away. In the autumn, Donata left. It was always a tense time for me when a good housekeeper moved on. Often I would have to run around all day, and without Donata making coffee for me, and sometimes a sandwich, I would have had nothing. She had always been quietly there in the background and was very thoughtful and kind. When I was at home having time off I heard Michael was interviewing people for the vacancy. That made me nervous, but when I returned he told me that he was going to give a Portuguese lady called Alice Pereira a trial run. Seeing my expression, he asked why I looked so surprised. 'Well, if it's the same Alice, she was housekeeper here for a little while not that many years ago and lived upstairs with her husband Joseph,' I explained.

Michael's jaw dropped and then he couldn't help but laugh. 'Oh yes,' he said. 'I think you might be right. I didn't recognise her on her own.' It was good to see Alice again. Joseph was going to stay in Portugal and look after their house there, and Suzette and Paula, their daughters, were studying in London. Returning to her work at Michael's meant that Alice could see them regularly. They were a close family and Alice was lovely. I could breathe a sigh of relief.

Christmas was nearly upon us again, and Geraldine went to Paris to spend a bit of time with her family before going to Barbados for a three-week holiday with Michael. One afternoon I was told to get ready as we were off to a couple of cocktail parties and then on to pick up Andrew and Madeleine Lloyd Webber before going for dinner somewhere near to their home. We went briefly to a function in Hyde Park and another hosted by John Witherow, editor of the *Sunday Times*. Michael rarely stayed long at events which did not include a sit-down dinner and so it was still early in the evening when we arrived at the Lloyd Webbers' home. Andrew appeared outside just as the Phantom pulled up and said for us to come in for a moment. As we approached the living room we spotted Evie and Leslie Bricusse sitting by the bar. I saw Leslie grinning from ear to ear. Michael was smiling with surprise and as we walked into the room Michael Caine looked up from his seat beside the crackling open fire. Michael began to chuckle as more and more friends appeared. They told him that he would not actually be going out for dinner that evening as they had arranged a thank-you party for him. It was of course a thank you for the trip he had orchestrated to mark his seventieth birthday. Almost everyone from his party was there. Michael looked very happy. He told me later that he actually felt quite honoured too. There were after all some highly distinguished people among his friends and he felt rather humbled that they had been so thoughtful.

I think Andrew must have noticed me gazing about me. The walls were heavy with paintings and other fascinating objects. He began to tell me about the picture I was looking at and soon I was on a tour of the house. It was on quite a grand scale, of course, but I think what struck me most was how warm and welcoming it was. It was colourful too, but not in any way garish or over the top. Just very homely. And when he talked about the pictures and things he had collected he was very animated and excited to tell their stories. Of all the houses I have been in, it remains one of the most magical I have seen. After dinner, most of us migrated to the sofas around the open fire and were having coffee and liqueurs. Michael and a few others were standing at the bar and I'm not sure what they were talking about, but one of them suddenly called out to everyone, 'Does everybody think that Michael should marry Dinah?'

A bit of a cheer went up and someone said, 'Michael, why don't you ask Dinah to marry you?'

Michael put his head in his hands and, in his best Jewish accent, said, 'Oy vey, tell them, Dinah, tell them how many times I have ask.' There was general laughter and it was pointed out that whenever they saw him I was at his side anyway. The people who did not know how long I had worked for him were aghast when they heard. I reminded them that I was already married and the conversation drifted onto other things. Later, in the car, Michael picked it up again. He knew I was becoming increasingly unhappy at home.

Not only had my mother died, but now also my friend Jackie. They had always been central figures in my home life. When I was working, Mum had always been happy to help Takis with the children and even took them on holidays when I had to work. And she had just always been around as part of the family.

Jackie's daughter Charlotte had been born within a few weeks of my youngest son Luke and we had been inseparable friends all through the time that we were bringing them up. But now she was gone and Luke was in his late teens and studying music and Daniel had a good job and had lived in Cheltenham for several years. Takis had continued to do his own thing, but instead of writing songs for a band he had become quite obsessed with learning Greek music. My world had changed.

In working for Michael I had always been aware that I walked a fine line and had always kept my wits about me. I say 'wits', but actually I have never seen myself as a clever person. Friends who know me best say I have good intuition and common sense. Anyway, I had long ago realised that it could be dangerous to let Michael know if there was anything going on that made me vulnerable. He might step in to help or he might just as easily exploit the situation for his own fun or gain. That was how unpredictable he was. Thoughts of a different life and even of divorce had begun to occupy my imagination more and more frequently. But it was unthinkable that I could share any of that with Michael although he knew I was not very happy at home. He also knew that I did not see big houses or large sums of money as the most important ingredients for happiness or a fulfilled life. Like most parents, the safety and wellbeing of my children was my Achilles heel. That must have been in his mind when he offered to put a million pounds in a bank account if I agreed to move into his house as his girlfriend.

He quickly pointed out that it was sufficient to ensure that Daniel and Luke need never have any real money worries in the future. By now I was used to Michael's matter-of-fact statements in areas that more usually are expected to contain some attempt at romance. Before, I had never given his proposals a moment's thought. His controlling nature or his temper alone had been enough for me to know it could not work. As I grew older I could see the value of being financially secure, but I couldn't be with someone *only* for that reason.

But this time I did find myself thinking things over. I wasn't considering his offer, but it did jolt me into pondering my situation. I had no security at all. And that was another conversation I could never have with Michael. If I showed any concern for my precarious existence he would say either 'Well, you could be my girlfriend and then all this would be yours' or 'Oh, don't be silly, dear, you know I'll always look after you'. That was all very well, but in real terms it translated to 'Do what I say and lump it, and I can drop you like a stone if it suits me', so it was never any comfort whatsoever. I knew any attempt to gently allude to the fact that he held all the strings would be seen as tantamount to calling him a liar, and a major explosion would be inevitable.

As usual, my pondering got me nowhere and life went on as before. Michael and Geraldine went to Sandy Lane, Barbados for Christmas and at the end of the week I went to Stonebank, Little Neston.

On New Year's Day 2007 Michael called to wish me a happy New Year. He did that every year, but this time he said he did not feel at all well. A little later he rang again. He told me that he was covered in blisters and had picked at them and then pooed everywhere. It sounded dreadful and I was spared no details. Now that I know the full extent of the illness he was suffering I am amazed he was sufficiently lucid to talk as he did.

Over the next few days I heard very little, but I did know that he was in hospital. On 7 January he called and told me that he was dying.

He also said that an air ambulance was bringing him home and he wanted me to go direct to the London Clinic in Marylebone and wait for him there. His friend Philip Green was in Barbados and had arranged the emergency flight for him and Geraldine.

It was a very large and rather empty room that I was shown into at the London Clinic. Michael lay on what looked like a low sunbed. He must have been given powerful painkillers, but was awake and half sitting up. Geraldine had been with him over the past few days, but I don't think even she was prepared for what we saw when the bandages were slowly removed. His left leg was black. The appalling smell was even more shocking. There were gasps of horror even from the assembled doctors. 'I'm dying, aren't I?' Michael said quietly to me.

No one knew exactly what he had. Specialists in tropical diseases came to look. Meanwhile his leg was washed and disinfected in a purple potash liquid. I didn't leave until eleven that night and Geraldine was given a room at the hospital. In the early days of his illness it remained a mystery as to what was attacking Michael and eating away at his leg. It really was like something from a horror story. Within forty-eight hours he was rushed to intensive care and we were told that blood poisoning had begun to damage his organs and they were beginning to shut down. I had never seen so many tubes and wires and bleeping machines. He was surrounded by what looked like glass walls and could see the other patients. Michael was being given all manner of drugs and painkillers, and our conversations were often quite strange. One evening he told us that the woman in the bed opposite had just died and floated out of the window. Another time he went into detailed descriptions of the spaceships that he could see. He stayed there for the next two weeks and Geraldine and I sat with him. At night she stayed at the hospital in case there was any kind of emergency. There was no let-up from the worry. It was constant and gruelling. Only when Michael was moved to his own room did it begin to feel that his condition might begin to stabilise. But it was just the beginning of the long and painful road to recovery. Over the next few months he was in and out of the operating theatre. First his leg had to be thoroughly cleaned and any decay removed.

But whatever it was that was eating it kept reappearing and having a bit more.

The exact type and dose of antibiotic had to be found. The repeated general anaesthetics and other treatments were taking their toll as well and it remained a very stressful and upsetting time. There never seemed to be a day when we could sigh with relief and be confident that Michael was out of danger and would make a steady recovery. Every problem the doctors faced could have signalled the end for him. Geraldine and I did our best to bolster up each other's shredded nerves and be ready for the next day. Mostly we went through those days side by side and took turns at being there through the weekends.

One of the most frightening times was one weekend when a nurse called me urgently to Michael's bedside. I was told that he seemed to be fading and asked if I could talk to him about anything which might trigger his mind back to the here and now. I went through anything and everything I could think of. I told stories from the recent past and all the way back to the early days of knowing him. The nurse, a male nurse called Calvin Moorley, was a specialist in intensive care and was watching the monitors as I talked. He could see when the signs improved and helped to guide me when he saw any response to my babbling. I mentioned the friends and girl-friends and even stars who I thought were most important to Michael, and told all the tales I could remember. After a couple of hours Calvin was confident that he was becoming more stable again and a few hours later he was able to answer simple questions and know who he was and where he was.

There were some terrible scares over the first month. According to his doctors Michael died several times, techni-cally speaking, and each time was revived. The doctors said he had a remarkably strong will to keep going. Without that they were certain he would not have survived his ordeal.

The days in the London Clinic were long, but there was usually plenty to do. It was to be a while before he could feed himself normally, so I would break up his food and spoon feed him meals. Then his teeth had to be brushed and his hair cut and combed and he needed help to and from the bathroom.

Geraldine and I had to develop the basic nursing skills. I had learnt over the years that family and friends are vital when someone is in hospital. They really can save a life that might otherwise be lost. Whatever the experts are doing, it is the close friends who best know the person being treated. A friend can sound the alarm when something just does not seem right and alert someone to a problem before a doctor has a chance to see it coming. After all, the doctors can't be at every patient's bedside day and night. With Michael's treatments it was very complicated, as so many specialists were needed. Each one had to be aware of what the others were doing at all times. Often it caused difficulties, as, for instance, the treatment for the infection could interfere with the care and medication for the liver or the heart. From the outset it was important to keep track of the daily conversations about Michael's progress and, as time wore on, I began to find it in some ways quite engrossing. Michael and Geraldine had nicknamed me 'Dirty Gertie' as apparently I showed little fear of facing the grim reality of everything and would roll up my sleeves and get on with it. But when my friend Diana was in hospital I had learnt that I could be most helpful if I braced myself to face anything, however grisly it might be.

It became gradually accepted that *Vibrio vulnificus* was the bacterium causing the problem. It may well have come from an oyster he had eaten. In most cases it can be quite easily eradicated, but for people with certain liver problems or increased blood sugar levels it can get into the bloodstream and wreak havoc.

Michael had both these conditions, which put him into the category where a high percentage of people do not survive.

A plastic surgeon called Dalia Nield had been overseeing

everything and it was she who began the skin grafts. It was not until then that the future began to look brighter.

Fortunately, Michael was a few weeks ahead with his *Sunday Times* articles.

When they ran out he reviewed the dinner provided by the London Clinic. It was not easy, as he discovered he could not properly hold a pen and his spelling seemed to have gone haywire. Geraldine took over the writing, with Michael doing his best to dictate in his most lucid moments. But I'm sure those articles were a lifeline for him over those months. Often when he emerged from an anaesthetic or deep sleep his first words were '*Sunday Times, Sunday Times*'.

Eventually a bit of a routine was established. Jim the chauffeur would pick up Geraldine and me from Woodland House at about 7.30 each morning and off we would go to the London Clinic. As Michael's condition began to improve, we would pick up whatever he fancied for breakfast. Croissants were the first things he requested from the outside world. Over the previous year he had put himself on a diet and managed to lose about three and a half stone – in fact he'd just completed a book about it: *The Fat Pig Diet Book*!

That was an achievement, but the timing was not ideal. The doctors felt he should try to put on some weight so his body had some reserves to fuel his fight. Jim spent all day every day waiting outside with the car in case there was any fetching and carrying to do or any errands to run. As Michael's condition improved, there were papers to bring backwards and forwards from the office and, most importantly, tasty titbits to be fetched to meet Michael's returning appetite. Jim would take Geraldine or me or both of us together to pick up a meal from selected restaurants in Marylebone High Street for Michael to review in his *Sunday Times* column. It was a while before we discovered Reubens on Baker Street, a kosher deli with restaurant downstairs, and it instantly became the favourite. Geraldine, Jim and I would go and sit at the little wooden table by the door and order whatever Michael wanted. Usually it was a salt beef sandwich, chopped liver or one of their beautiful soups. Perfect fare for building strength and very tasty too. While it was being prepared a bottle of wine would be brought out for the nursing team, together with a mezze of all manner of delicacies. It was all delicious, but it was the chips that I became addicted to. Chips and wine; fine European cuisine! And as we became regulars they always gave us the wine. We could not have found a friendlier and more perfect place.

When John Fraser had been in hospital for his knee and hip operations, the staff who had got to know him well would visit him regularly. The periods of convalescence and physiotherapy meant that this took place over quite a few months, and trips to see him became a regular part of our week. Before that, the ever-changing people who formed Michael's workforce had not really been very social outside the working day. After seeing John, and sometimes rather guiltily smuggling him a small glass of wine, a few of us would find a local place to have something to eat or a quick drink.

It had become known that Matthew the gardener had a boat near Tower Bridge. One day it was arranged that a few of us would go and see it. I had heard him talk about a barge and had got it into my head that it would be quite small and narrow. When Nicolanne and I found the St Katharine Docks we stepped into another world. From the City of London skyscrapers we were suddenly in the peace and quiet of a small marina. There were lines and lines of motor boats and yachts, but then we spotted a group of old black tarred boats with very tall masts. They were huge. I now know that they were Thames sailing barges. They used to carry cargoes to and from the ports on the east coast and also to France, Belgium and Holland. When we found Matthew's barge, Jim was standing at a varnished wooden bar 'down below' and Matthew was shaking margarita cocktails. I don't remember those first few minutes inside the barge, but apparently I walked around the big saloon saying, 'It's real, it's a real boat, it's wood, it's a real boat,' and was touching the iron beams overhead and thick wood planks along the sides. The look of everything and probably the woody tar smell had taken me back to my childhood. I remembered the cargo ships I had played on in Holyhead Harbour and the pilot cutters I had occasionally been allowed to go out on when the sea was not too rough. The most exciting trips were running stores out to the Skerries lighthouse keeper. I was usually made to stay below, but would peer excitedly through one of the little portholes. When I had walked into the St Katharine Docks marina I felt like I had left the city, and being inside the barge was like travelling back in time. I sat at the bar and gazed about as the others chatted and shook up more cocktails.

There was an open kitchen or 'galley' with a huge gas hob and oven and at the other end of the saloon was a small stage. This, I discovered, was used for theatre and live music events, and was also home to *Cabaret Cloche*, an eccentric once-a-month show set up by Matthew and his friend Peter Joucla, a theatre director. A Brazilian chef called Helio Fenerich did the cooking for those kinds of things. Matthew was attempting to perfect a few cocktail recipes that evening and we were all increasingly happy guinea pigs.

The margaritas were quite a sophisticated version made with agave syrup, a natural sweetener which gave them a subtle flavour. After two or three the subtlety was probably lost on us. But they went down very easily. We had all brought bits and bobs of food and put together a simple feast of French bread, cheese and crisps. As Michael often said in his more positive reviews, 'it was historic'. The barge more than the food, perhaps, but we had a nice evening in something of a time warp. I loved London, but still felt most at home in the countryside. When Michael was in the London Clinic I needed the fresh air more than ever, but could only get home every few weeks. Occasional trips to the boat became a welcome pick-me-up after long days in the sterilised hospital air. I'm sure the wind would funnel down the Thames and bring with it a salty seaside smell. I always felt rejuvenated after a few hours by the water. For me it was just what the doctor ordered. And the bar on the barge was always well stocked too!

It was nearly three months before there was talk of Michael being able to return home. He had been through hell. There was a time when it looked like he might have to lose his leg to save his life. His leg was saved, but his Achilles tendon and other balancing tendons had been damaged and had to be removed. A big boot was presented to him made of plastic or carbon fibre or something similar. It was called an orthopaedic boot and could be strapped around his foot and lower leg to protect the skin grafts as they healed. But every few days, just when he was preparing to face the outside world, another problem would flare up and delay his release. Eventually he was allowed out and, with help, he hobbled up the path to the house. For those who had not seen him for a few months it was quite shocking. He looked thin and pale and his legs and arms would shake when he tried to stand still. It was no surprise that his confidence also seemed to have taken quite a bruising. Michael still needed a lot of care and a lovely nurse called Claudette Williams would sleep on the landing outside his bedroom in case he had any problems in the night. A staff sister called Amparo Macera also called regularly to change his dressings. Calvin Moorley from the London Clinic had got on very well with Michael and he was also a regular visitor checking on his progress at home.

The lady from Drawing Down the Moon worked as secretary for six weeks and then was replaced by Rose Bryan. When she left, Calvin's boyfriend Nick took over. It turned out that Michael's temper, impatience and ability to shout and swear had not suffered as a result of his ordeal. Nick had very soon had enough and Ruby took up the hot seat.

Most days Michael sat on his bedroom balcony so his leg could get the air, but some of the grafts were not looking good. After a few weeks he had to be readmitted to the London Clinic. This time Geraldine and I took turns at tending to his needs and whims and generally keeping him washed and fed and his spirits up. He always put off any friends who wanted to visit. He said it exhausted him. That may well have been true, but also he probably didn't like to be seen in such an incapacitated state. While I was there, Shakira Caine and Terry O'Neill ignored the veto and I'm sure seeing friends did Michael a lot of good. Terry and Michael had spoken on the phone every morning for years and years.

Now more than ever he needed good conversation. For someone who feared boredom the months sitting inactive were doubly terrible. He had never been one to show much interest in reading, and throughout his long illness he still didn't turn to books. But often he was quite heavily sedated by strong painkillers that also helped him to stay calm during his slow recovery. His second stay at the London Clinic was not to be a quick one, as it was discovered that he had contracted MRSA. It was not just any old standard MRSA either. Oh no, this was the supersonic version. Everything was tried to eradicate it, but without complete success and in the end, with nothing really to lose, it was decided that the skin-graft operations would be attempted anyway. It was another long and nail-biting ordeal, but eventually Michael was able to return home once more.

Little by little he improved, but it was to be about a year before he could walk without the aid of a stick. He did as much work as he could and camera crews began to appear again to film interviews with him. Two or three times a week a lady named Heather arrived on her bicycle to give Michael half an hour of physiotherapy. I'm sure some of the exercises were uncomfortable and sometimes painful, but from the howls and screams that went on almost without let-up it sounded as though she was doing unspeakable things to him. It was quite a melodrama and the cries could be heard from the garden and out in the street. The jangling of her bicycle bell would signal her arrival for what soon became known as 'torture time'. Any member of staff who had recently been on the receiving end of one of Michael's blastings could sometimes be seen wearing a slight smile when they noticed the bicycle arriving!

It was 24 July 2007 when my own life took a new turning. After work I often stayed at the house and had a drink with Michael and Geraldine. This time Amparo Macera, the staff nurse, or 'Ampi' as everyone called her, was there too. She and I had been chatting about some detail of Michael's ailments and she walked down the road to Farley Court with me. As soon as she left I sat at a desk in one of the offices and called Takis. The first thing I heard was that he had been on his own all day and that I hadn't bothered to call. When Michael was ill I was often with him every second of the day or running some urgent errand, so calls home were sometimes not possible. The conversation didn't improve and I heard myself say I was leaving. I wasn't at home so I couldn't leave exactly, but he knew what I meant. Over several years the tension had been steadily growing and I had felt something snap. There was a tangled mass of problems and grievances, but even on a simple practical level things were not good.

The next morning I mentioned what had happened to Michael. It was against my better judgement in some ways, but there was no choice. He looked quite startled, but just said, 'Good for you, darling, you should have done it a long time ago.' I was about to ask if I could stay at Farley Court on my days off, but he got there ahead of me. His occasional chuckles were a bit unnerving, but he went on, 'Anyway, the flat's your home, dear, and you can clear out John's old office and use it as a lounge if you like.'

John's old office was the biggest room and had remained unchanged for many years. He had never shown any interest in computers and on his heavy, leather-topped desk sat a huge typewriter and several grey metal Rolodexes bursting with index cards. There was another large, dark wooden desk used for the cuttings book pasting sessions and this same desk was also home to the most modern equipment in the room, a motley collection of 1970s telephones in mustard yellow, red or black. Where the grey-green carpet had worn away there were areas of dark felt underlay bubbling up and khaki-green filing cabinets with tarnished brass handles stood in groups around the room. On the walls were a few colourful engravings of elaborate theatre costumes and one or two reproductions of watercolours depicting craggy mountain scenery. Dark rectangles on the faded walls indicated where others had once hung.

As usual with Michael, if something was going to be done it had to happen straight away. It was a few hundred yards from Woodland House to Farley Court and he walked slowly down the road with me. From the drawers and drawers of papers he picked out the files he wanted kept and the rest were to be chucked out. The room had not been painted 'since Adam were a lad', as my mother would say, and Michael said to pick a colour and he would pay the painters. He had been deemed well enough to travel at last, and was soon flying off with Geraldine to La Réserve in the south of France for two weeks.

He said he wanted the room smartened up and everything done before he returned. The challenge was on and I snapped into action. I knew that Nobby and Sid and their huge lorry were due to collect the garden waste in a day or two and asked Matthew the gardener to tell them they were needed at Farley Court first. When the call came I nipped up the garden path to inform them of my mission. Nobby said to jump up into the cab and they would give me a lift round the corner. I was a bit hesitant as it was quite a climb and Sidney already had a good collection of salvaged items on the passenger seat. I put on a brave face and found my footing on the little ladder as Nobby and Sid and Matthew and Jim stood grinning at me. It was a big lorry from the 1960s, but when Sidney clambered up behind me his bulky frame made the whole thing lean over. The double seat was only really large enough for him, and I'm sure his sweatshirt carried on it the history of more than just a day or two's work. After only a short rumble and a couple of lurches we stopped outside Farley Court and Sid swung himself deftly out of the cab and dropped to the ground. As I peered out, trying to see a way to climb down to street level, two long arms reached up and hands the size of dinner plates grabbed me. After a few undignified moments of flailing limbs, I found myself safely on the pavement. Michael had said all the furniture from the office could go, and go it did in what seemed like a few seconds. Michael liked Nobby and Sid for their fast and no-nonsense approach. Or, as he put it, 'They don't fuck about.'

Nobby opened the big window and everything was on the grass and then gone. I began to say that maybe the carpet ought to go too because of all the holes, but before I had finished my sentence Sidney had rolled it up, underlay and all, and thrown it out of the window. As the dust was still settling in the empty room I heard the rasping horn of the old lorry making its way back up Melbury Road to the house. It felt very strange for a moment as Sheila the accountant and I stood in the silence of the big empty room. I knew I was very lucky to have the flat as a home. But everything was happening so quickly and I had no idea as to what the future might bring. There was no time to mull things over just then. I had to run back to work in case Michael phoned.

When I walked in there was sniggering. Sidney had told

someone about my little lorry trip. It had spread through the house like a bush fire. It was not exactly as I had remembered it and his version of the story ended when he pulled me down from the cab. He added, 'Me 'ands were everywhere, but she weren't complainin'.' Even Alice had joined in with Shirley and Lani (the maids) and was ribbing me.

'Oh Dinah, you not waste any timey,' she said, setting off another shriek of laughter. I never did ask Alice where she learnt English.

She spoke fluently, but would pronounce lots of words with a 'y' at the end, and often put one on the last word at the end of a sentence too. I liked it. It made for a lovely tuneful way of speaking. Having worked for Michael before, Alice knew exactly what she was getting into. And she wasn't frightened of him, either. Sometime in her second week, Michael had shouted at her one evening about something. She told me about it the next day. 'Straight 'way I look at him in his facey an' I say to himy, I say, Mr Winner you stop nowy, you stop nowy. Then I tell himy, I not need *you*. I not need *you*. You need some a body, but I not need *you*. Don't forgety. You get no dinner from me if you shouty.' It seemed to work. I never did hear him shouty at Alice. I'm sure it helped that she was an excellent cook.

Daniel Jardim, the caretaker at Farley Court, had recommended some painters and they made a good job of freshening up the new lounge. More importantly, they did it very fast. Rolling up the old carpet had revealed a very dusty wooden parquet floor. When Michael saw it he told me to arrange to have it repaired and polished. He said it would be my birthday present. A week or so later I had a freshly painted lounge with a shining wood floor. All the staff had chipped in for two huge plants for my birthday and Michael sorted out an armchair from the house. Paola gave me a table, Gae provided the chairs and a television and Geraldine donated a coffee table. I felt peculiar and disorientated, but also very fortunate. The downside I knew only too well. I had always known that it was foolish to be in a position where someone else held the cards. And with Michael that could be particularly dangerous. But I didn't see much of a choice. It made me nervous, but I would just have to keep awake and see how things turned out.

*   *   *

Towards the end of the year Michael appeared on the Parkinson show. It was his first appearance on television since his illness. Having also lost a lot of weight through his diet the year before, he did look rather drawn and thin. He had always been known as quite a barrel of a man, so for many people I think seeing him was a bit of a shock. There were ongoing problems with his health which meant he often had to go to hospital for a night or two now and then, but he was through the really miserable and worrying time. Michael was back. He could get up and down the stairs now without help and had learnt to walk well despite the loss of important tendons. Perhaps the biggest change was that he no longer had quite the energy he once had and would sometimes have a short nap after lunch or at the end of the day.

When all the staff gathered at the house for champagne and canapés on the evening of the Christmas party he was on good form although he did not attempt to wander around with plates of food. Instead he sat and actually talked to 'ordinary' people, which was good to see. I heard him advising against smoking big cigars. He still regarded chain-smoking cigars as his downfall, rather than any oyster. He was probably right in saying that the nasty bacteria only got him as they did because of the damage he had already inflicted on himself by smoking and an overly rich diet. When it came to the ritual of the group photograph he was up and down to the camera just as he had been in previous years. The various partners, and even some of the staff, had not seen him all year; they had just heard the horror stories, so it felt like something of a family reunion. Michael had no real family except for some cousins, whom he showed little interest in keeping in touch with. His ex-girlfriends and the people who had worked for him for many years were the next closest thing he had to family, I think. He certainly referred to some of them as family sometimes. There was a particularly jubilant atmosphere when we all took our seats at the long table in the Bombay Brasserie that year. People who no longer worked for Michael, such as John and Zoe, were there, as well as some newcomers.

Keda Price-Cousins had worked on the television series *Kilroy* with Nicolanne, who had put her name forward when a stand-in receptionist was needed. She was a tall and lovely-looking young woman in her late twenties and had been PA to Robert Kilroy-Silk. On her very first day she was shown into the kitchen and told that all she had to do was listen out for the doorbell and report to Michael with the name of anyone who called. She sat at the table and talked happily to Alice, who was cleaning the oven and then beginning to prepare lunch.

I was in the office with Michael. When I heard the doorbell ringing several times I motioned to nip out to answer it, but Michael stopped me. 'No dear, we are paying someone an absolute fucking fortune to do nothing but open and close the front door. I can't think what can have gone wrong. Something terrible must have happened. The poor girl must have had an unpleasant accident or be trapped in the lavatory or something. We will go and see, let's go and see, shall we?' As he was saying this, he had got up and was walking out of the office. I followed, fearing the worst for Keda. And she had seemed such a lovely girl. The only ray of hope was that he did have a tiny flicker of laughter in his voice as he was making his way down to the kitchen. As he pushed the door open Keda looked startled and her chair clattered as she jumped to her feet, staring nervously at him. 'My dear, this is not really working, is it?' he began, in a matter-of-fact tone, but also with a slight smile. 'Our agreement was very simple. Our agreement was that when the doorbell rings you go and you open the door and you see who is there. And then you ask them what their name is and you ask them what it is that they want. And then you come and you tell me. That was our agreement, wasn't it my dear? BUT IT IS TOTALLY FUCK-ING POINTLESS IF YOU ARE DEAF AND INCAPABLE OF HEARING THE FUCKING DOORBELL OR HAVE SOME OTHER KIND OF FUCKING PROBLEM WHICH IS STOP-PING YOU FROM WALKING DOWN THE FUCKING STAIRS.'

Keda had been apologising as he was shouting and as Michael left the room he said quietly, 'Let's have one more try then, dear, shall we?'

When he had gone, Alice, who had stood holding a half-dried plate through Michael's little rant, turned to Keda. 'Oh my God, you must look at his facey and say to himy, "No you will not shouty," or always he will shouty.'

Alice was right, it did work for her, but I don't think it would have been a good idea at all for Keda. In fact, the most commonly agreed technique was to stand quietly with an apologetic look and wait until he had quietened down. Ultimately, everyone had to find what worked for them. As it turned out, he rarely if ever bellowed at Keda again. She worked on and off for several years and, after the hiccup on her first day, I could see that Michael quickly grew to like her. When she left he wrote her the most glowing reference I've ever seen.

The only employee who was *never* at the receiving end of one of his tirades was Pippa Neve. She was a very well-spoken woman in her early forties and took over from Ron as accountant when he retired. In Michael's eyes it seemed she could do no wrong. She even asked if she could 'buy some pictures', for heaven's sake, to 'brighten up the walls of her office'. He said *yes*. It was unheard of. She found some watercolours of Cornish harbours and Michael even paid to have them framed. Pippa's theory was that he might have thought she was even posher than she actually was. Her mother had worked as a secretary in the Queen's private offices and had often travelled with Her Majesty. Whatever it was, she worked for over a year without Michael so much as even raising his voice to her.

But as we sat down to dinner at the Bombay Brasserie, it was Sheila Gee who was the reigning accountant. Sheila was of similar age to Pippa, but other than that a very different person. She came from outside of London and seemed quite an earthy country lady. I think she had been a bit of a biker girl in her youth and probably still was. She was also a black belt in tae kwon do. As with Pippa, I quickly got to know her and like her. The accountant's office was in Farley Court, so it was crucial that I got on with anyone who worked there, especially now that I had left home and I would be there even on my days off.

Anyway, the Christmas dinner that year was as enjoyable

as ever. John had been on form with his stories and snippets of history and Zoe had performed a few pliés and pirouettes and a song or two. All in all, I thought it had been the usual kind of staff party. Well, that's the impression I was under until Zoe, Nicolanne and I got back to the flat. According to Zoe I had behaved disgracefully. I didn't know what she was talking about. 'You know very well, how could you, how could you, the poor man,' she was saying.

I soon discovered that she was outraged by the fact that I had tickled Matthew the gardener a few times. I had found it very entertaining. While we sat on sofas in the lounge area I had discovered that his ribs were particularly sensitive and yes, I had nearly made him spill his Cobra coffee once or twice. But I had only tickled him.

'What are you talking about, he was laughing!' I said.

'Yes, well, of course he was laughing,' Zoe told me, 'that's what people do when they get tickled. You were flirting with him and it was embarrassing.' I wondered if she was winding me up. Nicolanne agreed with Zoe. My behaviour had been childish and inappropriate and they both insisted I should apologise. I was amazed, especially coming from a couple of youngsters, both of whom had told me stories over the years that would make my hair curl. All I had done was tickle somebody. The next day Alice made one of her rice puddings and I smuggled a bowl of it out to Matthew. I also told him that I had been sent to apologise. He laughed, of course, and I felt like a real nitwit. When I told Nicolanne she just said, 'Oh my God, what are you like! Pull yourself together, woman. You flirt with him and now you're taking him rice puddings!'

*   *   *

Michael had taken a while to decide on whether or not to return to Barbados that Christmas. I had never known him spend it anywhere else. Eventually he had plumped for going and he and Geraldine flew off to the sun. He still had two ulcers on his leg and the hope was that the warm salty air might help them to heal. I had my own difficult decision that year. And in the end I too decided to try to make Christmas as usual. I couldn't bear the thought of upsetting Daniel or Luke and hoped it might be possible to be civilised and avoid unnecessary dramas. It was a little naive of me. We all got through it, but it was not a good atmosphere. I had made a mistake. The most cheerful thing was that I got to spend lots of time with the dogs, two black poodles called Bella and Chiki.

The New Year did not start well for me and gradually got worse. I knew my marriage was over and there was a lot that needed to be sorted out. Luke seemed fine and had lots of friends around him, but I didn't like not seeing him every week or so. I missed him, of course, but I wanted to keep an eye on him too. We were close and telephone conversations were just not any substitute for being there. On top of all my personal worries I was under ever-increasing pressure from Michael. I knew that there was no such thing as a free lunch and sure enough, the fact that he knew I was always just down the road was already leading to problems. Through the worst of his illness I had worked nearly every day and now it seemed he expected things to continue that way. I had always known both myself and Michael well enough to be clear about the fact that I needed regular breaks. There were always undercurrents and subtle games and scenarios going on. They were of his own making, of course, and often simply for his amusement. After time away, the slate would usually be pretty much wiped clean again. If he got up to any more mischief making I would have a break again before it became unbearable. For nearly thirty years it had worked that way and I was very clear about the fact that without those interruptions I would not have survived the job for long.

During his severe illness everything was different. It wasn't very pleasant sometimes, but was easy compared to what he could put me through when he was at full strength. Besides, they were frightening and difficult times so I wanted to be as helpful as possible. But now Michael was concerned about Paola and began to send me on frequent trips to meet her. I would go for lunch or accompany her to give a bit of support at some of the medical consultations she needed. I was then given some 'excuse' to pass on to explain how I was able to be absent from work. My trips to see Paola were frequent and the reasons he told me to give were ever more complicated or ridiculous. And I was going to the dentist so much that I could have had all my teeth replaced several times over. If I protested about anything he would fly into a rage and say, 'YOU WILL FUCKING WELL DO AS I TELL YOU OR YOU ARE FIRED, DO YOU UNDERSTAND?'

As far as I was concerned, all of that should have been kept as his own personal business and he should not have involved me. Michael knew exactly what he was doing and found it much more entertaining to include me when he played with fire. He would get me playing with petrol while he dropped a match in the mix whenever he felt like it. The upset and drama he caused would amuse him. That was the cruel side of Michael that I had always been very wary of.

He could behave like a two-year-old pulling the wings off a fly. A lack of empathy may be normal in a baby, but very disturbing in an adult who holds the strings that you dangle from. He knew very well that I could no longer comfortably go back to my home in the north and was enjoying the power he had, knowing I was trapped and under increasing pressure. I felt very foolish for having got myself into such a situation. His constant health problems and the limp he had been left with were increasingly frustrating him, I think, and I was the one he could most easily vent his anger on.

Things were not feeling good. Luckily, Ruby was secretary through that time and a pillar of strength when I most needed it. She knew just what to say to bolster me up if I got a chance to nip into her office for a few minutes. And if I called into Farley Court, Sheila did her best to lift my spirits and would sometimes pour me a gulp of wine to help take the edge off things. The staff could see that I was being put slowly through the mangle and showed their concern, but there wasn't really anything they could do. By the beginning of February my world was still miserable, and by the middle of the month I looked like I had some kind of allergy. One of the worst things to do in front of Michael was look upset and most of the time I managed to just about hold myself together. But I was spending a lot of time in tears when I was on my own and my eyes looked permanently sore and puffed up. On 14 February, Valentine's Day of all days, I could take it no longer.

Michael put the phone down having spoken to Paola and immediately he was screaming at me for telling her or not telling her some detail I should or should not have divulged. What he expected of me had gradually moved from being very difficult to downright impossible. I told him I could not do it any more and was leaving. He was shouting at me to come back, but I kept walking and marched out of the house. When I got to Farley Court the phone kept ringing and I said to Sheila to tell him I had gone. Throwing a few things into a bag I went out into the street and stopped the first cab I saw. Not having any idea where I was going, I just asked the driver to take me to the river. I was desperate for air after my weeks of claustrophobia, but when the cabbie saw the state of me and the tears tumbling down my cheeks he looked very alarmed. I could see him glancing at me in his mirror. After a minute or two he asked, 'Whereabouts on the river are you going?' I said I didn't know and that anywhere on the Embankment would be fine. After another pause he said, 'You are obviously very upset and I really don't feel I can leave you on your own by the river. Do you have a friend anywhere who could meet you?'

His kindness and concern made it even more difficult for me to stop sobbing and then I thought to call Matthew. The Thames was now on my right and we were headed towards Westminster. Matthew answered immediately and had already heard that I had walked out. News always travelled fast at Woodland House. He said I could go to the boat and he would leave work and be back in less than an hour. I began to wipe away the tears and the cabbie was happier to be given a place to go rather than simply 'the river' as a destination. I told him briefly about my nightmare at work and that I had just walked out. There could be no mention of Michael Winner, of course. We pulled up under the hotel in the St Katharine Docks, and the driver insisted on carrying my bags along the pontoon and up onto the deck of the barge. I said I would be

OK now and was trying to pay him, but he wouldn't take it. Instead he said he would walk me to the coffee shop on the quayside and I should call my friend again and see how near they were. Knowing Matthew would be on the Tube without a signal, I called Nicolanne. She was working at a production company in Old Street and would come straight away. The cabbie had heard my conversation and finally seemed satisfied that I was not going to attempt to drown myself. I knew I must have looked a terrible mess of mascara and was still finding it difficult to pull myself together. He paid for my coffee and wouldn't take a penny from me. Wishing me well, he disappeared. In all the cabs in all of London I was very glad I had stepped into his. It was as if he had been sent by the gods. I realised later I had no number for him and so no way to thank him. But thinking of it, angels probably don't have telephones.

Once on the boat we made hot coffee with toast and brandy. An odd mixture, but it usually worked to pick me up and I knew I had to get my strength back pretty fast. The fact that Nicolanne and Matthew both knew Michael's ways and understood my situation exactly was already helping me feel less alone.

Michael had been phoning Nicolanne to see if she knew where I was. She had simply told him that she had heard I was upset and was worried about me and said she would call him after she had spoken to me. Matthew showed me to a cabin I could stay in as long as I liked and it was good to be in a world so far removed from Michael's. Kitty, the ship's cat, a very handsome grey tabby, brought me part of a mouse in the early hours of the morning. The poor little thing had been rather chewed up. I felt a bit chewed up too, but I did still have a head. It was a reminder that I had to quickly get things into perspective.

The next day I was in better shape to look at the future and decide what my options were. If I walked away from Michael, I would need to find a place to live and a whole new way of making a living. I was in my early fifties and Michael had always assured me that if I worked for him until I was sixty he would give me a pension. Unusually for him, he had actually put that in writing. I felt foolish for having let myself slip so much into a position where he held all the cards and there seemed no way out without facing an unknown and probably financially rather grim future.

It had never been in my nature to see a doctor unless something was badly and obviously wrong, but friends told me that I was in quite a state and highly stressed and I should go, if only to show them that I was taking my health seriously. In the end I agreed and came away with a note recommending that I rest for several weeks. I also had a prescription for Valium. Now and then I had taken it in the past, but in very small doses. A friend had given me some and very occasionally, when things were rough at work, I had broken a tablet in half and swallowed it. I found that it just seemed to help me bite my tongue and survive a difficult day.

Having said that, though, I mentioned it once to one of Michael's nurses and she assured me the amount I took would probably not even calm a small rodent let alone a whole human being. Perhaps it was a placebo effect, I don't know; it only mattered that it did the trick.

Michael had been calling anyone he could think of to find out where I was and what I was up to. Telling him I was on the gardener's boat was not exactly going to help my situation. Nicolanne and Matthew understood that very clearly so we kept it under wraps. Nicolanne called him and said that I was stressed and upset and would ring him in a day or two. I knew I had to go back and get on with it and in a few days I hoped I would be able to admit that to myself without the miserable feeling that came with it. When the time came, Michael showed more concern for my wellbeing than I was expecting.

He already knew exactly what my grievances were and thought I should simply be thicker skinned. I told him that if I was to be put through week after week of bombardment then we would soon be back in the same place.

Something had to change. When he kept repeating, 'We are all very worried about you, darling, and hope you will come back very soon,' it did not feel good.

When it got to, 'Yes, well, come back, dear, and we will see what we can do,' I felt a ray of hope. It was agreed that I would have the rest of that week off and return to work on Monday.

Monday arrived far too soon. Friends had always said that when I was having a rough spell at work they noticed it took about a week for me to get back to my normal self when I had time off, and I would begin to grow tense and irritable four or five days before I was due back. I'm sure they were right.

Some people seem able to leave their stresses and strains behind them as easily as flicking a switch, but I never managed to do that. Fortunately Michael was in 'tiptoe' mode when I saw him next. That was not going to last long – he would quickly find it boring – so I made the best of it while I could. I made it clear that if he wanted me to see Paola it could only be when I was not at work. Then it would be as a friend to her and a clear line would be drawn.

I needed that to preserve my sanity and hoped it would bring an end to the lies and subterfuge that I felt bullied into. Paola had been given the all-clear, but still needed some operations. Also, she had been told it would be ideal if she put a bit of weight on before then. Michael said he thought it a good idea for her and me to have a bit of a holiday so we could both recharge our batteries.

He booked the Hotel Royal Riviera on the Beaulieu–Cap Ferrat border. The suite was fabulous, overlooking the pool and the beach. It was May and every bush and tree was in full flower. We swam in the mornings and after lunch went on long winding walks through the exquisite landscape and the port of Saint-Jean-Cap-Ferrat. During the week, Michael would phone several times a day to find out where we had been and tell us more places that he thought we would enjoy. He was always excited and wanted to hear every detail of what we were doing. Paola asked him about Monte Carlo, as she had not been there before. 'Don't bother, darling, it's like a fucking council estate,' was all he really had to say about it. 'You are in the most beautiful place in the world, why waste time going to Essex?' Paola insisted that he must know somewhere good to eat there. 'You can probably get a pizza or kebab, but I really wouldn't risk it,' he told her, chuckling. He had dropped the gauntlet as far as Paola was concerned and we got a cab to Monte Carlo that evening.

When Michael next called he must have nearly fallen off his chair. We were having cocktails at the Hotel Metropole and Paola had booked a table for dinner. After his initial shock he seemed to find it very funny. 'Typical, just fucking typical, I should have known, and your kebabs there will cost me a fucking fortune,' he said through gales of laughter. It was a very relaxing and beautiful holiday for both of us. Because of her operations, Paola was still not allowed to drive and on our return I found that Michael had arranged that Joanna Kanska would take her to any appointments she had. It was kind of him and also showed that he was being much more thoughtful to me. He was making the long overdue step of not so readily putting me between a current and earlier girl-friend. Things were looking up.

Things were looking even more up when my youngest, Luke, said he was moving to London. He had friends in Muswell Hill that he knew from his music studies at university and he could stay with them. I had a strong feeling that, at his age, he could only benefit from seeing something of the cosmopoli-tan life of a big city. I had been worrying about him still being at home in a small village and it was good to see him finding his way forwards without any pushing or prodding from me.

Michael had cause for celebration too. He announced his engagement to Geraldine and, to mark the occasion, there was to be a party at the Ritz on 28 October 2008. And it was to be a very big party, too. He had also made it clear that he was indebted to Geraldine for standing by him and nursing him through a very long and miserable illness. All the stops were to be pulled out. Alongside his oldest and closest circle there would be Geraldine's friends and fam-ily and also people that they had more recently struck up friendships with. Even Sir Terence Conran and his wife Lady Vicki were invited. I say 'even' because Michael and Sir Ter-ence had been enjoying a long-standing feud in the papers over a fish. But Michael had recently seen Sir Terence and Lady Vicki at the Cipriani hotel in Venice and gone over and talked to them. Michael was very good at upsetting people.

Well, in many ways he was famous for it, of course. But it is not so widely known that he was also quite good at burying the hatchet. I think he expected everyone else to be like that too and could be very disappointed if he found someone was not.

The longest stand-offs seemed to be when he felt he was owed an apology. But if that was forthcoming then all was usually forgiven and forgotten as far as Michael was concerned. We all have baggage we carry around, but if you rummaged through his I don't think you would find many grudges. However, when *he* made some brash, insensitive or just plain thoughtless and rude comment about someone he knew, or even considered a friend, he seemed to expect that they would not be offended. He seemed to assume that it would be like water off a duck's back to them and that they were absurd if they took umbrage. He could get quite irritated and be very slow in making any kind of peace offering and might even prefer to let a friend drift away. So he didn't always live up to his own standards. But it did seem that at least he was not one to lock doors behind him.

Michael grew quite panicky as the big day approached. He had invited over seventy people and he could not rest easily until he knew who had accepted. A problem with having celebrity friends is that they have a tendency to lead busy celebrity lives. But all was well and the seven round tables were filled.

Michael and Mary Parkinson were more recent friends and were seated with Michael and Geraldine. Shakira Caine was next to Michael Parkinson and on her right was Andrew Davis. Andrew owned the heliport in Battersea and many hotels and both he and his partner, also called Andrew, were very exuberant characters and were known for being hugely entertaining. Geraldine was seated between Michael Parkinson and Michael Caine and Michael between Mary Parkinson and Evie Bricusse.

Andrew and Mary Lloyd Webber were also at their table and so too, of course, was Leslie Bricusse, Michael's oldest friend. I was seated with Ruby the secretary and also Emile Riley. Emile was a very long-standing friend of the Caines and always very good company. Also on my table were Roddy Gilchrist and his wife.

Roddy, a journalist who often wrote for the *Daily Mail*, had known Michael for some time. Roddy lived quite near and when Michael began walking regularly around Holland Park, as part of a routine to bring strength back to his leg, Roddy often accompanied him. Vanessa and her partner had been invited too and were on a table with Simon Cowell and his mother, Julie.

When Ruby and I nipped outside for a cigarette, Simon asked me about Paola.

I had always found him a very friendly and straightforward person and he seemed to have stayed just the same despite being rocketed to stardom. He said to let him know if he could do anything to help and gave me his own and his PA's number should we want tickets to go to any of the shows. Paola and I did take him up on that offer occasionally, first when Leona Lewis was in the final of *The X Factor* and later when Paola's daughter got through to the live shows. If we went backstage afterwards he would be very welcoming and, although his dressing room was as busy as Euston station, he always made time to chat with us for a while.

When dinner was over, the music from the adjoining room began to entice people to drift slowly onto the dance floor.

I danced with Henry Wyndham, the chairman of Sotheby's, whom Michael had known for many years. He had also been at Michael's seventieth birthday party in Venice and I had always found him a very charming and interesting man. At one point it became very crowded so I imagine that virtually everyone was up there. It was quite surreal to be gliding past Sir David Frost and his wife Lady Carina, Bill and Suzanne Wyman, and all the other famous people. Henry and I may have looked quite surreal too, perhaps, as he was a very tall man. And I do mean tall. In heels I must be nearly six foot, but even so he towered above me.

I didn't see Michael on the dance floor, but I'm sure Geraldine would have inspired him to take part. He had made a remarkable recovery and the only downside for him was that 'having a bad leg' could no longer work as much of an excuse. It was good to know that somewhere among the dancers he might well have been doing the soft-shoe shuffle.

In 2007 Michael had been replaced by an animated mouse. But when Esure sponsored the weather on ITV 1 and Channel 4, he was invited to return to his role in their adverts and was very happy to accept. Once again Ron Purdie began to appear regularly at the house in his usual role as co-producer, and Diane Chittell was the production coordinator. I was listed on the call sheet as hair stylist, but was under strict instructions that I was only to attend to Michael's locks and act as his assistant. I was to stand behind him at all times holding his script and throat lozenges and run and get him fruit tea with honey or whatever else he might require. There were to be three days of filming. On the first day Michael was in a lounge with French windows. It was a perfectly ordinary lounge except for the fact that it was full of water and fish and

Michael was standing in the middle of it with bubbles rising from his mouth. Lorraine Doyle played the lady standing and staring in surprise through the French windows at Michael. It looked like he was standing in a very large aquarium. Of course, it turns out that it's not real water and they're not real fish. As far as I remember, that day's filming was smooth and uneventful.

The second day did not go quite so well for me. We were in a street in Willesden Green, north London, very near to where Michael was born. A particular kind of background was needed and he knew it would be ideal. Halfway through the morning Michael told Kate, the runner, he wanted her to stand in as an extra. He asked her to take off her coat, but she then complained she was cold. Michael turned and snapped at me, 'Dinah, give her your top.' We went into the nearby house we were using as a unit base and I gave her the grey cashmere sweater I was wearing. I put my thin raincoat back on with nothing but my bra underneath. After about an hour and a half the scene was finished and my teeth were starting to chatter. I asked Michael if I could go and put my jumper back on. 'Yes, yes,' he snapped again and I nipped back into the house.

It could only have been a minute or two before I re-emerged. Just as I was stepping back into my designated place a few feet behind him he turned and launched suddenly into a completely unexpected tirade. 'WHAT THE FUCK ARE YOU DOING FUCKING ABOUT, HOW DARE YOU WANDER OFF, YOU ARE A FUCKING DISGRACE, IT IS COMPLETELY FUCKING UNPROFESSIONAL...' He went on and on repeating himself at full volume for several minutes. Ruby and I had begun to use a scale from one to ten to refer to Michael's shouting. This was certainly a nine. There was real rage and cruelty in his eyes and in his voice. Some of the crew had gone off for lunch and the remaining ones looked at their toes as he was screaming at me. First I was shocked and embarrassed, but then gradually felt more and more humiliated.

When at last he stopped it was lunchtime: he went off to the Rolls-Royce Phantom and I made my way to the butty wagon, or catering bus, as some people call it. Although I was feeling very shaken, I was determined to try not to let it show and managed to get my shoulders back and my chin up. Tamlin French, the costume supervisor, and Tricia Cameron, the make-up artist, came over to see if I was all right, but there wasn't really much to be said. I had begun to carry some Valium in my bag for this kind of happening and took one with my coffee. After lunch the filming continued a little further down the street. Between takes Michael would call me to do his hair and send me to get hot drinks for him. He was also putting his script down willy-nilly and expected me to always find it and bring it to him when next he needed it.

Once again, out of the blue, he exploded, 'YOU FUCKING USELESS IDIOT, CAN'T YOU DO ANYTHING I TELL YOU...' It went on and on and then he was yelling at me for his script. Marcia Gay, the first assistant director, tried to help by passing him hers, but Michael's was in capitals so he could read it without his glasses. I picked up his script and handed it to him, but he was off and had no intention of stopping.

...YOU CAN'T EVEN PASS ME A FUCKING PIECE OF PAPER WHEN I NEED IT, YOU ARE A FUCKING WASTE OF TIME AND COMPLETELY AND UTTERLY FUCKING UNPROFESSIONAL. YOU SHOULD NOT

BE ON ANY FUCKING FILM SET, YOU ARE A FUCK-
ING DISGRACE, DO YOU FUCKING UNDERSTAND,
YOU ARE A FUCKING DISGRACE...

The crew stood silent and the two advertising agency people
looked at the floor. I bit my lip as he kept screaming, but the
feeling of humiliation grew and grew until I had to fight back
tears. I could sense the shock of the assembled crew and the
atmosphere was something like that of a school playground
when a child is being terrified by a bullying teacher. Part of
my humiliation, I think, was that I felt ashamed that everyone
knew I had worked for him for so long. I felt very foolish to
find myself trapped into having to tolerate his behaviour. As I
stood there with tears beginning to well up I knew that however much of a monster Michael might look, I was probably
seen as a strange and pathetic wretch, standing there silently,
apparently too feeble to stand up for myself or walk away. I
could sense the embarrassment of the crew. And I could feel
how it must have looked like some kind of perverse power
struggle or game of ritual humiliation that was being played
out in front of them. It certainly must have been clear that
his horrendous outbursts had no connection to what I was
actually doing or not doing. But I didn't have any clear idea
of what had really provoked his venomous attacks. When the
roaring subsided I fumbled in my bag for more Valium. Over
the next few hours he threw several more fits of rage at me.

I stopped hearing his actual words – the booming in my
head replaced them with:

YOU ARE TRAPPED. YOU ARE COMPLETELY
TRAPPED. I CAN FIRE YOU ANY TIME I LIKE AND

YOU WILL HAVE NOTHING. NO PLACE TO LIVE. NO PENSION. NO JOB. I HAVE MADE SURE THAT YOU HAVE NO SECURITY AND YOUR LIFE HANGS BY A THREAD THAT I HOLD. YOU HAVE TO STAND THERE AND TAKE IT. I CAN RUIN YOUR LIFE IF YOU DO NOT DO EXACTLY WHAT I TELL YOU. HA HA HA HA HA.

By the end of the day I was quite a wreck. It was cold, but I don't think that was why I was trembling. I knew I looked terrible as I had not always been able to keep back the tears. I also knew I had to go back to the house with Michael in the Phantom. Jim rushed off to get me a cup of coffee so I could take another Valium. I did my best not to look upset as that only ever irritated Michael and would make things worse. When we got out of the car he said, 'Come in at the usual time tomorrow, you won't be on the shoot.'

The next day was the last day of filming and was in the garden at Woodland House. I stayed out of the way as much as possible and any of the crew who saw me showed concern as to how I was, but as usual there was nothing I could say except the usual 'OK, thank you'. I noticed everyone was particularly quiet and humourless. That seemed to be how Michael liked things; with everyone tiptoeing about as if in fear. When normal working days returned Michael was irritable and there was tension in the air, but nothing I had not been through before. About a week later I got a letter.

Apparently it had been sent to every member of the crew. It asked simply that anyone 'who found Mr Winner's treatment of the hairdresser Dinah May very disturbing please consider offering their support should she need it in any formal appeal'.

The letter went on to give details of the union BECTU and appealed to the cast and crew to 'do whatever you can think of to prevent this happening again to anyone in our industry'. There was no name or signature at the bottom. Michael's first response was to stomp about saying he knew who it was and it was just troublemakers. He told me that he had 'severely bollocked' the camera crew just before he attacked me. He had not worked with them before and said he was worried afterwards that they might decide to walk out. He thought that they were responsible, but it was only a hunch and he had no evidence to support his theory. Over the next few days he made lots of calls trying to flush out the culprits. I was very nervous that the letter might make him direct more anger at me, but I also found it heart-warming that some kind of acknowledgement of the events had been made. Of course my situation was complicated and no one from the film crew could be expected to know the bigger picture. I was not as clear about it then as I am now, but my choice was to either attempt to survive whatever Michael threw at me or walk away and see what settlement Michael or the legal system might bestow on me. I didn't feel that would be much. And the thought of finding a friend to stay with while I fought Michael Winner in the courts did not exactly help to lessen the stress I felt. I knew I had to soldier on if I could.

Michael muttered about the letter every day for a couple of weeks. I imagined he might be hatching something. Sure enough, in mid-December 2008 an article appeared on the Richard Kay page of the *Daily Mail* under the title 'Calm Down! He's My Friend'. I presumed it was written mostly by Michael. It was clearly his agenda, anyway. Perhaps the most hurtful part referred to the letter I had received, with me quoted as saying 'How dare someone write this? They certainly never asked me.' Well, I could say the same about that article. I was not consulted in any way, shape or form.

I found it very disturbing that an offer of support could be belittled and squashed like that. If the writers of the letter read this I would like to say a very clear 'thank you'. And also, of course, that I think you are a *great* credit to your industry. What I could see, even at the time, was that no one could risk stepping forward in protest. If anyone had stood up for me they would almost certainly never have been asked to work for Michael again, or anyone he had influence over, for that matter. A film crew is usually composed of lots of small units and most people are self-employed. Any whiff of trouble from anyone and they may not be given work next time around, and everyone has a family to provide for or rent to pay. There is certainly no incentive for anyone to stick their neck out.

That episode had somewhat soured my connection with Michael. At some level I knew that I was being bullied because Michael needed to vent his frustrations and anguish on somebody and I was the safe and available target.

I can't be certain what side of his character it came from. Perhaps it was all some kind of demonstration of his power. But any kind of understanding was no real comfort. I still found that side of him disturbing. I noticed that I was often dreading the next working day in a way that I had never done before.

Fortunately Ruby was still secretary and most days could be broken by meeting her for lunch somewhere. And life outside work was improving.

With Luke now in London I saw him regularly, and sometimes he would stay at Farley Court. One day, out of the blue, he mentioned the dogs, Bella and Chiki. He knew how much I missed them, but I had felt that it might be heartless to leave Takis without them. Also, of course, I knew that Michael might have erupted with rage if he knew they were with me at the flat. Luke felt that his dad would be happy to be able to come and go to Greece without the added complications they brought.

Any dogs I had ever owned had always come from my mother's friend, the well-respected breeder Penny Jones of Clopton Poodles. Apart from looking beautiful we always found that all her dogs had such lovely natures. She agreed to give them a bath and haircut and Luke whizzed up to Neston one day to pick them up. I could not believe it when they stood blinking at me in the lounge at Farley Court. Other dog lovers will understand how difficult it had been not seeing them for months.

Sheila the accountant had said she was happy to let them out now and then during the day when nature called. If I was with Michael for lunch then Matthew would nip to the flat and take them for a walk. Bella and Chiki worked their charm and quickly had him wrapped around the dog equivalent of their little fingers.

Michael continued to be dogged by health problems. He and Geraldine went for their winter break and, shortly after their return, Michael had to spend a few nights in hospital with cellulitis. The feverishness and flu-like symptoms, together with the strong antibiotics he was on, meant that he was not in good enough shape to work for a while. But whenever he had the strength he would pick up where he had left off. Alongside his weekly 'Winner's Dinners' articles, Michael was putting together a book under the same name. His ability to get through bout after bout of gruesome illness was remarkable on its own, and he showed no inclination to put his feet up or slow down. After the unpleasant episode on the film set there had been quite a cool atmosphere on the days I spent with him in his office. It began to thaw during the times that he was most ill. Partly I think because I could not help but have a human concern for his wellbeing, but also perhaps it reminded him of how much he leant on me sometimes. I had hoped that his brushes with death might have made him a little more compassionate or sensitive towards others. Instead I began to see that, if anything, his continued health problems often frustrated him and that could boil over as anger. I was possibly the person he could most easily direct it at and so I began to try to keep that in mind and not take it all too personally.

When summer arrived, he and Geraldine went to La Réserve de Beaulieu for three weeks. Geraldine wanted to spend the middle week of the holiday with her family in Spain so I flew out to join Michael for those days. In the past if I joined him on holiday it was simply because he never wanted to be on his own. That still held true, but now there were practical considerations as well and it made good sense to have someone with him who was aware of his complicated health problems. At 6.00 on the dot we would go for an afternoon stroll along the coastal paths and enjoy the spectacular views. But between breakfast and 6.00 were the taxing times for me. Michael would allow me a quick swim in the sea in the morning, but after a few minutes would be standing up by his sun lounger and waving his white towel, shouting, 'DINAH, DINAH, DINAH.' He was very happy to spend the day chatting or dozing and expected me to stay at his side at all times.

When I thought he was asleep I might nip off back to the sea and dive in. But it seemed that as soon as I surfaced I could hear 'DINAH, DINAH, DINAH' and looking back there he would be, waving his white towel. I don't know how he did it. It was like he had some kind of 'killjoy radar'. I did get a little respite that week as luckily Barry McKay was there with his wife and children and I could sneak off sometimes when Michael was chatting with him.

I knew Barry was a businessman whose work took him all over the world. Only recently I learnt that he had managed the band Lindisfarne in the 1970s.

Michael had met Barry at Sandy Lane one Christmas. Well, it might be more accurate to say that Barry had seen and heard Michael that Christmas. Their first proper meeting very nearly took place in a courtroom. He had watched Michael being waited on hand and foot and then kowtowed to by Grant McPherson, the executive chef, and then after all that attention Michael still got to his feet to shout and swear and generally throw a noisy tantrum.

Barry was not impressed. In the usually friendly atmosphere of Sandy Lane he made sure not to mingle with Michael. Once home, Michael continued to hound Grant McPherson in his 'Winner's Dinners' column and Barry, who knew a lot about Grant and had great respect for his talents, was growing increasingly appalled and stood up in his defence. Letters and emails began. Grant was thinking to sue Michael for the things he said in his articles but Barry advised against it. Michael dictated long emails for Ruby to send to Barry and increasingly they involved talk of legal action. The balloon grew bigger and bigger until one day Barry stuck a pin in it with a funny letter and the whole thing exploded into laughter. Lawyers and barristers must have wept. Barry, it turned out, travelled a great deal and knew many of Michael's favourite hotels. He also paid a lot of attention to the quality of service in the places he stayed in and, added to that, had a reputation as someone with a very fine legal mind. They had things in common and a friendship soon sprang up. Barry and Michael exchanged emails regularly and their paths often crossed when Michael was on holiday.

Their conversations ranged from serious legal matters to places to visit or avoid, interspersed with frequent shaggy-dog stories of the kind Michael really enjoyed. I had first got to appreciate Barry as the man who could distract Michael for a few minutes while I ran off to the sea. But all the family were charming and I really enjoyed chatting to his wife Fleur, who was such a warm and lovely lady.

When Geraldine returned I flew back to London. And there was excitement building. ITV had commissioned 12 Yard Productions to make a new television series. It was to be called *Michael Winner's Dining Stars*. And the first filming was to take place in the last days of Michael and Geraldine's stay at La Réserve de Beaulieu.

It was in the spring of that year that Michael had first told me that Jimmy Mulville, one of the co-founders of Hat Trick Productions, had approached him with the idea for a television series. The basic premise was that Michael, the feared god of food criticism, would go to the homes of ordinary folk and judge their cooking. Of course, to make it interesting these home cooks had to be people whose family and friends felt they were exceptionally gifted in the kitchen. During the dinner Michael would make notes about the food and then disappear into a back room to record his thoughts about the whole dining experience. The cook and their friends would then be invited to the Coronet, a recently restored cinema in Notting Hill Gate, London, to be told Michael's honest, and sometimes quite brutal, assessment of their endeavours. The climax would come when the host was told whether they had won three, two or one Michael Winner Dining Stars – or nothing at all. The first filming I was aware of took place during Michael and Geraldine's last few days at La Réserve de Beaulieu. First off, a pilot episode had to be made and it was essential that this meet with the approval of the top brass, Peter Fincham, the director of television for ITV, and Alison Sharman, the director of factual and daytime television. Michael clearly had great respect for the big bosses and, as it turned out, they liked the pilot and were enthusiastic for the show to go ahead.

He was not quite so respectful to Matt Walton, the executive producer, or Nic Guttridge, the director. For my part, I was not complaining that he had found other people to pick arguments with and rant and rave at. The disagreements started early on and continued right through the editing process. It probably did not help that Michael was a director himself and may not have liked being told what to do by people in their thirties. If that was true, he was certainly not going to admit it and after each blasting Matt and Nic would drift away and discuss how difficult he was. I say 'difficult', but actually they had quite a few other words for it.

A series of four programmes were to be made as a trial run. Joan Hills, the make-up artist, and I got on well from the start, which was fortunate as together we would be traipsing round after Michael for the next few months.

I was put down as hair stylist as usual and, also as usual, I would be his general assistant and dogsbody. What was not so usual was that, it being something of a reality show, Joan and I would appear in the programme from time to time. Michael wanted us to be within a few feet of him at all times so if we were not scampering after him in the street we were usually squashed behind the camera in the corner of a kitchen or dining room.

My heart sank when one morning at a quarter to ten the phone rang and it was Michael.

WHAT ARE YOU FUCKING DOING PICKING UP THE PHONE? YOU ARE NOT MEANT TO BE THERE PICK-ING UP THE FUCKING PHONE, YOU WERE MEANT TO BE HERE FIFTEEN FUCKING MINUTES AGO. I DON'T FUCKING BELIEVE THIS, YOU NEED TO GET ALL MY CLOTHES PACKED AND...

I tried to interrupt and tell him that he had told me 11.00 that morning, but he wasn't listening so I put the receiver on my dressing table and ran around quickly doing my own packing. Michael continued bellowing, but through the telephone it sounded like a tiny man trapped in a box. When I heard the muffled little outraged voice saying, 'DINAH! DINAH! DINAH! ARE YOU THERE, DINAH? WHERE ARE YOU, DINAH?' I picked up the phone again.

'Yes, yes, I'm just getting my things, I will be there as soon as I can...' But Michael was off again so once more I left him venting his spleen.

HOW DARE YOU BE SO FUCKING LATE? THERE IS SO MUCH TO DO AND WE HAVE TO FUCKING WELL

LEAVE AT ELEVEN SO YOU BETTER GET HERE NOW,
I SAID NOW, DO YOU UNDERSTAND? I SAID DO
YOU FUCKING UNDERSTAND? ... DINAH! DINAH!
DINAH! ARE YOU FUCKING LISTENING? DINAH!
DINAH! DINAH! WHERE ARE YOU? DINAH? DINAH?

I knelt on my suitcase and struggled to get it zipped up and
the tiny trapped man was still shouting as I dashed out of
Farley Court. 'DINAH! DINAH! HOW DARE YOU? WHERE
THE FUCK ARE YOU? DINAH, DINAH, DINAH, PICK UP
THIS FUCKING PHONE NOW, DINAH, DINAH, DINAH,
DINAH!'

Sheila had heard the commotion and I asked her to replace
the receiver when the little man fell silent. It had always been
part of my job to pack Michael's suitcase before he travelled
anywhere, but Geraldine was gradually taking over that side
of things. When I got to the house he continued his shouting
and was still not listening when I reminded him that he had
told me to be there at 11.00.

Being completely confident that the mistake was his, I added
that I had never been late and he would not be employing
me if I *had* ever been late. It shut him up eventually and in
the Phantom to the heliport he stayed silent and sulky. We
boarded a helicopter which was to take us to the Lake Dis-
trict and then on to Scotland. As London shrank to a toy city
below us we put on our ear defenders and sat looking out of
our windows like spoilt children in a huff. Somewhere over
Leicester he offered me a barley sugar and I took it without
a thank you. A little later he tried to talk over the noise of the
engine, but he was still going on about my being late so I just
shouted, 'I CAN'T HEAR YOU, I CAN'T HEAR YOU.' A little

while later he offered another barley sugar, but snatched the bag away just as I was about to take one. The second time he tried that trick I was ready and my hand shot out lightning fast and I grabbed one. That made me feel better, but I did my best not to smile. I noticed Michael was chuckling and gradually, like the barley sugars, our stand-off dissolved. Somewhere near Sheffield we were talking and by the time we landed we were friends again.

Something very good happened in the first weeks of filming. Michael returned to his earlier self. He seemed to become more and more like the good-humoured man I had met in the early '80s and was fun to be around.

Admittedly, he was still shouting sometimes and making other people's lives a bit difficult, but thankfully not mine. When we were visiting a new place, and out and about in the streets, his mischievousness and curiosity were blossoming. Joan and I had to stay close at hand at all times in case he needed something and having her there was a real bonus. When Michael was being particularly boisterous or absurd I had someone to roll my eyes at and she had a knack of exploding into laughter at just the right moment. Early on we had been to Wilmslow in Cheshire and I was carrying more and more of Michael's clobber. Apart from the throat sweets and jar of honey and scripts, I now had tissues and towels and even a hairdryer to lug about. In one shop Michael had gone into I saw a row of wheelie bags and suggested that one might be ideal for me to pack with all his stuff. He agreed and gave me the usual six seconds to pick one out. I chose a glossy pillar-box red one, knowing it would be easiest to spot in a flash. If I had known at the time that it would occasionally appear in the final programmes with me scurrying in front of it, I might have made a different choice.

Each episode showed the chosen cook preparing the dinner, but also some fly-on-the-wall filming of Michael talking to local inhabitants. He had a whale of a time and would just get carried away with enthusiasm and idiocy. The people in charge had suggested that he should appear 'menacing' – I imagine because of his reputation as a harsh critic they were looking for maximum tension and dramatic effect. However, left to himself, Michael was much more naturally a kind of ridiculous and endearing pantomime character. He loved going into shops and trying things on or just being plain silly, and with the film crew there he felt he had licence to do anything he liked. In Essex he got himself togged up in archetypal Essex gear and in Scotland he blundered into a shop selling traditional tartans and was soon standing in kilt and sporran. Also, he had good radar for anything surreal, childish or kitsch. In Solihull, for example, he found a shop where he could record his own message for a talking teddy bear. He made a panda for Geraldine which said 'Geraldine, you are the most wonderful person in the world' and the teddy he gave me screamed 'DINAH! DINAH! WHERE ARE YOU, DINAH? FOR HEAVEN'S SAKE, WHERE HAVE YOU GONE, DINAH?'

As filming commenced, Michael told me that if the series was successful his next catchphrase would be simply 'DINAH!' I cringed a little at the thought, but quickly realised it could be a lot worse. Joan and I had got used to scurrying after him at all times, whether filming or not, and his bad leg was becoming less and less noticeable. The constant walking was probably the best thing he could be doing.

As the camera crew packed up after filming an incident, Michael would already be striding off looking to find or create more lunacy. In Kingsand in Cornwall there were lovely cobbled streets lined with little cottages. Michael had tried knocking on doors and was disappointed to be told that most of them were holiday homes and would probably be empty until the summer. He wanted to find another local to act as a judge on the show and he was not giving up. First he told me to look through the letterboxes to see if there was any sign of life. I was hesitant and said, 'I'm not sure I like…'

But he crouched down saying, 'Oh for fuck's sake, it's not rocket science, look, you just push the fucking flap up.' The camera crew were having a short break so Joan and I ambled up the hill as Michael peered through letterboxes into people's houses. When a dog leapt snarling from behind one of the doors, nearly biting his nose off, he staggered backwards in fright.

'Right, we are meant to be a fucking team,' he snapped. 'Dinah, it's your turn now. See if you can see any sign of life.' I began tentatively pushing open letterboxes. In one cottage I saw boots and shoes and called to Michael to come and look. 'Any sign of dogs?' he asked cautiously.

When I said 'no' I thought he was going to knock, but instead he tried the door and it swung open.

Without a pause he marched into the little hallway. Joan rolled her eyes in horror and put her head in her hands and I ran after him saying, 'No, Michael … we can't just … it's somebody's house … we can't…'

But when I got along the corridor to the kitchen Michael was pulling a chair out and sitting himself at the table as he yelled out, 'HELLO … IS ANYBODY THERE?' Then he turned to me and said, 'See if you can find things to make a cup of tea.'

I was whispering 'No, no, we can't do this, we've got to go, what are you doing?'

Just then a door at the back of the kitchen opened and the head of an elderly man appeared, looking rather alarmed. Michael said immediately, 'Ahh, hello, I'm Michael Winner, good to meet you. I've got rather a bad leg and needed to sit down for a moment.' Stepping into the room the man said, 'Well, it's lucky I don't have a bad heart or we'd have made a right pair!' We all laughed and Michael quickly explained what we were up to and soon the kettle was on and all was well.

When the film crew caught up with us they had found a local fisherman called Malcolm who had agreed to be one of the judges. Michael had also asked Doll Jago, a 96-year-old lady whose door he had knocked on. After the filming, when he saw the rushes, he admitted he found it rather disconcerting as she came across as being about the same age as him. There were two finalists and each was to cook dinner for three local people acting as judges as well as Michael, Joan and me. Zoe, being a local girl herself, had recommended Polhawn Fort as an ideal venue for the 'bake-off', and Michael had appointed her as one of the local judges too. The lucky winner would then cook for a dinner party at Michael's house. The researchers had done well to find not only some excellent cooks, but also some very lovely people.

Jane Bennet and Justine Forrest were the two women pitted against each other. Michael found it very difficult to choose as they were clearly both superb cooks and charming people too. Jane had cooked a passion fruit and orange pudding that I found absolutely out of this world, but Justine was to win the day. When she saw the guest list for the dinner she was to cook at Michael's house she must have been fairly daunted. There was Geraldine, Sir Roger Moore and his wife Lady Kristina, Andrew Neil, Christine Bleakley, Kym Marsh from *Coronation Street* and the chef Giorgio Locatelli, who was running his own restaurant, Locanda Locatelli. They proved to be the perfect guests as, despite the filming going on, everyone was quickly relaxed and jovial and put Justine at ease once she got going. It was a genuinely enjoyable evening and the food was fabulous. Also, unbeknownst to Justine, Michael had smuggled her family down from Longridge, Lancashire, and into his house. There was her husband Chris and children Alex, Millie and Christopher. My only part in the night's proceedings was to usher them into the dining room at the allotted time after the meal. Cooking aside, the Forrest family had made a huge impression on Michael. Two of the children had serious ailments, but the closeness, courage and plain good-heartedness of all of them was an inspiration. Michael kept in touch with Justine and was very happy when she set up her own brownie-baking business. Michael liked cakes and desserts and one of his favourites was a good chocolate brownie. Of Justine's he said, 'The best brownies I've ever tasted. An exceptional, superb brownie! Historic beyond belief, a taste experience – perfection.'

They moved Sir Roger Moore to comment too and he went with the altogether simpler, but equally complimentary, 'bloody lovely'.

The programmes were first aired towards the end of February 2010. A week or so before that, Michael threw a private screening and dinner party at Woodland House. Alice the housekeeper had returned to Portugal and a Filipino lady called Lulu Brown was in charge of the kitchen.

Ruby had also stepped down from her job in the hot seat

and Natalie Wright now worked in the little office next to Michael's. Fortunately for me, Ruby still appeared occasionally to work as receptionist or stand in for Natalie when she was away. She came in that day to help Lulu prepare the food and serve the guests. I cooked a version of chicken Marengo that my mother had taught me and also helped prepare the main dish, beef Stroganoff. Ruby was frying the strips of steak when I added the brandy for the sauce. I had been a little overgenerous, as, when she put a match to the pan, I thought the sheet of blue flame would take all her hair with it, and possibly the whole kitchen too.

When our hysteria died down we found that only her fringe and eyelashes had been neatly singed. I thought Ruby might have been angry, but she just quipped that even my cooking included a bit of hairdressing. The last whiffs of burning hair were nearly gone just as the first people arrived. The guest list included Sir Michael and Lady Caine, Lord and Lady Lloyd Webber, Sir David and Lady Frost, Mr and Mrs Archie Norman, Mr and Mrs Adam Crozier, Mr and Mrs Charlie Brooks, Adam Kenwright and Lucy Prebble, Andrew Davis and Andrew Onraet and Alison Sharman. I had met Alison a number of times at various meetings and lunches and when Michael was engaged in other conversations we chatted about anything except television.

We got along easily and talked mostly about our personal lives. She knew I had left Takis and that my hopes for an amicable settlement and a fifty-fifty split of our little house had been dashed. I had to get a lawyer and was doing things the slow, miserable and expensive way. But other things were happening to reshape my world. I had got to know Matthew the gardener a little better. When he first started at Michael's

I had told my mother and my friend Jackie that there was 'something of Clint Eastwood about him'. I was never one to have crushes on actors, but they knew only too well that I had always carried a torch for Clint. Of course Matthew did not exactly look like Clint Eastwood, but there was something about his manner. And maybe the look in his eyes. It was strange as I had known him for about fifteen years before we really talked about anything except Michael's instructions for the garden or how he got the roses to bloom so well. But through the Christmas parties, visits to see John Fraser, and occasional evenings on his boat, I had slowly got to know him. He could make me laugh like no one else and was very good natured and kind. When I had to go away he began looking after Bella and Chiki. I had thought that impossible because of his cat, but Kitty would keep up on the table or bar top and look down on the dogs with slight disgust as they pottered about below him. When Matthew was away he would leave Kitty at Farley Court or I would take the dogs to the barge and stay there.

Not long after I had left home Michael had asked about Bella and Chiki and if I missed them. In a moment of bravery I told him straight out that they were with me at Farley Court. His eyes came out on stalks, but once they were back in their sockets he just shrugged and said, 'I don't fucking believe it, they better not put hair all over the office.' I assured him that as poodles they didn't shed any hair. And that was that. It was a great relief. A few months before the filming of *Dining Stars* had begun, Bella, who was only twelve, began to have fits. It usually happened in the early hours of the morning and was extremely horrible and heart-breaking. Several times I had rushed her to the 24-hour vet in Victoria and Matthew would meet me there. Her fits became more frequent and although various medicines were tried I was told that there wasn't really anything more that could be done. In those times I dared not leave the dogs alone and Michael knew that Matthew had looked after them whenever I had to work. I was staying on the boat when Bella went into her last fit at about three o'clock one morning. When she wouldn't come out of it we rushed her to Victoria, but the vet said it really was the end of the line. It was completely heart-breaking. Bella had the most beautiful nature and I had lost such a beautiful friend. I couldn't even think where to bury her. I didn't know anyone in London who had a garden except Michael, but it was too personal a tragedy to involve him and everyone at the house. In the end Matthew and I drove to Faversham in Kent, where he had friends with a fishing boat moored by a little peaceful woodland, and we laid her to rest there.

I didn't tell anyone except Ruby about my romance with Matthew. And I had no idea where it might be leading anyway. We knew there were suspicions among the staff. If I went out with boxes of papers for the garden tip I often saw Shirley or Lani busily cleaning a window when I looked up at the house.

There were eyes everywhere and sometimes it was quite comical, but I was certain it was better to leave a question mark in the air. But even Michael began to make little comments. Once he asked what I was doing at the weekend and I told him I was going to look after Matthew's cat. 'I've not heard it called that before!' he said, quietly chuckling to himself. I felt myself going a bit pink and pretended I hadn't heard. Gradually he made it a bit of a running joke. As I was leaving on a Friday he might say something like, 'I suppose you'll be "looking after the cat" this weekend.'

I would try to ignore his quips, but he would roll his eyes and bark with laughter. Matthew had stopped his work as the gardener just before filming for *Dining Stars* had begun. I was very lucky to have the flat in Farley Court, but because of the office there I could never feel totally away from Michael's world, and I needed that so I could be fresh and ready for whatever the next chapter in his life might throw at me. Whenever I had time off I would go to the boat and that was very like going to the country. The boat itself was, as my friend Diana put it, very 'Pirates of the Caribbean'. As the spring weather arrived there were decks being caulked with hot pitch, sails spread out and dressed with wax and ochre red pigment and always the smell of fresh paint. Also there was a good community of barge folk who worked on the river and in and out of the dock and as I got to know some of them I quickly felt at home.

Whatever people may think of his other skills I'm sure that Michael's greatest talent was for self-promotion. And he certainly worked hard at it and took it very seriously. He knew that in the modern world, if you wanted money and fame, it was perhaps the most important thing and he didn't need to employ a publicist. With his new television series about to go on air he had pulled out all the stops. As well as his 'Winner's Dinners' column in the *Sunday Times*, he pushed for as many newspaper and magazine articles as he could. That was all well and good until he set me up for an interview. A young journalist called Jenny Johnston was going to arrive at Woodland House to talk to me about my years of work with Michael. An article was to appear in the *Daily Mail*. I was nervous. In the past when I had been asked to comment I soon found that anything I said would be wrong and I would get days or weeks of hell from him afterwards. Also, over the years I had learnt that if he gave me credit for anything in the papers it could lead to trouble for me from the girlfriend he was with. Eventually I had managed to persuade him to just leave me out. The day before Jenny Johnston was to call, Michael began listing all the things he wanted me to say and all the things I was definitely *not* to say. He had sometimes given me printed sheets to remind me of the things I should mention to any journalist. I got some more of these with everything typed out in capitals.

THE SERIES HAS BEEN GREAT. HE YELLS AND SCREAMS FOR THE CAMERA AND SOMETIMES HE YELLS AND SCREAMS IN REAL LIFE, BUT MICHAEL, JOAN (HIS MAKE-UP LADY) AND ME HAD LUNCH AT RESTAURANTS ALL OVER THE COUNTRY AND IN SCOTLAND. JUST US. THE FOOD WAS USUALLY DREADFUL BUT IT DIDN'T MATTER, THE COMPANY WAS SO GREAT.

He did some name-dropping ones too.

I'M ALWAYS INSECURE. IF I HAVE TO GO SOMEWHERE POSH WITH HIM I SAY, 'I DON'T LOOK GOOD ENOUGH, I'M NOT WELL DRESSED. I'LL STICK OUT LIKE A SORE THUMB.' HE SAYS, 'DINAH, YOU'RE ABSOLUTELY BEAUTIFUL, YOU'LL BE THE BEST LOOKING PERSON THERE. SHUT UP AND GET ON WITH IT.' I DON'T MIND WHAT I DO REALLY, AS HIS ASSISTANT.
IT RANGES FROM GARDENING TO HOSTING

MAJOR STARS LIKE ROBERT MITCHUM, JACK LEMMON, MARLON BRANDO, CHARLES BRONSON. HE TOOK ME TO TRAMP DISCOTHEQUE WITH CHARLES BRONSON AND JILL IRELAND WHEN HE WAS BETWEEN GIRLFRIENDS. I WAS HIS WALKER. WE'D GO OUT AND PEOPLE WOULD THINK THERE WAS SOME BEDROOM BUSINESS GOING ON BUT THERE WASN'T, I WAS MARRIED AND HE RESPECTED THAT. NOW I'M NOT MARRIED HE'S WITH GERALDINE WHOM HE ADORES. SHE'S A GREAT LADY. I'M PART OF THE FAMILY.

So I had sheets of some of the stories he wanted me to mention, but there were lots of other things too. I was to say that he had never tried to seduce me or asked me to marry him and that I was a great admirer of Geraldine and she and I were close friends. There were also lots of events from his past and previous girlfriends that I was forbidden to talk about at all if I was asked. Just for good measure, he bellowed more instructions at me the morning before Jenny arrived and told me I would be fired if I dared to say anything other than exactly what he had told me. When Jenny Johnston and I sat down in the cinema in the basement I was not exactly feeling relaxed and cheerful. In fact my head felt like it was full of hot scrambled egg and I could hear a low hum in my ears. I did my best to regurgitate everything I could remember, but Jenny had a job to do and, surprise, surprise, kept asking awkward questions. I would be babbling on, trying to remember Michael's typewritten sheets and other instructions and she would interrupt with things like 'has he ever tried to seduce you?' or 'does he bully you, he bullies you, doesn't he?'

I couldn't even say, 'Well, can we ignore that subject or I'll lose my job.'

After an hour or so Jenny Johnston left. I imagined she might well have got the impression that either I was a bit of a nutcase or was in a very difficult position. Both maybe! Anyway, I tried not to think about what her article might contain. To put it mildly, it made me very nervous. On the morning of Saturday 20 February 2010, I went and bought the *Daily Mail*. There was a double-page spread with the heading 'Calm down dear, it's only the worst job in Britain'. Apart from that I thought all might be well. I was quoted as saying things like 'Michael was fabulous' and there were lots of positive comments about Geraldine too. I thought I was in with a good chance of him being happy. Boy, was I wrong about that! I had only just finished reading the article when my phone rang.

Michael had something to shout about in nearly every paragraph. I was a nervous wreck before I even got into work the following Monday. Jenny Johnston had got a few names wrong, which Michael was furious about, and he also told the editor of the *Daily Mail* that I was very upset as well. There were phone calls and angry emails and Michael demanded to be sent a transcript of the tape recording of my interview. I think he hoped that his anger over the mistakes coupled with saying that I was upset by the article would give him the clout he needed to find out exactly what I *had* said. He was ranting and raving at me and telling me that if he found out I had mentioned this or that I would be 'FIRED, DO YOU UNDERSTAND, FIRED'. I was back in the horrible and impossible place he would put me from time to time. As far as I know, Michael never got a complete transcript of my interview, but bits and bobs were sent to him by email. Whatever incriminating evidence he was looking for he didn't seem to find, and over a few days his shouting tailed off.

The following week I was told I might be interviewed again. This time it was in connection with his appearance on the television series *Piers Morgan's Life Stories*. He had mentioned it several weeks earlier, but after the *Daily Mail* article he had said he didn't think I would be needed. But then, all of a sudden, I was to be under the spotlights after all. I was briefed by Michael once more on what a charming and generous man he was and how lucky I was to have such interesting and exciting work. This time he also told me what to say if I was asked to comment on his childhood and added that Geraldine would be talking to the TV people and he didn't really see why they would want to bother much with me. I remember thinking that if he stopped shouting orders and threatening me I would quite happily tell the world about the good times we had and give examples of his generosity. But Michael had his own agenda as usual and preferred to bash me over the head with it rather than have a normal conversation. I took some Valium. Michael kept me in his office until I was called and then I trotted down to the cinema without even getting a moment to powder my nose. The programme was aired in April 2010. I looked a bit like a rabbit caught in the headlights, but I assumed I had done all right as there was never any mention of it afterwards. But I don't think I had been gushing enough in praise of him as for the next few weeks I was treated like an irritating idiot. If I had to take anything up to his office he would then flap his hand and say, 'Get out, get out, you're fucking useless.' I had been through periods like that before and found it was not exactly brilliant for my self-esteem. And self-confidence had always been a sensitive area for me.

It often didn't take much criticism to make me feel pretty insignificant and Michael could keep up an unrelenting barrage of niggling and disparaging remarks which I could feel gradually pushing me towards a miserable hole. And I had seen him do it to more robust people than me. Ruby had managed a year and a half in the hot seat, but by then his constant negative and nasty comments had ground her down to the point where she knew she had to leave. The energy it took to steel herself through each day left her increasingly drained and her doctor told her the various ailments she had started to suffer from were all stress related. But having people who had worked for Michael as my friends was a great help. They knew what it could be like and reminded me that perhaps I was not actually 'useless'.

Through Matthew I had met David Hockney's assistant, Jean-Pierre Gonçalves de Lima. I had got to know him well over a few years and discovered he had a knack of getting me back on track when I was nearing the end of my tether.

His work with David meant he was mostly in Bridlington and not often in London, but he had a habit of appearing out of the blue with very little warning. By some happy coincidence it was often just when I was struggling most with life in Winner's world. He also happened to be an amazing accordionist and played mostly '30s jazz and musette. If we were at the boat he would pull out the accordion he kept there while Ruby his Jack Russell scampered about the saloon and Kitty watched from the safety of the chart table or bar top. Jean-Pierre would listen to the story of my latest pressures and dilemmas and then, like a magician shuffling cards, lay everything out in front of me in a new and encouraging form. And I'd never met anyone so good at making light and laughter of something and also keeping sight of the underlying weight of it. After those evenings I sometimes had a slight hangover, but always felt recharged and ready for whatever might be thrown at me next.

I made a point of telling Michael about people I knew if they were in any way in the public eye. It was a good reminder to him that although I didn't talk to journalists, his bouts of unpleasant behaviour were not entirely invisible. It did make him more respectful for a while and he stayed true to form in that he was always very happy to hear I was out and about enjoying life.

Through all the busy times of filming *Dining Stars* I had seen Paola when I could. She had been doing very well, but then discovered she needed the exact same operation as I had had a few years earlier to free a blockage in her digestion.

There was nothing sinister about it, but I knew it was a horrible ordeal to go through. Although in the past I had managed to persuade Michael to stop sending me as his envoy, he did give me two days off to go and see how she was. Michael often wrote about how he kept in touch with many of his ex-girlfriends, but what people didn't often know was that, especially during any health problems, he often reached into his pocket to look after them as well. It took a few months, but Paola made a good recovery.

When the decision was made not to film a second series of *Michael Winner's Dining Stars*, Michael was very disappointed. The viewing figures had been good, but apparently not good enough. Personally I don't think Michael had done himself any favours by giving some people involved in the programme quite a rough time. But I have no idea if that had any bearing on the decision to axe the show. Michael blamed himself for criticising the way women in the north of England cook and dress. He wished he had been told earlier that northern women form a high percentage of the viewers of ITV1. He also felt it would have been better to concentrate on his talent for being a nincompoop rather than a hard-nosed critic. I knew that side of him well and had enjoyed seeing him being silly on camera. He had a humour all his own sometimes and when he talked to people in the street or shopping arcades something quite absurd would often quickly evolve. For instance, when he met the town crier in Shrewsbury, a man about seven feet tall, Michael was soon wearing his tricorn hat and the town crier began ringing his hand bell and calling out, 'MICHAEL WINNER IS HERE AND HE DOESN'T WANT ANYONE TO KNOW.' It could be schoolboy silliness, but when he kept it up even the most highbrow people often couldn't help but eventually sag with laughter.

Michael was understandably glum for a while after his hopes of becoming a bigger household name had been dashed. I think he really missed the fun and tomfoolery it had allowed him, too. The energy he had found during the filming was remarkable and, although he had health problems still niggling at him, he looked better than he ever had since his severe illness. He started to work shorter days again, but he had plenty of writing to occupy him. *Unbelievable* was published in 2010 and then he immediately began working on *Tales I Never Told*. His autobiography, *Winner Takes All*, had been published in 2004 and since then Michael seemed bitten by the writing bug and was prolific. He would tap away on his laptop at great speed and let secretaries and editors worry about spelling and punctuation. Being impatient by nature, he was only really excited to get the stories down. I got used to reading over his shoulder when he asked me and knew to only mention a mistyped word when it was unclear what he meant. Sometimes, when the mood took him or speed was of the essence, he would talk into a Dictaphone and let his secretary take it from there. His books were a perfect platform from which to demonstrate his wit and humour, and name-drop extensively, of course, as he told tales of his extraordinary life.

And whatever anybody thinks of Michael, there was no side to his life that could be described as humdrum. But I think it's true to say that writing each new tome became, at least in part, a necessary irritation to get to the real reward – a book launch. Michael found ways to make the launching of a book very exciting and enjoyable. Certainly for him, and probably for some of the invited guests, too. For me, they became occasions that I grew increasingly to dread. Over the years I had learnt that Michael's shouting could take me by surprise at any time and I had gradually come to terms with that. But on book launch days Michael-the-Not-Very-Nice was certain to turn up with his fiery dragon of a temper, largely because he was nervous. Ironically, the events usually took place in the calm and airy beauty of the Belvedere in Holland Park and, as with all Michael's literary excursions, the publisher was the Robson Press. When I first met Jeremy Robson I found him to be quietly spoken and amiable and couldn't help but wonder at how he coped with the outbursts and tantrums. It seemed Jeremy could ride the punches and find the humour in the situation, which often served to calm Michael down. He was never fazed by Michael, though I did hear later that at one point he told Michael to only deal with him on the phone as the hallmark gruff and often aggressive manner could be alarming and unpleasant for his staff, who were not in a position to hit back. The editing of a book, I would imagine, is normally a rather quiet and contemplative process, but with Michael, unsurprisingly I suppose, it could be a pretty noisy business.

Fortunately, I had very little to do with any of that side of things, but the launch day itself was when the clamour and racket would often rise to a crescendo. In the early days it was in line with Michael's usual levels of uproar, but that changed with the first of his *Winner's Dinners* volumes, based on his articles in the *Sunday Times*. He had come up with the idea of giving his own 'Winner's Awards' in conjunction with the launch of the book. They managed to be serious and tongue-in-cheek at the same time. There was Best Restaurant in the World, given to Harry's Bar, Venice, and Best View from a Restaurant Table for La Tour D'Argent, Paris, joint winner with Delfino in Portofino; Best Jelly went to the Mirabelle and Phoniest Restaurant Line for the phrase 'Your main course will be with you in a minute, sir'. There would be at least a dozen of them and sometimes more. He asked friends of his who were very famous to present these awards, such as Sir Michael Caine and Andrew Lloyd Webber and Simon Cowell, and also wooed other household names when possible, such as Joanna Lumley and Barbara Windsor. All that was well and good and made for a jolly evening, especially with the crates of champagne supplied by the publishing house. But I don't remember enjoying any of those evenings myself. I was usually set some task so trivial it was almost unnecessary, and then snapped at, screeched at and finally roasted in front of the assembled company.

Through the years I had begun to recognise just some of the complicated patterns that influenced Michael's behaviour and an event he had organised himself, stirred with guests he wished to impress and garnished with celebrities was not a cocktail I was likely to enjoy.

I was usually the closest human and an easy target, but now and then I shared the privilege with some of the staff of the Robson Press. I had met Jeremy's lovely wife Carole at book launches, but did not know her well. I got to know her a little better when one year she came across me in the ladies as I was pulling myself together after a particularly scalding attack. She was understanding and sympathetic and did her best to calm me down. The following year James Stephens, sales director of the Robson Press, also showed his concern as I fought back tears. I had been passing up the awards certificates to Michael, who in turn passed them to the appropriate celebrity to present to whichever restaurant manager or owner had been deemed worthy of the accolade. No doubt I had made some monumental error. James asked if there was anything he could do and nipped off to get me a drink when I said it might help me to pull through! The reality was that on celebrity-presented Winner's Awards book launch days it was just a matter of keeping my head down and hoping I could survive the evening with a little dignity still intact.

Anyway, as I said, they became occasions that I grew increasingly to dread. It was not a rare sight to see Michael lording it over people, but perhaps through his books, particularly those connected to his 'Winner's Dinners' articles, he had found a world where he really did feel supreme. I knew Jeremy had developed a good-humoured shield that was almost impervious to Michael's tirades and which Michael liked and respected, but when the Robson Press joined forces with Biteback Publishing, Michael-the-Not-Very-Nice found a new adversary in Iain Dale, their managing director. Iain was fresh to the battlefield and, after witnessing sobbing staff and accusatory letters in angry capitals, he closed the castle gates. To be more accurate, he closed the gates, raised the drawbridge and read Michael the riot act too. Michael's eyes were on stalks when he got an email from Iain which pulled no punches. I knew his look when he was accused unjustly of something or misrepresented in the press. His hackles would rise. But I had also got to know the look he had when arrows of truth were cutting into him. When his hackles were up he would set to work in a fury, but on the rare occasions that someone stood up to him and he felt backed into a corner by his own poor conduct he behaved very differently. His eyes widened and his cheeks flushed as he read. Then there was coughing and muttering of obscenities. Next came the barks of disbelief as he slumped back in his chair and then leant forward again to peer at the words as if in the hope that they would change or disappear. That was my cue to say, 'Is everything all right, Michael?'

He had been so transfixed by whatever the letter contained that my voice startled him and he looked up suddenly. 'Oh nothing ... fucking ... I don't believe it ... how dare he ... fucking publishers ... who the ... just look at this ... listen.' He began to read extracts, and as he read I could see that the tone carried a gravity and weight which clearly troubled Michael.

I thought his face could not get any redder, but it did as words like 'disgraceful', 'abusive' and 'bully' jumped out and would set him off coughing again. As I said, it was a long letter and drew to a close with sentences such as 'Let me make it clear. I will no longer tolerate your abuse and bullying to my staff...' and 'You make a complete fool of yourself by your insulting and intemperate behaviour'. In my experience it was a very rare occurrence to see someone standing up to Michael so boldly. Michael's knowledge of law and readiness to use the courts was well known and, along with his influence and wealth, would frighten most people into keeping quiet, but clearly not Iain Dale. From where I was standing it actually felt very good, to be absolutely honest, when someone had the strength to say 'enough'. I'm sure it was good for Michael as well, although of course it would not have *felt* very nice at the time.

He was about to leave for a holiday in Switzerland and sent a short sharp note to say that he refuted everything and that he would answer Iain's letter on his return. The mulling over would have continued and Michael no doubt saw that he had met his match. On his return, he did his best to defuse the episode with a light-hearted reply. It was still short and he joked that Iain had accused him of pretty much everything except kicking his dog and emptying the water from his goldfish bowl. When he realised he had stepped over the line and it was not going to be tolerated, Michael often used his sense of humour as the first line of defence. He had backed down with quips, but everyone concerned remained on guard as the next volume of *Unbelievable Tales* was being penned, for which, of course, he needed a publisher.

He seemed to have burnt his boats with Iain Dale and the Robson Press, but he also can't have got anywhere in his search for another publisher. I was in the office one day, many months later, as he began tapping a number into his desk phone. 'I'm just calling Jeremy, dear. Watch me eat humble pie. It doesn't matter who you are, everyone has to eat humble pie at some time or another.' It wasn't the first time that Michael had waved the white flag of truce, and on this occasion too Michael was charming and apologetic and good relations were eventually restored. And I was perfectly happy with all that until I saw the date of the next book launch approaching.

The most hands-on part I played in Michael's writing and publishing process was the carrying of many boxes of his books from the hallway of Woodland House up several flights of stairs to the office. I would then unpack them and, when they had been signed, pack them up again and carry them back down to await collection. There were hundreds and it could take days.

Receptionists always seemed to vanish when a new mountain of heavy boxes appeared.

The books that were to be signed and sent individually to people were put in a jiffy bag, taped up and the appropriate stamps put on ready for posting.

Michael usually did all this himself. He could have instructed his secretary or told me to do it, but he didn't. I'm sure that was because he enjoyed it. All jiffy bags that were received at the house or office were kept for reuse. I don't think Michael was especially concerned with recycling for the good of the environment, but that's what he did anyway. If the envelope was large he would put the book into it and then cut through the fluffy padding to make it the appropriate size. This done, he would fold the raggedy end over as I stood ready with the sticky tape dispenser. When I went to put a strip of tape where I thought he wanted it he would be saying, 'No, not there, there. Look, there, you idiot,' and he would nod his head, using his nose to point to the place he wanted stuck. He was mostly good humoured when books were being wrapped, so after being called a bloody idiot a few times I would tape his fingers to the envelope in an accidentally-on-purpose kind of way to let him know he was getting irritating.

There would be laughter and more swearing and I would take over the task of holding the end of the folded envelope while he became commander-in-chief of the tape dispenser. There would still be a lot of swearing and I would still be a bloody idiot, but that way round was usually the most productive if there were lots of books to be posted. But once wrapped and correctly addressed, the second-hand envelopes needed their stamps. That was Michael's favourite part. Stamps were kept in the second drawer down on the right-hand side of his big writing desk. There were new stamps and also 'second-hand' stamps.

If a letter arrived bearing a stamp that had escaped a noticeable post mark he would cut it out and save it for reuse. He expected the staff to be vigilant and do the same. If he saw me throw an envelope into the waste paper basket with an unmarked stamp on it he would notice it immediately and snap, 'What the fuck are you doing? Get it out get it out, give it to me, don't you know how much a fucking first-class stamp costs?' The rescued stamp would join the growing pile in his desk drawer. When there was time Michael would send me off for a glass of water and from that fill a little Wedgwood bowl he kept especially for the purpose of soaking off stamps. Once a few were happily immersed he could get on and wrap another book or whatever he was doing.

As the gum softened and the stamps peeled away they would be left face down dotted about the desk top. Michael liked his office very warm at all times so the little damp rectangles would soon be perfectly dry and ready for stage two.

Now free of gum, a substitute glue was needed and, as

with the cuttings book, Pritt Stick was the preferred brand. Seeing the stamps being carefully regummed and pressed into place on an envelope was like watching a small boy playing at post office. As I heard Woody Allen say in an interview when asked about his constant writing, 'Busy fingers are happy fingers.' Michael always seemed very jovial and absorbed when he was cutting and gluing. I thoroughly enjoyed those days too.

It was always best to be cheerful around Michael even when he was irritable or morose. I would bounce into his office in the mornings and he would say, 'What have you got to fucking smile about?' or, 'It's OK for you, skipping around, but what have I got to look forward to? I'm a fucking cripple with only the grave to look forward to, that's all I've got.' He wasn't looking for sympathy, but had to get his moaning out of the way before the day could properly begin.

In fact, if I showed any sympathy he could get quite annoyed so I had to try something else like, 'You have, you have got plenty to look forward to … you've got … umm … well, you've, err … well, you've got a lovely milkshake to have at 10.30.'

Then he could laugh and snap at me that I was 'really fucking funny' and the day would start. My divorce was proving to be long and stressful and Michael enjoyed poking his nose into that. In the early days he had been very helpful and phoned his lawyers whenever I had any nagging questions. But he found it all very interesting and entertaining and began sending long emails to my solicitor. In my naivety I didn't think much of it until I saw the bill for her replies. He always put my name at the bottom so in the end I had to ask her not to reply to any emails she received that were written entirely in capital letters.

In July, Michael announced that he and Geraldine were

planning their wedding. It was to be a very simple ceremony. He said the grand celebration had been the engagement party and they were to have the simplest possible wedding. Natalie and I were asked to be witnesses.

Nearer the time he talked with Sir Michael and Lady Caine, and it was settled that they would be witnesses, and the day before they would have a celebratory dinner at their home in the country with just a few close friends. When the big day came, I got to Woodland House at the usual time. At about ten o'clock that morning Geraldine asked me to go and help Michael to get ready. He had taken to wearing cotton pyjama trousers almost every day, even when he went out, as they were most comfortable for his leg. He wasn't getting away with that on this occasion. We laughed a lot as I got him smartened up. My divorce had only recently been finalised and I couldn't help but tease him about how the tables had turned. If anyone had eavesdropped they would have imagined it was a groom in his twenties getting ready, not someone in their seventies. We were giggling like children. He wore black silk trousers, his black boots with a bit of heel that made him look a little taller, a dark blazer and crisp white shirt. I tried to persuade him to wear a tie, but he wasn't having any of it. As it was he looked smarter than I had seen him in a very long time. When he was done I rushed to the downstairs loo by the kitchen to quickly get changed myself. When I emerged Michael had just passed the bathroom door. He looked quite dashing, but also very sombre as he concentrated on making his way slowly down the stairs. 'All dressed up and ready for the oven,' I called out brightly and without really thinking, as I headed to the kitchen. I saw Michael stop abruptly. Then he turned and came back up one stair to where I was standing.

'What did you say, dear?' he said, looking up at me. I began to repeat it cautiously and as he turned back to the stairs I heard him wheeze with laughter. His shoulders were shaking. I grabbed my bag from the kitchen and got down to the front door to open it for him. He was chuckling to himself as he stepped out into the sunshine. Jim was waiting with the Phantom just outside the gate and once Geraldine and Michael were off, Natalie and I, along with Julien and Fabrice, Geraldine's sons, followed in a black cab. We were headed for Chelsea Old Town Hall and the simple ceremony was carried out in the Rossetti Room on the first floor. Sir Michael and Lady Caine had been in very good humour from the moment we arrived. And they teased Michael a little too.

When the wedding party emerged on the steps of the Town Hall there was quite a gathering of people and lots of paparazzi snapping away. But one photographer was not there to get pictures. He was much more excited about throwing confetti. Yes, Terry O'Neill and his wife Laraine had appeared to congratulate the newlyweds and wish them well. We ambled around, or 'ponced about' as Michael would say, for nearly an hour before Sir Michael and Lady Caine headed off and Mr and Mrs Winner were driven home. From the morning right through to our return to the house there had been a reporter and photographer doing the official photographs for *Hello!* magazine. All of the staff had clubbed together and bought Lladró china figurines of a bride and groom and they were placed on top of the wedding cake. The photographers took pictures of the cutting of the cake and then they left us all to have a bite to eat and drink champagne. Jim had been invited in and Ruby was working as receptionist that day and of course Lulu and Lani were there too. Michael disappeared to have his usual afternoon nap and Geraldine, Julien and Fabrice and Ruby, Natalie, Jim and I went and sat out on the terrace.

We were all chattering and laughing when I heard the intercom buzzing in the kitchen. Michael was back in his office and wondering what Ruby and I were playing at. Natalie had gone, as she always left at 4.30 to pick up her little boy. I did try to remind Michael that it was his wedding day, but he just said, 'Never mind that, there's work to be done.' Geraldine rolled her eyes knowingly and we finished the day as per usual. A few days later Michael and Geraldine flew off for their honeymoon in Portofino on the Italian Riviera.

Having some time off, I caught the train to Faversham in Kent. The barge was moored on the quayside while some repair work was being done. The little station reminded me of Michael's story of when he went and met Marlon Brando there. Marlon was staying with friends nearby and I think Michael thought he had been invited for the day. He whizzed down in his Ferrari to their agreed meeting place at Faversham station, but as soon as he arrived Marlon said he was ready to get straight back to London. He may have tricked Michael into giving him a lift, but it backfired on Brando when Michael's driving scared the living daylights out of him. When Michael admitted he had been a bit crazy and next time he would drive more carefully, Marlon assured him there wasn't going to be any next time.

I walked down through the town and along Abbey Street. Most of the buildings are lovingly cared-for medieval timber-framed houses and looked beautiful in the autumn evening light, the window boxes and baskets still full of colour. At the bottom, just before the turning to the quayside, was Ray Walton's workshop. I had met Ray on the first trip I did on the barge and then later at Goldsmiths' Hall in London when he was showing his work. He was a silversmith and had recently won the Jacques Cartier Award for an amazingly beautiful leaf-shaped serving bowl. Thinking of something to get Michael for Christmas and birthdays was never easy. Once I had discovered how much he liked antique silver photograph frames I always kept a look-out for those. One year I found some small silver moccasin shoes just like he often wore and I was surprised by how much he seemed to love them. He kept them in pride of place by his desk. When his seventy-fifth birthday approached, I talked to Ray about the idea of making a little director's chair in silver. I got him all the photographs I could of Michael's favourite one and he made the chair a few inches tall and perfect in every detail. I've always been amazed by that level of craftsmanship. Even the back had the texture of leather and of course Michael's name was engraved on it, just like the real thing. It looked good with the silver shoes next to it and he sat a crystal bear in it that Geraldine had given him.

On the quayside there was plenty of craftsmanship, but on a whole other scale. The ancient wooden sheds were still home to shipwrights, boat builders and riggers and the quay itself lined with sailing barges. Arriving always felt like stepping back in time or into a museum. But during the day it was a hive of activity. The barge had been in a dry dock there and had a few great lumps of timber replaced by a shipwright called Tim Goldsack. In the two months in dry dock I had spent my weekends under the barge with a great big roller and buckets of paint. An old friend from the north, Michelle Monroe, came down to help for a few days. She had once been a lodger with my mother as a teenager and had grown to be part of the family. Michael had met her a few times and liked her. And he could see she was the kind of person that it was better not to get on the wrong side of too. One evening she was wandering along the quay with Chiki on a lead. I was on the deck of the boat changing my shoes when I glanced up to see her walking up a gangway to a dry dock.

Just then I saw Chiki step off the edge and hang by her little neck for a moment before dropping about ten feet into the water below. I shrieked at Michelle and went rushing over just in time to see Chiki surface and start swimming off down the creek. Her eyesight was not very good, but she was a tough and healthy dog and as she was the grand age of nineteen, I was particularly protective of her. Without thinking I slid down the bank and plunged into the water. Matthew had heard the commotion and came running just in time to take little Chiki from me, grab my hand and help pull me back to dry land. I was a soggy, muddy mess, but once I saw Chiki was safe I set off after Michelle. She had sensed my fury and had got off to a head start. Luckily Matthew was there to call out that it may be better to get the dog warm and dry first and look into disembowelling Michelle later. As it turned out, Chiki had enjoyed her little swim, but my mobile phone was not so happy. In my hurry to jump in after the dog I hadn't thought to empty my pockets. I had spoken to Michael earlier that day when he was fresh back from Portofino. I called him on Michelle's phone and gave him her number in case he wanted to get hold of me. But I got no sympathy from him when I told him about my dip in the creek. He knew only too well my love of being in water. He just laughed and said something like, 'Don't try and blame the dog or anyone, you would jump into my fish tank if it didn't have a fucking lid on it.'

Michael and Geraldine had returned from honeymoon

looking happy, healthy and very suntanned. I thought I had gone rather a good colour too, after my time on the barge, but it turned out to be mostly mud or red ochre from the sails. Michael had got straight back to his work routine and would be at his desk at 9.30. On Wednesday mornings everyone knew he would usually be busy on his *Sunday Times* article and no one would disturb him. And he didn't disturb any of us either. I could usually sit in the kitchen and talk to Lulu or Lani or Jim. Apart from those mornings, Michael usually wanted me in the office. Often I was just fetching files he needed or taking papers backwards and forwards to Natalie next door. If he wanted coffee or a milkshake I would nip and get that too. He would talk about whatever he had been writing or have me peering over his shoulder to read something on his laptop. The mornings tended to be when most work was accomplished and gradually in the afternoon it would tail off into general chatter.

By the end of the day he would be more interested in Twitter. Once hooked he had become pretty fascinated and really enjoyed it. First thing in the morning, Michael would do a few tweets to say what he was up to and show me who had tweeted what back. But he didn't really start tweeting in earnest until the end of the day. Michael liked the banter, but would get the odd wave of horrible remarks. When that happened there would be a flurry on the keyboard as he deleted or banned people, or whatever Twitter maestros do, and then he would slam his laptop closed in disgust. I would get a short lecture on how a bit of fun can be spoilt by a few obscene idiots. Michael didn't always bother to mention to me the times that he himself was stepping outside the boundary of good clean fun, but Ruby followed him on Twitter and would fill me in. I think the closest shave he had was with Victoria Coren, but by the time I heard about it the dust had settled. Michael had drawn attention to her 'bosoms' and seemed not to realise that his schoolboy attitude might appear more than a little inappropriate and offensive in the global community of Twitter. He clearly did not know who she was, either, not that there was any excuse to be found in that. He certainly didn't know that Giles Coren, whom he knew and liked, was her brother, or that she was the daughter of the great humorist Alan Coren, whom he had known. Michael happily dug himself into quite a hole and I think he was lucky that Victoria had the grace not to bury him in it. When he finally told me about the drama he became quite agitated and red faced. He knew it had been a close call. I could almost see the steam of relief escaping from his shirt collar. But it was quickly defused and he and Geraldine went to dinner with Victoria and Giles. What I grew to like most about Twitter was that it could so engross Michael that I was able to look out of the window or perch on the arm of the sofa and take the weight off my feet for a while.

Soon after the honeymoon, Geraldine went to Paris to have some time with her family there. I stepped into the hall one morning and Lani appeared immediately. 'Please, please,' she was saying, 'Sir's collapse on the bed we not know what to do.' I ran upstairs and had to shake Michael gently before he opened his eyes. He said he didn't feel good and just wanted to rest for a while. I got him back into bed and kept an eye on him, but felt there was something not quite right. When I asked Natalie to phone Geraldine, she said to check if he had taken Night Nurse. She said if he had he may just need to sleep it off, and to keep her informed. Sure enough, he admitted

324

he had taken some in the early hours of the morning. After letting him sleep for an hour or so it worried me that he was still not stirring. What alarmed me most was that he showed no interest at all when the phone was ringing next to his bed. I knew that, however weak he felt, he *always* answered his phone. He wouldn't drink any water and I thought he seemed rather hot so took his temperature. It was high and he seemed to be drifting in his speech. I ran down to Natalie and she called the doctor. I sat with Michael trying to keep him awake by talking and making him sip iced water. It was suddenly very frightening as I found I could only just keep him conscious. I was just about to call an ambulance when the doctor arrived, but after a quick look at Michael he called one straight away. I went with him to Chelsea and Westminster Hospital. Alerted to the situation, Geraldine immediately came back from Paris and was at the hospital early that evening. Michael was in good hands, but it was not until the next morning that they told us he had an *E. coli* infection. Michael had always liked steak tartare and had prepared it for himself for lunch each day that week. He remembered that on one of those days he had left it on the side in the kitchen for a little while before eating it.

For many people the infection need not be very serious, but because of Michael's weakened condition from his earlier illness it was a terrible setback. With powerful antibiotics he felt recovered in about a week and returned home. But his liver especially was not good, and with a weak immune system and water retention problems he often had to return to hospital. He had often been advised to slow down and work less and have a more leisurely life. Now, he listened. The theory was good. But in practice I think he only knew how to be who he had always been. He and Geraldine returned to Gstaad for Christmas that year. Michael said afterwards that some days he did not leave his room. He was often not feeling strong enough. But he did say that the views over the mountains were so breathtaking that it was the best place he could be.

In 2012 he had to slow down whether he liked it or not.

Of course he didn't like it at all, but he was surprisingly philosophical. If he was going out for the evening he would have an afternoon nap to charge his batteries. He accepted that long-haul flights were not a good idea, but would go on regular trips to Europe with Geraldine. She made sure he exercised each day and would also get him walking to Holland Park and round and about as much as possible. He often showed little enthusiasm, but a poke from a stick or her umbrella would get him moving along. As she said, it was all for his own good.

When I got to work one morning he told me he had gone for a walk on his own and come across a couple of peacocks in the street. They often seemed to wander out from their Holland Park home and occasionally they would appear in Michael's garden or at Farley Court. He liked seeing them and would sometimes try to guide them back to the park gates. On this occasion it was early evening and he was in his pyjama trousers. He wore them all day if he could, and Geraldine had sewn fasteners on them to reduce the risk of involuntary exposure. Michael never really gave much of a damn about his appearance unless it was important to him to be showing his respect. Those times were quite rare, such as occasions involving royalty, Police Memorial Trust events and that kind of thing. Apart from that, he seemed pretty unaware or uninterested in how people saw him. Anyway, he said that the peacocks had picked up pace along Melbury Road and he had to shout to an approaching couple to stop still so the peacocks might turn up into Ilchester Place. 'The couple saw me waving my stick and shouting "stop there, stop" or something, but then I looked and the fucking peacocks had disappeared,' he said. He knew they must have gone through one of the gates and into a garden and when the couple reached him he was peering over the walls. They looked concerned and asked him if he was OK and as Michael told them he was looking for the peacocks it slowly dawned on him that they had not seen them at all. The female peacocks, or 'peahens' I think is the proper word, are brownish grey and would have been very pavement-like in colour in the evening light. 'They looked at me like I was a right fucking lunatic,' he said, roaring with laughter. I told him that if he was going to go out in his pyjamas chasing peacocks, it might be safer to be with someone who looked sane.

Michael found incidents like that hilarious and it was rare for many days to pass without something ludicrous cropping up. He just seemed to attract it without effort. I always enjoyed his eccentric streak. And maybe when someone is so unselfconscious it makes it easier for people around them to be themselves too. His sense of humour and of the absurd had helped him through some very difficult times and 2012 was bringing more of the same. Hardly a month went by without him having to go to hospital for a few days. Each time the strength was knocked out of him, but each time he got through it. His ability to recover and get back up was remarkable. He always managed to get out for dinner at least once a week and write his *Sunday Times* article. And there was a new book taking shape, *The Hymie Joke Book*. That was ideal, as it involved talking to friends and emailing people in the search for stories and didn't require long periods of concentration.

If he had the strength to stand up, Michael would be at his desk at 9.30. With a very weak immune system he was plagued with unpleasant afflictions, but he battled on. He might be in shorts or pyjamas, but it didn't matter. He would get to his office and plod onwards. The staff in the house had got used to helping to look after him. Shirley had left as he felt he no longer needed two maids, but Lani, Lulu and Natalie were always there and sometimes Ruby too. There were grim times, difficult times and frightening times, but he knew everyone well and, like him, I think we all kept our sense of humour as far as possible. He continued to be insistent that the cuttings book be kept up to date and if he was writing I would get on with that on the kitchen table. But now if he buzzed me it was quite likely to be about some health-related matter. And everything was still loud and dramatic.

As I said, these were grim times, but he was able to laugh through most things and that helped inspire us all to do the same. I had learnt how to change dressings from Ampi, Calvin and Claudette so I could be more helpful. There were times, especially during the period he had MRSA, when he had needed a good wash and Geraldine and I would don swimsuits and wellingtons and help him in the shower. We got on with the practicalities, and the absurdities and hilarity seemed to look after themselves.

One day in November, Michael showed no sign of wanting to get up. He was not in good shape and doctors were not optimistic; they said just to keep him comfortable and give him whatever he wanted. We feared it might be the end of the line and after a few days Geraldine called the rabbi.

He came the following day and she showed him into the bedroom. Michael had seemed a little stronger that morning and after a few minutes we heard him calling 'Dinah, Dinah'. I went in and, reading Michael's expression, I asked the rabbi if he could leave the room for a moment so I could attend to Michael. Once he had left Michael said under his breath, 'What's he doing here? I really don't need him here.'

When I went back out to the rabbi he looked at me and with a gentle smile said, 'He doesn't want me here, does he?' I smiled back at him and Geraldine whisked him away to the lounge. On my return to Michael's bedside he made it clear that he wanted me to promise that no rabbi would be returning. I gave him my word and it wasn't spoken of again. Michael had always seemed ambivalent about his Jewish roots. I rarely if ever heard him talk about it, but I had once seen a paper on his desk which showed he was being financially supportive of a synagogue in Israel. At the time I didn't know that it was the synagogue in Yemin Orde Youth Village that his parents had built. It was not something I talked to him about and I noticed he avoided anything that clearly identified his links with Judaism. But having said that, true to his contradictory nature, his last book was *Michael Winner's Hymie Joke Book: 50 Shades of Oy Vey*.

The visit of the rabbi, however, did coincide with Michael making something of a recovery. He had done it again and was getting his strength back. Then one night Fabrice went down with something horrible. Fabrice or Julien often came for a few days to give Geraldine some moral support as well as helping her with looking after Michael. It turned out to be norovirus that Fabrice was suffering from. We realised then what had been attacking Michael. And one by one we all got knocked down by it. Only Lulu escaped. Although he had pulled through again, Michael was not strong. On good days he would sit at a desk next to his bed and run his life from there. He also managed trips to restaurants so he could continue his articles, but he needed a fair bit of help. I began to spend more and more time in a chair next to him in his bedroom. In the mornings Michael was most lucid and would greet me with a broad smile.

His courage continued and he enjoyed each day as he could. Often we would just chat about the things we had been through together. In the afternoon he would be more tired, but if he closed his eyes I found he liked me to keep talking so I would fill him in with any news. Now and then he would smile or open one eye as if to check he wasn't dreaming. I told him about Daniel, my eldest son, who had just moved to London and was living nearby. Michael seemed very pleased to hear that. He knew that after my divorce I was frightened my world might be difficult or fragmented, but instead almost the opposite was true. I was no longer rushing backwards and forwards between two places. I went through all the ins and outs of what was happening and told him how lucky I felt that the boys wanted to be in London. 'Sometimes you worry too much, my dear,' Michael said quietly and smiled. Luke had found work and I was glad his flatmate had a piano so he could keep at his music too. We talked about the times he and Geraldine had invited Luke to the Ritz for Christmas dinners. Michael was quietly generous like that and would show people a world they might otherwise not get to see. The first time, Leslie and Evie Bricusse were there and could not have been better company for putting Luke at his ease in the rather overwhelming splendour of the Ritz.

Luke loved it and I was very glad that he could have the experience of eating out with Michael. But in an ideal world he might have been spared also having a taste of Michael's driving. Afterwards, I heard Luke telling a friend about the journey he had, sitting with me in the back of the Bentley. He thought Michael was having a lucky run with the lights as we whizzed along Bayswater Road, but then noticed the next light we went through was in fact red. 'I think that was red, Mr Winner,' he said anxiously.

'Traffic lights, waste of fucking time,' said Michael in a matter-of-fact tone as we sped onwards to the background racket of screeching brakes and car horns. When I retold the story to Michael he chuckled. I also reminded him that it was not just Marlon Brando who had refused to get into a car with him again. Sir Roger Moore had politely declined a lift with Michael once too. We were in the silver Bentley and were headed to somewhere in Mayfair to pick him up and go on to a nearby restaurant for dinner. He was standing in a one-way street and looking out for Michael. When we drove along it the opposite way and came up behind him he nearly jumped out of his skin. He got into the car and began explaining to Michael about one-way streets and road safety, but Michael was just finding it all hilarious. Mercifully, the restaurant was not far away. When dinner was over he offered him a lift back, but Sir Roger made it clear that he would prefer to get a cab rather than risk being cut down in his prime.

When Christmas arrived, Michael would sit in his chair for an hour or so, but was becoming happier to stay in his bed. Some of Geraldine's family arrived and the house was full of new voices. I was to have a few days off, but would only be down the road if I was wanted. It was a quiet time, but Luke came for Christmas Day and Daniel called in before going north with his girlfriend. And I felt very lucky that they both got on with Matthew and everyone was happy. When I next saw Michael, after Boxing Day, he was sitting up in his huge bed. He smiled and waved at me as I walked in. The mornings were always best for talking as by lunchtime his mind seemed to start wandering or he would be tired and want to sleep. Lulu and Lani were amazing with their help. Over the months they had gradually taken on any extra duties without a murmur of complaint. In fact, the very opposite. They both seemed as concerned for Michael's wellbeing as they might be for any friend or relation. Also Lulu had worked as a carer before and so was very good at knowing how to do things.

Michael had taken to Lani helping him with his lunch and so she took an earlier break so she could be back at one o'clock. He was still quite a stickler for timekeeping. A carer would come in at the end of the afternoon and stay through the night. At the weekends another carer came in case Geraldine, Lulu and Lani needed help. During the week I would sit with him and we would watch a film or continue our rambling talks. I had not had long, quiet conversations like that with him before. It was a whole new experience.

During his stays in hospital there had been all the comings and goings of doctors and nurses, and Michael was often in work mode whenever he had the strength. Now he was more amused by stories from the past or would want to know what was going on in my world. Having moved out from my home in Little Neston I had been sorting through the boxes and boxes of photographs I had collected over the years. Lots were from my modelling days.

Fortunately my mother had been quite a hoarder of press

cuttings too or I would not have half so many. But over the years I had also picked up old photographs that caught my interest or had some kind of magic about them. I took some in to show him one day and what he knew and remembered was remarkable. A few weeks earlier I had bought a press photo of Marilyn Monroe at the London Photo Fair. She was getting out of the bath with a big white towel wrapped around her. I had just liked the picture and all the newspaper stamps on the back showed its history. But there was no caption.

Michael knew immediately which film it was from and all kinds of other details about it. We went through quite a few photos and he named the films, the stars, and often the directors and producers, and threw in the odd anecdote or funny story as well. He had been very obsessed with film as a youngster and I think a lot of his knowledge stretched back to those times.

Apart from the hundreds of photographs in his home cinema, all of Michael with film stars or other famous people, the pictures I think he was most proud of were his collection of illustrations for children's books. These were beautifully mounted and framed and bore the name of the artist and the title of the picture in small, gold-leaf lettering underneath. It was a truly remarkable collection. There were Edmund Dulac illustrations for fairy tales, humorous drawings by Heath Robinson, Beatrix Potter watercolours for the Peter Rabbit books, other pen-and-ink drawings and watercolours by Arthur Rackham and several drawings by E. H. Shepard for A. A. Milne's *Winnie the Pooh* stories. One of my favourites was the pencil drawing on the landing leading to Michael's office showing the young Christopher Robin holding Pooh's leg as he absent-mindedly bumped the long-suffering bear down the stairs.

Perhaps in that picture I could somehow empathise with poor Pooh, although generally it was Michael who identified with 'Winnie'. He certainly had a lot of teddy bears and they were arranged along the window sill in his bedroom. The one most in favour would sit on the pillows on his bed during the day. Vanessa had given him a very splendid bear which often sat in pride of place. The first bears dated back to when he first met Catherine Neilson and from then on other people began to buy them for him too. I had bought him an Asquiths bear which lounged around with him when illness confined him to bed.

One lunchtime just before Christmas I had returned to the house just as Catherine was leaving. I had not seen her for a long time although I knew that Michael spoke to her on the phone a great deal. She was tearful and holding a very big teddy bear with the name 'George' on his jumper. She said she had brought him for Michael as she knew how much he loved his father, who had been called George. I discovered she had not been able to see Michael as he was sleeping. Catherine had been one of the constant threads through Michael's life and it was heart-breaking to see her so upset. I'm glad to say she did come back and see Michael a week or two later.

They were sad times for everyone and sometimes very difficult too. Over those weeks lots of Michael's friends called at the house to see him. Geraldine would show them in and I would leave them to talk. Paola and Georgina knew they could not call at the house and now that Michael was no longer using his phone I was their only link to him.

He had put me in some impossible positions over the years, but now I only cared about doing whatever seemed helpful. But each time a visitor left or a phone call was over I felt a heavy wave of sadness. And each time I did my best to keep myself together so I could breeze back into his room as cheer-fully as possible. Michael had a calm strength about him and seeing his courage helped me to keep my spirits up. Sometimes I could feel I was weakening and would nip out for a glass of water or on some other pretext. Occasionally he stopped me from leaving and told me not to be so silly. I'm not sure he fully understood that I was so sad and fearful to be los-ing him and the world that I had known for so long. In many ways I suppose that had already gradually been happening and I had simply not noticed it very clearly. But it must have been a part of the cloak of sadness I was feeling. He said I had good friends and knew how to be happy and everything would be all right.

And he said I knew he had made sure I would be well looked after. As with most other things, he had never been shy of talking about his will. He had left me the flat at Far-ley Court, enough money to live on and also his Suzuki jeep. But I was never sure he really knew how much I was going to miss him for who he was. And my years with him were a big and living part of me. Without him those times would be cut off suddenly as memories. Everything would be differ-ent. Everything would change for me and I couldn't possibly know what the future might hold. Over those few months with Michael I had grown used to just dealing with each day as it came. And we had got quite good at finding cause for laughter. We laughed about the jeep when he said he hoped I would learn how to reverse it. I had slowly conquered my fear of driving around London, but would still get Jim or someone to reverse it into the garage. But to be fair to myself, that was mostly my horror at the thought of lurching into the Bentley or one of the other cars.

As our stories wandered through the years Michael increasingly mentioned 'the book'. The thought of writing about my times with Michael had been mine originally, but his enthusiasm for it grew and grew until it almost felt like it was his idea or even his book. Over a year or more, if one of us recounted some incident, whether funny or shocking, intriguing or absurd, he would sometimes follow it by saying, 'Put it in the book, dear, put it in, put it in.' Sometimes it would be something that I would have imagined him to prefer kept under wraps, but if I looked at all surprised he would just say, 'Of course you should put it in, put it *all* in, who cares, who cares, tell them everything.'

Once when the reality of the task of writing had hit me I had said, 'But I can't really write a book, can I?'

Michael smiled at my lack of confidence and insisted, 'Of course you can fucking write a book, dear, you just say all the stories you remember. And you're in the art world now so it should be a piece of fucking cake,' and then bellowed with laughter. He started joking about my being 'in the art world' when he first heard that Matthew was an artist and photographer and knew I had gone to openings and concerts and things like that. I think he might have felt it was a little out of keeping with my earthy, northern, country-girl side. But when I told him I was going to the private view of David Hockney's big exhibition at the Royal Academy, Michael had hysterics. I knew he had also got an invitation, but it turned out that he was going to the official opening whereas Jean-Pierre had arranged it that I went the day before to the less formal evening for friends and family. I half expected Michael to be a bit peeved.

Instead he coughed and wheezed and choked with laughter.

When he could speak he said, 'You're fucking unbelievable, you've only been in the art world five minutes and you're already poncing about at the top.' It was a great evening. Jean-Pierre had put Diana's daughter Lara on the guest list and Luke as well. The show was a huge and beautiful eye-opening experience and so cheerful I soon felt quite euphoric. It wasn't just the champagne. When we left the colourful woodland and headed for the food being served in the restaurant, the sound of an accordion was drifting up the stairs. François Parisi, Jean-Pierre's friend and teacher, was playing away happily. Just to hear him was amazing in itself. The exhibition was in early 2012 and with more than a little 1930s bohemia in the air.

Michael did not have quite such a good time. The night of the official opening was very, very crowded. He said he could see David Hockney, but didn't have a hope of pushing through everyone to get to him. They had last seen each other in Holland Park a few years earlier. I knew Michael found him an impressive person and liked the constant lively twinkle of humour in his pale blue eyes. The painter Michael saw most was Lucian Freud. That was simply because they both really liked the Wolseley restaurant in Piccadilly and I often saw him there when I was with Michael. They would doff their caps at each other, so to speak, and occasionally exchange a few words.

As the days passed Michael would sleep longer and his hours of brightness in the mornings grew shorter. I would talk to him quietly unless I felt he was deeply asleep. It felt cold sitting still in the huge room and the last weeks I look back on as though something of a dream. But so often, just when it seemed he was fading away, he would be back and sitting up and waving and blowing kisses to me when I arrived in the morning. I think it helped me to only gradually have to face the fact that soon he would not be there. I was able to do that slowly and in my own time. So many friends had been to the house and perhaps his nearest neighbours were the last to say their farewells. I remember Jimmy Page coming in and the gentle smiles of Don and Shirley Black when they called. Michael knew so many really lovely people.

Of course I knew that these were goodbyes, but I couldn't let myself completely take that in. The worst moment was when a small metal bed arrived. Geraldine and the palliative nurse had arranged it, as it was becoming very difficult to sit him up or help him out of bed. It arrived on a Wednesday, just as Geraldine and her daughter-in-law and the baby were about to leave for Paris. I think the most difficult time for me through all this was having to explain to Michael why we needed him to be in that little bed. However necessary, it was completely heart-breaking.

The weather was bitter cold again the next day and the snow heavy at times. With Lulu often having to be out on her errands as housekeeper it was soon clear that it was too much for Lani and me to lift Michael when needed. I called Stephen, the builder who had been working at the house now and then. He and his son Sam managed to drive through the snow and stayed the whole day. Michael had known them both for most of their lives and they were like family. They worked out how to fit the sides to the metal bed and made light of helping as well as keeping the atmosphere less gloomy. Lani always left at four and Stephen and Sam stayed on with Michael and me until the carer arrived at six. When Natalie had left she was concerned as to how I might cope the following day, as the worsening weather was already making road and rail chaos.

Sure enough, the following morning she could not get into work. But Stephen and Sam had said they would help again and somehow they got through. For me that was a huge relief. Together we could lift Michael when needed and they helped keep my spirits up after the various phone calls to doctors. Geraldine returned that evening, and on Saturday when I called she said she thought he was growing weaker. On Sunday lunchtime we spoke again and she said he had drifted into a coma so I went up to the house to see him. He seemed to be in a very, very deep sleep. The carer and Lulu were there and I suggested to Geraldine that we get some air. We walked the streets for a while with thick coats on against the cold. The sky was heavy and there were flecks of snow in the air as we made our way towards the warmth of the Scarsdale Tavern.

On Monday morning, Lani helped me to change dressings on his arms to make sure he was comfortable and I had learnt through looking after my mother that someone in a coma could often hear everything around them so I talked to Michael quite normally. But seeing him in the little bed made me feel that he would not want to wake again now. I kept hold of his hand and began to talk to him about the people I knew had meant so much to him but who were no longer around. And often I told him he had said all his good-byes and he could now go happily and join his old friends. It must have been an hour or more that I talked quietly to him and then he began to take short breaths. I found myself calling out to Natalie, who was just down the stairs in her office. When she came in and saw Michael's breathing she ran to find Lulu. Together we spoke to him for a few moments, but it was soon clear that he had gone. Natalie phoned Geraldine and also Lani, who had just nipped to the high street.

When Lani rushed in she was immediately in tears and set me off again, but Natalie gave me a bit of a shake and I pulled myself together. We stayed with Michael until Geraldine got back and then left the room so she could be with him. Wandering down the stairs to the office I looked out into the branches of the big old oak tree. They were swaying gently and sunlight sparkled through them. After my mother had died I had taken to standing by the tree sometimes and talking to her. Michael teased me about a lot of things, but not about that. I never heard him draw a line through any of life's great mysteries and now and then, if I was in a quandary over something, he would nod towards the oak tree and say, 'Well, my dear, maybe you should go and ask your mother.'

ACKNOWLEDGEMENTS

I'VE BEEN A LITTLE WORRIED at the thought of writing these acknowledgements as there are so many people I must thank that it may begin to look as though I have actually made very little contribution myself. The truth is that this book really *couldn't* have been brought into existence without the encouragement, guidance, advice and assistance of many others.

I will start at the begining and that means, of course, with Michael. His excitement and badgering proved to be a great source of encouragement and, in his own way, he built up my belief that writing something was a real possibility. Ruby Snape and Diana Morgan-Hill, both of them friends and both writers too, continued to spur me on until I did eventually get out all my notebooks and diaries and look to making a start. Once at that stage it was another friend and writer, Peter Joucla, who, in those early days, cycled across London one or two mornings a week helping me to get all the stories and incidents into some kind of order and begin to actually put words on paper. His guidance and good healthy discipline prepared me for the path ahead.

Once up and running, the next person I leant rather heavily on was Matthew Houston, my partner and, I should really say, *collaborateur*. As Matthew had worked for Michael for quite a few years he knew many of the people and stories and general day-to-day goings-on at Woodland House. Yes we argued, in fact we argued quite a lot, but I'm glad to say we laughed even more. I'm certain I could not have got through everything without him around with his good humour and plain hard work. Even now he is going through boxes and boxes of photographs and scanning the best of them for inclusion between these pages. We have been through the whole bookwriting process together and it is testament to his patience and kindness that we still talk, let alone remain the best of friends.

Next I must say how lucky I was to be able to talk to so many people who had stories about Michael. I am especially grateful to the friends of Michael's I spoke to and for their encouragement as well as the reminder that he would want me to 'tell it like it is'.

Some of Michael's ex-girlfriends and the many other friends I have made through my work all proved helpful in recounting incidents, some of which had, for a long time, been lying in dusty corners of my memory. With their help I could bring the episodes to life once again and compare my notes with their versions of events. I am very grateful to them all for their support and their cheerful tolerance through all my questioning. In

no particular order whatsoever I must thank John Fraser, Zoe
Vigus, Georgina Hristova, Pippa Neve, Keda Price-Cousins,
Jenny Seagrove, John May, Paola Lombard, Nicolanne Cox,
Lalaine Meneses, Pat Wooll, Jim Sharkey, Nobby Clark, Cheryl
Baker, Sheila Gee, Vanessa Perry, Lily and Dante Yuson and
Joan Hills.

I would also like to make special mention of Gae Exton, Ian
and Ingrid Houston, Jean-Pierre Gonçalves de Lima, Sarah
Malet and Margaret Watson for their unwavering support
and offers of financial help in the thin times, not to mention
the many good dinners and evenings out. Without their aid I
could not have remained buoyant and cheerful and certainly
not so well fed and watered. Also, along with Diana, Ruby,
Nicolanne, and Robin Day-Viaud, they read chapters as they
rattled out of the printer, and their thoughtful comments and
encouragement were a huge help to me through some long
winter months.

I realise there are far too many other people to mention by
name who have been so important in supporting me through
the past year or so. It is probably just as well that I began this
book with no idea of how time-consuming and all-engross-
ing the task would be. My sons Danny and Luke and other
close friends have been encouraging, understanding and also
respectful of my need to be so often immersed in 'Winner's
world'. I am lucky to know such good-hearted people and I
am very grateful to them all.

And last but of course by no means least I would like to say
a big thank you to all at Biteback Publishing and the Robson
Press. It was a whole new world to me and I found everyone
very friendly and welcoming. As editor, Olivia Beattie's sharp
eyes and intelligence have been invaluable in checking every

detail, particularly, I think, my grammar. And, although I have never pretended to be a proper 'writer', Jeremy Robson himself has remained gentle and respectful towards my own way of putting words on a page. Not only that, but he has been reassuring in my times of worry and can never know quite how helpful his emails were in keeping me going, especially the ones which ended simply with the word 'onwards'.

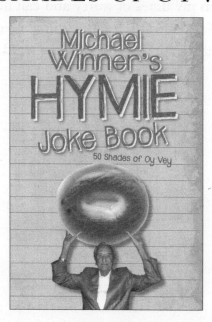

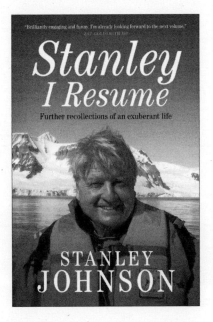